Theorizing Nationalism

Theorizing Nationalism

Graham Day and Andrew Thompson

Consultant Editor: Jo Campling

First published 2004 by
PALGRAVE MACMILLAN
Houndmills, Basingstoke, Hampshire RG21 6XS and
175 Fifth Avenue, New York, N.Y. 10010
Companies and representatives throughout the world

PALGRAVE MACMILLAN is the global academic imprint of the Palgrave Macmillan division of St. Martin's Press, LLC and of Palgrave Macmillan Ltd. Macmillan® is a registered trademark in the United States, United Kingdom and other countries. Palgrave is a registered trademark in the European Union and other countries.

ISBN 0–333–96264–8 hardback
ISBN 0–333–96265–6 paperback

This book is printed on paper suitable for recycling and made from fully managed and sustained forest sources.

A catalogue record for this book is available from the British Library.

A catalog record for this book is available from the Library of Congress.

10   9   8   7   6   5   4   3   2   1
13   12   11   10   09   08   07   06   05   04

Printed in China

Contents

Acknowledgements

In writing this book we have accumulated debts of gratitude to a good many individuals who took the time to read through drafts of the following chapters. Thanks, therefore, to: Deborah Cook, Paul Chambers, Catherine Davies, Howard Davis, David Dunkerley, Ralph Fevre, Richard Jenkins, Robert Holton, John Hutchinson, Dominic Pulera, Tony Spybey, Zlatko Skrbis, Charlotte Williams, Chris Williams, Steve Williams, Howard Wollman and Neil Wynn. Particular thanks go to Paul Chambers who advised on a number of chapters. Sociology students at the Universities of Bangor and Glamorgan also road-tested drafts of chapters.

Thanks, too, to Zlatko Skrbis for information on the interesting project he and colleagues at the University of Queensland are undertaking on cosmopolitanism.

Jo Campling helped us to develop the initial idea for the book and steered us – eventually – to the finish. Thanks, also, to Anstice Hughes and Emily Salz at Palgrave for their time and help.

Andrew Thompson would especially like to thank Cerys and Llew for their love and patience, and Graham Day would like to acknowledge the support and encouragement he has had from Daphne, Matthew and Tamsin.

The authors and publishers wish to thank the following for granting permission to reproduce copyright material in the form of extracts: Craig Calhoun (1994) *Nationalism*, by permission of Open University Press; Emile Durkheim (1964) *The Rules of Sociological Method*, by permission of Simon & Schuster; Cynthia Enloe (2000) *Bananas, Beaches and Bases: Making Feminist Sense of International Politics*, by permission of University of California Press; George Fredrickson (2002) *Racism*, by permission of Princeton University Press; Ernest Gellner (1983) *Nations and Nationalism*, and Michael Mann (1988) *States, War and Capitalism*, by permission of Basil

Blackwell; Ivan Hannaford (1996) *Race: The History of an Idea in the West*, by permission of Johns Hopkins University Press; Doreen Massey (1994) *Space, Place and Gender*, by permission of Polity Press; Carol Swain (2002) *The New White Nationalism in America*, by permission of Cambridge University Press; and, finally, Howard Winant (2001) *The World is a Ghetto*, by permission of Basic Books.

Every effort has been made to trace all the copyright-holders, but if any have been inadvertently overlooked the publishers will be pleased to make the necessary arrangement at the first opportunity.

Preface

These are tumultuous times for nations and nation-states. Many contend that the world is changing in ways which challenge them, or even threaten to undermine their very existence. The talk is of 'globalization', and the emergence of new 'multicultural' and 'transnational' identities which supersede the old national loyalties. Unprecedented levels of international migration and global travel mean that new diasporic populations are spreading around the world, separated from their original homelands by vast distances, and yet often still owing some allegiance to them, or at least to their memories of what they used to be. To varying extents, these migrant populations are integrating with their host communities, bringing about in doing so new mixtures of cultures, ideas and values which break with former traditions and with established histories. In many ways, national frontiers and boundaries no longer seem able to cope with this endless flow of people, symbols and material resources. The equation which once held true, that individuals would identify themselves most fiercely with the territories from which they originated, and with the political authorities that controlled them, no longer appears so self-evident. Perhaps the historical period during which nationalism was the most powerful of political ideologies and nation-states the strongest of actors on the world stage is drawing to a close. Yet, looking back over a troubled history of two centuries or more, from the time when nations began to establish their dominance as the key political units, we might ask when, if ever, things were really settled. Ever since nations came on the scene, and national identities began to be promoted as the prime focus of collective identification, they have been associated with controversy and frequent upheaval, as their limits have been questioned, and efforts have been made to replace existing versions with competing alternatives. In the contemporary world, we might see the

Middle East as the region in which the 'national' question remains most volatile and dangerous; but events in places as various as Taiwan, Kashmir, Chechnya and Kosovo show that problems to do with nations are by no means confined to that area alone. Indeed, issues of nation and nationality are rarely far from the centre of the world's political hot-spots.

Whilst resolving such problems might seem to be the job of political scientists and experts in international relations, the nature of nationhood and national identity is clearly something close to the heart of modern societies. It is not surprising therefore that social commentators and theorists have had a good deal to say about it. A case can even be made to the effect that the rise of modern social theory, and sociology in particular, is intimately connected to the development of the nation-state, and in some ways has been helpful to it. Numerous sociologists have worked to provide particular nation-states with help in understanding and dealing with what were seen, from their varying national perspectives, as the critical problems of the day, and few have been altogether immune from engagement with nationalistic aims and aspirations. At least until quite recently, most sociology has been carried out within national confines, and there are still very distinctive national varieties of sociological theorizing. In many ways, the oddity is how comparatively little attention this has attracted. In the development of sociology as a discipline, the nation and matters related to it have received a great deal less systematic discussion than questions of class, 'race', and, albeit latterly, gender. It is only relatively recently that the sociology of nationalism has entered the standard curriculum, and that texts have begun to appear examining its significance. For much of the time when 'nation building' was at its height, the meaning and purpose of nationhood was taken more or less for granted, and nations were treated as providing the fixed context within which social processes could be examined and analysed. It was as if social relations occurred naturally within the boundaries of nations, while political or diplomatic relations happened between them.

We have therefore something of a paradox, in that the critical examination of nationalism and national identities seems to get going only when their continued importance has been put into doubt. Undoubtedly the volume and calibre of writing about nationalism has risen vastly in recent decades, so much so that some would contend that it represents a new beginning, as topics and difficulties that were previously neglected are now given their due attention. This is not to deny that the classic contributions to sociological theorizing made some effort to understand the importance of nations, although this was often by implication rather than through explicit analysis. However, for a good part of the twentieth century, mainstream sociologists were producing theoretical and practical reasons for predicting an eventual decline in the significance of nationalism as an aspect of social organization, and therefore as a topic for social theorizing. In the long run, it appeared to many to be incompatible with the drift of modern development. The upsurge of nationalistic feeling and action around the Second World War, and the continuing instability and political reorganization that followed it, led to a reassessment, and sparked a continuing debate as to whether or not this view was correct, since the potency of ideas of nationhood and nationalistic discourses seemed to remain undiminished. New national divisions appeared in unexpected places, and questions of national identity took on a new relevance in the context of debates about ethnicity and new forms of political representation, emerging both above and below the national level. In Europe, for example, the expansion of the European Union leads to fierce arguments about the future of national sovereignty, while at the same time claims are made for greater regional autonomy within nations. Such developments fuel debates about whether or not national divisions are a necessary and inherent feature of human society, or destined to be overtaken by supranational forces and the rise of new kinds of identity politics.

What is certain now is that any comprehensive analysis of current economic, cultural and political developments cannot avoid addressing the attendant role of nations and nationalisms. Likewise, as is evident from political rhetoric, media debate, public emblems and ceremonies as well as prominent aspects of popular culture like sport, music and the arts, the discourse of nation-ness and the symbolism of nationhood continues to occupy a focal position within our daily lives. It is highly dubious that the impact of such forces is decreasing in general terms, even if among certain social circles or groups there is a feeling that national loyalties are outmoded. Consequently a growing number of scholars from a wide range of academic disciplines have been encouraged to explore the reasons for the continuing strength of the nation as a social force, and they have produced an ample, and increasingly sophisticated, literature which needs to be critically assessed and made available to a wider audience. Up until the 1980s, writing on these themes appeared to be a relatively marginal academic exercise of interest to only a few. Now it has moved nearer to the heart of the social and political sciences, as well as figuring prominently in other fields such as cultural and media studies and literary criticism. In this we find a reflection of the political and intellectual temper of the late-twentieth and early twenty-first centuries, when at least as many have discovered an enthusiasm for the nation, and nationalism, as have sought to criticize or denigrate them.

Our aim in this book is to understand this literature, and to distinguish among the main approaches taken within it. We are particularly interested in evaluating it in terms of what it has taken from, and added to, social theory. To aid our exposition, each main approach is illustrated through detailed consideration of the work of one or two key social theorists, who have made major contributions to moving the discussion forward. Because our principal concern is with the sociological analysis of nations and nationalism, we have devoted some space to placing this literature in relation to other leading contemporary sociological preoccupations, with class, gender, 'race' and ethnicity, which constitute the other main forms of identity with which nationality might seem to compete. More likely, as our arguments show, these kinds of identification blend with one another in increasingly complex ways. There is little about the contemporary political scene to suggest that this is about to change; instead, there are many signs of 'born again' nationalisms taking root, while at present it is difficult to conceive of conditions in which states will not feel compelled to act in the 'national' interest, and to be seen to be doing so, in the eyes of most of their citizens. Compared to the power exerted by ideas of nationhood, fledgling attempts to construct notions of 'global' citizenship and to build transnational institutions and movements, including those which are avowedly anti-nationalist, seem comparatively feeble, and attract the adherence of the few. Therefore we have no reason to expect that the analysis of nations and nationalism will lose any of its urgency in the years to come, or that it will cease to play an important part in the progress of social theories.

CHAPTER 1

Theorizing Nationalism: Contrasting 'Classical' and 'Post-Classical' Social Theory

Surprisingly, nationalism does not feature prominently as a topic in the history of social theory. Taking some of the general overviews as a guide (see Elliott, 2001; H. Anderson and Kasperson, 2000), it would seem that none of the key figures dwelled at length on nationalism as a specific matter for investigation. Compared with the attention given to other social phenomena, such as class, religion or the state, nationalism has been curiously neglected. As Billig (1995) points out, it rarely gets more than a passing reference in undergraduate sociology textbooks, which can be regarded as barometers of what constitutes the mainstream of work. Nevertheless it would be disingenuous to suggest that social theorists have wholly neglected nations and nationalism. Since the 1960s, and especially from the 1980s, there has been a marked growth of interest in theorizing nationalism. This has been fuelled by political changes taking place across the world in which nationalism has played a prominent role. It has also been encouraged by academic developments, notably the efforts of a number of important scholars who have given discussions of the sociological dimensions of nationalism a much-needed impetus.

However, Billig's assessment still stands. The study of nationalism is not yet part of the mainstream of social theory. A few studies, such as Billig's own, and that of Benedict Anderson (1983), have made the crossover into the mainstream, but a good deal of the content of the discussions among those working directly on nationalism has not. In turn, participants in these discussions, especially in what we term the 'classical' debate, have often been cautious, even sceptical, about the relevance of mainstream social theory for their work. So students of social theory turning to the study of nationalism for the first time will rarely encounter writers with whom they are already familiar. They may find it difficult to fit the issues at the heart of most discussions of nationalism into the theoretical frameworks acquired as part of their wider grounding in social theory. Consequently, the study of nationalism can appear esoteric, requiring a specialized knowledge and using a language and conceptual apparatus entirely its own. This is especially true given the impact of an enormous range of historical and case-specific literature, the general outlines of which are often buried within a mass of detailed erudition.

A main concern of this chapter is to show that this need not be the case. There may be truth in Anthony Smith's (1983) observation that the study of nationalism requires an inter-disciplinary training; nevertheless students of social theory ought to feel at home within this field. Nationalism, along with the nation and national identity, are thoroughly sociological phenomena, and how we think about them should not differ greatly from how we think about other aspects of society. As with any other subject studied by social theorists, analysis of nationalism as a social phenomenon involves, among other things, consideration of the structural forces that contribute to its occurrence, and reflection on the ways in which people use the category of 'nation' to interpret the social world, just as they might use other familiar categories, such as 'class' or 'gender'. Of course, the content of the discussions is rather specific, but still we can employ knowledge gained in other areas of social theory (and, indeed, other disciplines) to make sense of nationalism.

This chapter provides a broad introduction to the study of nationalism by social theorists. At the outset, we ask why, unlike scholars in other disciplines, social theorists came to discuss nationalism only relatively recently. Given its impact on the lives of so many people, this lack of theoretical attention is perplexing. We suggest this relative silence is a consequence of particular ways of theorizing 'society'. Thereafter, our main aim is to provide a guide to some of the broad developments in theoretical studies of nationalism. In particular, we will distinguish between 'classical' and 'post-classical' approaches to nationalism. In doing so, we will show how debates on nationalism parallel, and sometimes are explicitly informed by, broader currents of social theory.

Developments and consequences

It was historians and scholars of international relations, not social theorists, who emerged as the prominent figures in the early development of the study of nationalism. In the first half of the twentieth century, historians such as Hayes (1931), Kohn (1944), and, in the period after the Second World War, Snyder (1954) and Shafer (1955) provided encyclopaedic surveys of the differing forms of nationalism found across the globe and throughout history. Others like Cobban (1969 [1944]) and Carr (1945) were preoccupied with exploring the significance of nationalism for contemporary international relations. Although sociologists such as Ginsberg (1962 [1935]), Wirth (1936) and Znaniecki (1952) made significant contributions during this period, undoubtedly the real advances were being made within history and international relations.

The reception given today to these early scholars is largely critical. Introducing his revised edition of *Imagined Communities*, Benedict Anderson dismisses their work, on the grounds that additions made to the literature since the early 1980s 'have, by their historical reach and theoretical power, made largely obsolete the traditional literature on the subject' (1991, p. xii). Anthony Smith (1996a, 1998) is more generous in acknowledging the contribution of this early generation of scholars, although he too criticizes the absence of general theoretical models from their work. From the perspective of the social theorist, much of this early work on nationalism is deeply unsatisfying. The studies are concerned mainly with analysing the ideology of nationalism, rather than with determining what might have led to its rise and spread. Some refer to the social or sociological influences on the type of nationalism claimed to exist in different countries. For instance, Kohn's (1955) conceptualization of 'eastern' and 'western' nationalisms accords some explanatory significance to the relative strength of national bourgeoisies. With the exception of E.H. Carr, however, whom Gellner (1994a) cites as an inspiration for his own work, none of those writing in the first half of the twentieth century offers anything approaching a general theory of nationalism. Reading this early work leaves one with little sense of what happened to transform people's sense of the world so fundamentally that they came to identify with, and be moved by, the idea of the nation.

Nor do we get a great deal of assistance in addressing these issues from the more sociological contemporaries of these early writers. Our intention here is not to engage in any detailed discussion of the limited contribution made by the classic social theorists, whose work is discussed extensively by Anthony Smith (1983), Guibernau (1996) and James (1996). However, it is necessary to note that, like so many of their generation, Durkheim, Weber and Pareto were influenced in their writings, to varying degrees, by nationalist thought and politics. Richter argues for example that Durkheim's life and thought 'take on added significance when they are related to the events of the Third Republic' (1960, p. 172). Yet, despite living through a period in which nationalism was emerging as one of the most powerful forces of the modern age, these writers had relatively little to say about it. James refers to the 'poverty of theory' in this area (1997, p. 83). Much the same can be said of later generations of social theorists, who also were plainly aware of nationalism's impact. Many were critical of its 'aggressive' elements, yet shared with Durkheim and Weber a view that the nation was a sociological reality, and that, with some qualifications, groups of people could be referred to as sharing a 'national character'. Writing in the 1930s, for instance, the British sociologist Ginsberg spoke of the need to overcome nationalism but remarked that 'no doubt national character is a reality in the case, at any rate, of long-established nations' (1962, p. 252). Elsewhere, he seemed comfortable to speak of populations as if they formed unified, homogeneous nations. Contemporaries of Ginsberg, such as the 'critical theorists' of the Frankfurt School, were touched more directly by nationalist excesses, yet displayed no interest in investigating nationalism as a general phenomenon.

It is impossible to say with certainty why social theorists neglected nationalism, even when they were so conscious of it. Perhaps they underestimated its appeal for the masses, and thought its influence would dissipate quickly. The tendency to treat nationalism as a passing phenomenon, with shallow roots in society, has been a recurring feature of sociological analyses (Hastings, 1997). Berlin notes this, in relation to the social theorists of the nineteenth century (1998, p. 599). In his view, with the exception of Durkheim, the 'prophets of the nineteenth century' failed to anticipate the impact of the progressive 'centralisation and bureaucratic rationalisation' which industrial progress required and generated; against the upheaval and disaffection brought about by this change, the appeal of the 'old, traditional bonds' was powerful (1998, p. 600). Marxists, who have routinely dismissed attachment to the nation as a form of false consciousness, are especially vulnerable to the charge levelled by Berlin.

However, if this assessment fits some of the thinkers to whom Berlin refers, it does not apply to them all. Berlin concedes that Durkheim understood correctly that fundamental changes to social structure and social values 'deprived great numbers of men of social and emotional security' and created a need for 'psychological equivalents of the lost cultural, political, religious bonds which served to maintain the older order' (1998, p. 601). Undoubtedly Durkheim (1979) appreciated the capacity for increased individualism and weakening of collective values, and advocated policies (for example, in the field of education) to promote the cohesiveness of the nation. Max Weber also held that the turn to ideology, including nationalism, could be understood as an attempt to escape the emergent rationalization of society (A.D. Smith, 1983; P. Anderson, 1992a; Imhof, 1997). Smith remarks that, for Weber, nationalism was an antidote to 'the soulless and mechanical rationalisation which threatened to engulf the world' (1983, p. 33). While Berlin's comment was not intended to stretch to twentieth-century social theorists, we do find some who espouse the views to which he refers. Ginsberg reflected the opinion of many liberal thinkers when he expressed his hope that people might recognize the 'need for diverting the rush of its [nationalism's] crude and primitive emotions into a calmer and deeper current of feeling towards the rational good of humanity' (1962, p. 256). Similarly, in the aftermath of the Second World War, Cobban writes, in memorable terms, that there were many for whom nationalism was 'like a survival of a dead age, the ghosts of Garibaldi, Mazzini, Byron, Bolívar, come back with a faded scent of nineteenth century liberalism to haunt an age in which all that they stood for no longer has any right to exist' (1969, p. 13). Berlin's strictures do not apply so strongly to the theorists of the Frankfurt School, since although their work on nationalism was confined largely to studies of Nazism and its origins, they made it a primary concern to grasp the mass appeal of this type of ideology (Held, 1980; Calhoun, 1995).

A more persuasive argument is that social theorists have been guilty of taking nations and nationalism for granted. Anthony Smith attributes this tendency to the fact that sociology's origins can be traced to national societies in which there existed a 'firmly entrenched sense of nationality' (1983, p. 25). Only in countries such as Germany and Italy, not unified until 1870 and 1871 respectively, and therefore in which the existence of a coherent national identity was arguably more problematic, did sociologists afford nationalism greater consideration. Smith adds that while sociologists have studied 'society' as a bounded territorial unit – the 'nation-state' – they have failed to acknowledge that the 'study of society was always *ipso facto* the study of the nation' (1983, p. 26; see also McCrone, 1998). His charge finds direct resonance in the more recent work of Billig, who suggests that sociologists do not bother generally to define what 'society' is, assuming that readers of sociological texts already know the answer. In the few instances where the concept is defined, it is done in such a way as to be difficult to distinguish from the concept of the nation, namely 'as peoples with a culture, a limited territory and distinguished by bonds of interaction' (1995, p. 53).

The gist of the argument put forward by Smith and Billig is that sociologists – and, though they do not say so, we would include social theorists more broadly – have failed to recognize the nationalism of the national societies in which they live and write. Nations and nationalism become a focus for research only when the 'society' they are studying is (*a*) not their own or (*b*) where rival nationalisms are openly to the fore of social circumstances, a situation usually regarded as 'pathological'. Billig describes this attitude in characteristically pithy terms: 'if sociological nets are for catching slices of social life, then the net, which sociologists have marked 'nationalism', is a remarkably small one: and it seems to be used primarily for catching exotic, rare and often violent specimens' (1995, p. 43). Maybe Billig's work, which has received more attention than Smith's earlier contribution, will encourage greater self-reflection on the part of social theorists as to how they write about 'culture' and 'values' in relation to 'society'. Ironically, however, as we will argue below, even some of the writers who acted as torch-bearers for the study of nationalism, at a time when it remained at the margins of social theory, can be accused of reifying the idea of the nation.

Smith and Billig go some distance towards explaining why the study of nations and nationalism has remained a minority pursuit among social theorists. The explanation can be supplemented by the suggestion that, among leading social theorists, nationalism was not viewed as being linked directly enough to the key forces of change that brought modern societies into being. Sociology emerged as a discipline dedicated to the study of modern, industrial society, and from the beginning one of its central concerns was to explain the structural processes giving rise to this new society, and the human consequences of the transformation. Nationalism became a notable feature of this new landscape. Indeed, Heilbron (1995) argues that, following the French Revolution, social theory in England and France acquired more of a national emphasis. Yet nationalism itself was not considered to have played a significant role in bringing the industrial society into being. According to Guibernau (1996), many of the early theorists were concerned with building general theories of social evolution, and nationalism was not seen as being integral to the main vehicles of change identified by Marx (the mode of production), Durkheim (the division of labour), and Weber (rationalization). Although Guibernau does not refer to Parsons, a similar argument might be made in relation to his modernization theory. Equally, for Marxists, whose concern has been with capitalism rather than industrialism, nationalism is located within the superstructure, and is not identified among the principal forces of change even by those, such as Gramsci and Althusser, who attribute relative autonomy to the ideological sphere.

Social theorists, therefore, have not been terribly helpful in making sense of nationalism, at least not until the last thirty years or so. In some senses, contemporary theorists are still addressing questions to which earlier generations, especially early modern sociologists, failed to attend satisfactorily. To adapt a familiar phrase, they are engaged in a debate with the ghost of classical social theory. Thus, the 'classical' debate surrounding nationalism mirrors concerns and modes of talking about social phenomena that were characteristic of the work of early social theorists such as Durkheim and Weber. Given the absence of a substantial legacy from these earlier generations, perhaps it is not surprising that the concerns of the first theorists to come to terms with nationalism as a sociological phenomenon should shadow those of early modern social theory. Later scholars have had to establish an appropriate sociological framework for thinking about the conditions that contribute, in general terms, to the rise and spread of nationalism, and about what explains the appeal of the idea of the nation. The extent to which they have succeeded in doing so is reflected in the influence of the 'classical' debate within general textbooks on nationalism (see A.D. Smith, 1998; Özkirimli, 2000). What, then, are its principal features?

'Classical' approaches to the nation and nationalism

After a lengthy period of neglect by social theorists, the second half of the twentieth century witnessed a burgeoning interest in the sociological dimensions of the nation and nationalism. Nevertheless, this has progressed in fits and starts. The 1950s and 1960s saw the publication of a number of broadly sociological studies, some of which stand the test of time better than others. Deutsch's (1966) *Nationalism and Social Communication*, originally published in 1953, and Kedourie's *Nationalism* (1960), stimulated some discussion, but their contemporary influence is negligible. Others fared better. Many regard Gellner's essay on nationalism in *Thought and Change* (1964) as marking the real beginning of the modern study of nationalism. Yet even allowing for its impact, it did not immediately stimulate more concerted social theorizing, and the 1960s and 1970s remained a largely fallow period. The notable exception is the work of Anthony Smith, whose prolific studies (1971, 1973, 1976, 1979) represent the most substantial contribution to general social theory during this period.

The 1980s marked the turning point. By the middle of the decade a number of studies had emerged that, taken together, gave form to what is now recognizable as the core debate within the 'classical' approach to the nation and nationalism (Armstrong, 1982; B. Anderson, 1983; Gellner, 1983; A.D. Smith, 1986). These studies were consolidated during the 1990s by further works integral to the core classical approach (Greenfeld, 1992; Llobera, 1994; Guibernau, 1996). This body of writing has greatly enriched our understanding of the nation and nationalism as social phenomena. To assess the collective legacy of the classical approach from the perspective of social theory, three core questions about nationalism can be considered: when and how it developed, and why it remains so significant.

Arguments about when nationalism developed are marked by a fair degree of consensus among classical theorists. Most hold that nationalism is a relatively recent phenomenon, dating from the late eighteenth and early nineteenth centuries. The central elements of nationalist ideology, among them the assertion that the world is divided into nations and that ultimate loyalty must be given to the nation, seem to have arisen only from the eighteenth century. Similarly, most classical theorists would date the nation's existence as a mass phenomenon, in which a national community is conceived as transcending social divisions, from the same period. Only rarely is it suggested that earlier social groups, in the medieval era or before, perceived themselves in this way. Anthony Smith (1995a, p. 54) argues that the ancient Jews may be regarded as the 'significant exception' to the rule. Where significant differences of opinion do arise is over the issue of whether or not the *roots* of nationalism can be traced back to earlier periods. Inevitably these disputes are underpinned by contrasting accounts of *how* nationalism develops. Answers to these questions give the core debate amongst classical theorists of nationalism much of its substance. In broad terms, they fall into one of two camps: 'modernist' or 'ethnicist'. While most commentators apply the term 'modernist' to one of the competing positions, the label given to the other varies. Anthony Smith (1998) refers to this group – which includes himself – as 'ethno-symbolist', a usage shared by Özkirimli (2000). Gutiérrez (1997) describes Smith's approach as 'historical-culturalist'. Our preference for 'ethnicist', a description borrowed from Hutchinson (1994), is merely arbitrary.

Modernists view the nation and nationalism as phenomena whose roots do not extend back beyond the period associated with the major socio-economic processes of modernity, such as industrialization, capitalism, the rise of the modern state and major related political changes, notably the French Revolution. The leading figure in this approach is Gellner, whose work combines elements of Durkheim, Weber and the social anthropological tradition in which he was trained. In contrast to ethnicists, who hold that nationalism has roots in pre-modern ethnic identities, Gellner argues that nationalism derives from the requirement of industrial economies for a workforce with at least a basic, generalized education, such as is provided by the centralizing nineteenth-century state. The new public culture that is created and reinforced by the state becomes, for the majority of the population, their national culture. Because industrialization does not proceed evenly, groups of a different culture who reside within a recognizable common territory (such as a region of a larger territory or a country within a multinational polity) but who are excluded from the benefits of modernization on the grounds that they belong to the wrong culture or 'race', or who resist assimilation into the dominant culture, counter-nationalism becomes a tool of resistance. The twin focus on economic and political forces found in Gellner's work is shared by other modernists, such as Giddens (1985) and Mann (1986). Others focus less closely on the rise of the nation-state, but place the accent on similarly modern forces such as capitalism, or, in Benedict Anderson's case (1983), 'print-capitalism'.

Ethnicists do not necessarily take issue with the modernity of nationalism or nations as such. Their leading exponent, Anthony Smith, maintains that while nations may be modern, their origins are not, but can be traced to earlier *ethnie*, to use his preferred term. For Smith, the maxim is that the forces described by modernists transform these *ethnie* without destroying them. Many survive the long haul into modernity, to become the basis upon which modern national identities are built. Modernizing processes, such as the development of a bureaucratic state and accompanying economic and cultural 'revolutions', may convert ethnic cultures into national cultures (A.D. Smith, 1991), but it is never the case that nations are 'invented', as some modernists claim. This argument has been subject to considerable criticism, as we shall see, but also has its supporters. Llobera, for instance, arguably bolder than Smith in speaking of the existence of fledgling national identities in medieval Europe, maintains the ethnicist line when he argues that nations 'cannot be created or invented *ex nihilo*. However, national identity may be submerged by the vagaries of history and may have to be re-created by an active intelligentsia in the modern period' (1994, p. 220).

Differences of opinion between modernists and ethnicists over the 'when' and 'how' of nationalism also inform their approaches to why nationalism attracts such widespread support. It is possible to point to a loose federation between certain modernists and ethnicists in the way they refer to how nationalism meets needs for security and 'community' (see Giddens, 1985; A.D. Smith, 1995a), but further probing reveals characteristically different takes on the matter. For ethnicists, the appeal of nationalism is that it draws on the familiar. Though the mass of the population may need to be 'reminded' of their historic identity, in times of uncertainty, or in situations where economic and political resources are distributed unevenly, 'peoples will fall back for comfort and inspiration upon those ethnic ties and symbols, memories and myths that have so often in the past supported and guided the historically separate populations of our planet' (A.D. Smith, 1986, pp. 225–6). For a theorist like Smith, nationalist movements generate support only because they draw on myths, 'memories' and symbols that are already present. In numerous publications, he stresses the limits to how far nationalists can convincingly rediscover and reinterpret the past.

For modernists, in contrast, nationalism's appeal is rooted in the forces that bring nations into being. In Gellner's case, the culture produced by a centralized education system provides people with their ticket to participate in the economic and social life of the national society in which they reside. The increasing significance of such cultures in industrial society contributes to the growing importance of national identity. As he argues:

> If a man is not firmly set in a social niche, whose relationship as it were endows him with his identity, he is obliged to carry his identity with him in his whole style of conduct and expression: in other words, his 'culture' becomes his identity. And the classification of men by 'culture' is of course the classification by 'nationality'. It is for this reason that it now seems inherent, in the very nature of things, that to be human means to have a nationality (Gellner, 1964, p. 157).

So having a national identity comes to be valued in modern societies due to sociological forces, rather than because of any desire for stability and a sense of belonging. As Gellner says: 'men do not become nationalists from sentiment or sentimentality ... they become nationalists through genuine, objective, practical necessity, however obscurely recognised' (1964, p. 160). The argument that national identity becomes important through the impact of certain novel forces is typically modernist. We might go further, and say that for modernists the appeal of nationalism stems from the social forces that enable the nation to be felt as a horizontal community (B. Anderson, 1983), rather than from the ethnic content of nationalism. In Anderson's case, nations, first and foremost, are 'print communities'. There are parallels between Anderson's statement that 'print-language is what invents the nation, not a language *per se*' (1983, p. 122) and Gellner's insistence that culture be understood 'anthropologically', and not normatively.

These writers are discussed more fully in later chapters, but for now let us emphasize two particular contributions they have made. The first is of a more general nature. Arguably the most significant 'classical' contribution has been to illuminate the sociological dimensions of nationalism. Compared with the earlier work on the ideology and politics of nationalism undertaken by historians, international relations scholars and political scientists, these social theorists have stressed that we must locate the rise and development of nationalism within a wider sociological framework, dealing with the structural forces and institutional developments that shape social relations. This has enabled them to generate theoretical models that, with very few exceptions, were missing before their intervention. The second contribution is concerned more specifically with social theory. As mentioned at the outset, how we theorize nationalism is not radically different from the way in which social theorists explore many other social phenomena. Classical theories of nationalism address quintessentially sociological preoccupations. Just as the foundations of sociological theory were laid with the examination of the rise and consequences of industrial society, so, too, this transformation has been at the heart of classical debates about nationalism.

Still, these works are not without their critics. In anticipation of our later discussion, let us point to something that unites modernists and ethnicists alike, and which, in large part, distinguishes both from what we will refer to as 'post-classical' approaches to nationalism. It is the manner in which classical theorists speak of the nation as a sociological reality. The core debate about whether or not nations are modern is founded on the supposition that there are indeed human populations today that we can describe accurately as nations, in a way we could not have done two or three hundred years ago. The question is not whether such nations exist, but when they come into being. Anthony Smith, for example, is highly critical of those who would deconstruct away the sociological reality of the nation. For him, as for most classical theorists, nations exist because certain groups of people share elements of a common culture, history and attachment to a 'homeland'. That they do so is regarded as a consequence of the interaction of various sociological forces over time. Whether ethnicist or modernist, classical approaches tend to refer to the nation as a real and unified social group. In speaking of the nation in this way, classical theorists continue a mode of thinking about the nation that stretches back to Durkheim and Weber, and which is characteristic of how mainstream sociology theorizes social groups (see Brubaker, 2002). It is an approach that is being called increasingly into question.

'Post-classical' approaches to nationalism

The period since the early 1990s has witnessed the emergence of a body of work characterized by concerns markedly different from those central to the classical debate. Indeed, in many cases there is very little direct engagement with classical theories, and what commentary there is on them tends to be critical. In Özkirimli's words, the 'common denominator of these studies is their belief in the need to transcend the classical debate by proposing new ways of thinking about national phenomena' (2000, p. 191). These studies can be termed 'post-classical' because the theorists involved seek to redefine the terms of the debate, and pose new and different questions. Even so, ideas at the core of the classical debate still constitute their starting-point, and while many post-classical theorists challenge its methodological and epistemological tenets, this is not universally the case. To give some background to this newer work, we will address three questions. From what areas of social theory do these newer approaches draw? What are the distinctive features of this work? What is the general contribution made by post-classical approaches?

Contemporary approaches to nationalism draw upon three main external sources. The first is research on gender, sexuality, and, most especially, feminist social theory. Feminism has had a significant impact on the way we conceptualize social phenomena across many areas of social theory. In particular, feminist theory has thrown light on the different social experiences of women and men, and also on the ways in which social theorists have been complicit in reinforcing these differences. One of the most original contributions of feminist social theory to the study of nationalism has been to highlight the relationship between nationalist discourses and symbolism and patriarchal practices and ideology. Research in this area has also produced illuminating studies of the connections between nationalism and gendered discourses of sexuality and sexual morality. A growing body of relevant work can be found in journals such as *Feminist Review* and *Gender and History*. While classical theorists such as Anthony Smith (1998) have begun to take on board some of these issues, their handling of this work serves to illustrate the gulf in approach between classical and post-classical theory.

A second source for post-classical approaches, and the most broadly influential, has been 'new social theory' (Seidman and Alexander, 2001). This comprises approaches such as critical theory, cultural studies, post-colonial theory and structuralist/post-structuralist theory. Drawing these different strands together, Seidman and Alexander contend that they have two common features. The perspectives to which they refer are 'post-foundational', in that they make 'decisive breaks from the classical vision presented by the founding figures and, in doing so, have drawn considerably from traditions that were previously viewed as their antagonists' (2001, p. 3). They are marked as well by a shift towards normative issues, in that the 'abandonment of foundational scientific theory has involved a turn to moral reasoning' (2001, p. 9). Students of contemporary social theory should recognize some of the elements involved: an emphasis on difference over universalism, a rejection of 'grand narratives' and a corresponding stress on contextual knowledge, and a move towards discourse and practice at the expense of sociological realism. For Seidman and Alexander, it is a virtue of the new social theory that it marks a 'downward shift', directing social theorists towards 'socially situated' theory (2001, p. 2) rather than metatheory. They refer for example to Brubaker's (1996) 'eventful' account of nationalism, which examines how the state has operationalized the category of the nation. From our perspective, another virtue of new social theory is that it locates nationalism more firmly alongside debates about race, multiculturalism and gender.

While the idea of 'new social theory' encapsulates much of the general tenor of the theoretical work of those operating outside the limits of the classical tradition, it is necessary to make two brief points about its applicability to post-classical theorists of nationalism. Seidman and Alexander draw a definitive line between new social theory and earlier theoretical traditions. Yet some more traditional approaches have shown themselves capable of assimilating epistemological and methodological aspects of the new social theory. Thus, we might point to studies that meld, to differing degrees, aspects of ethnomethodology and phenomenology with themes Seidman and Alexander view as characteristic of new social theory (Day and Thompson, 1999; A. Thompson, 2001; Brubaker, 2002; Hester and Housley, 2002). Secondly, not all post-classical theorists fit neatly within the descriptor of 'new' social theory. Some, such as Billig and Brubaker, are influenced more directly by post-foundationalism than by the 'normative turn'. For others, the emphasis is more definitely on the normative.

This brings us to the third influence on post-classical arguments, which comes not from within what might be viewed conventionally as social theory, but from political theory and political philosophy. We have included theorists working in these fields (Tamir, 1993; Kymlicka, 1995; Miller, 1995) in our discussion of social theories of nationalism because they engage in precisely the kinds of debates that now increasingly concern many social theorists. Even though nations continue to be regarded by many as normal and inevitable features of social life, the existence of multicultural, multi-faith societies raises profound questions about the continuing relevance of ideas of national cultural homogeneity. Virtually all academic commentators now accept that the nation is not a natural and unavoidable feature of social life. Arguments about whether or not it retains heuristic value therefore must involve examination of its normative significance for multicultural societies. Again, links can be made between such examinations of the value of the nation, and the morality of nationalism, and some of the concerns of classical theorists, such as Anthony Smith's 'defence of the nation' (1995a).

What then are the main features of post-classical approaches? Firstly, post-classical writers are less interested in developing the kinds of general historical-sociological theories of the rise and development of nationalism that characterize much of the classical work. This is not to imply that they eschew historical sociology altogether. In an essay on nationalism and democracy, for example, Calhoun (1995) outlines the significance of nationalist discourses for the development of democratic government since the late eighteenth century. Nevertheless, post-classical theory is less focused on the long-term. Billig (1995) notes debates about the origins of nationalism in passing, but his prime concern is with the day-to-day, rather than the broad sweep of the *longue duree*. Elsewhere, Brubaker (1996) adopts his 'eventful' approach to nationalism, rather than one that is 'developmental', as found in the work of Gellner and Anthony Smith. Thus his concern is with:

> Nationness as an event, as something that suddenly crystallizes rather than gradually develops, as a contingent, conjuncturally fluctuating, and precarious frame of vision and basis for individual and collective action, rather than as a relatively stable product of deep developmental trends in economy, polity, or culture (1996, p. 19).

Such approaches to the temporality of nationalism have been influenced by the turn against 'grand narratives' characteristic of new social theory, with its origins in deconstructionist theory. The contributions by Billig and Brubaker are also products of critical reflection on the practice of social theory, in general, and, in particular, on the way in which previous social theorists implicitly reify the nation. Billig's emphasis on the daily reproduction of 'banal nationalism' stems from a concern to show how sociologists have missed the nationalism of their own societies. Brubaker counters the conventional developmental treatment of nations as real entities by showing how they are subject to continual renegotiation across time.

Sensitivity to the danger that social theorists may reify the very categories they are analysing gives rise to studies that treat nationalism as a form of 'discourse'. Rather than reflecting reality, as its proponents claim, nationalism helps instead to organize people into groups, so creating the very boundaries between nations that are regarded often as 'common sense'. Others point similarly to how nationalist discourses naturalize the differential treatment of men and women by the state (Walby, 1996; Yuval-Davis, 1997). These writers prompt us to busy ourselves with unravelling the different histories and different ways of speaking that attach to the 'same' national identity. Such discussions are typically 'post-foundational' in that they (a) reject the idea that we can point to discernible nations, bounded, for instance, by a common culture and (b) concentrate instead on determining how the 'nation' is constituted in various times and places, often via competing discourses of the same nation.

There is another dimension to this reflection upon the 'reality' of the nation. Far from drawing on deconstructionism, it is concerned instead to address the normative value of the idea of the nation as a real community. Miller (1995) argues that even if nations are not real in the same way as volcanoes and elephants – that is, having an existence independent of people's thoughts about them – it is still possible to conceive of a 'common public culture' shared by members of a nation. For this reason, like some classical theorists, Miller believes it is possible to speak of nations as substantive entities. Even so, he considers nations to be 'created and sustained by active processes of thought and interchange among the relevant body of people' (1995, p. 6). Hence a nation is a form of community whose values and identity are the subject of ongoing negotiation and reflection. The very fact that Miller can write of 'defensible', as opposed to 'indefensible', versions of nationality underscores his concern with a type of nationalism that is capable of accommodating individual choices. As he says, '[r]ecognizing one's French identity still leaves a great deal open as to the *kind* of Frenchman or Frenchwoman one is going to be' (1995, p. 45). This advocacy of a conception of nationalism as something that people create together, rather than as a phenomenon over which they have no control, is typical of the post-classical stance. In contrast to classical approaches, there is a broad emphasis on the active role of people in interpreting and making sense of nationalism and national identity. Thus, rather than the 'grand theories' of the classical variety, post-classical approaches are characterized by the 'socially situated' or normative theorizing to which Seidman and Alexander refer.

In the chapters that follow we will return in greater depth to these various ways of thinking about the nation and nationalism. Often, as we have tried to set out in this chapter, they reveal radically different styles of theorizing. Our concern throughout will be to show how the dialogue that develops between these different approaches serves to enhance our understanding of nationalism as a complex social phenomenon. In each chapter, we will take the contribution of one or more key theorists as our point of reference, seek to locate it within the broader current of theory to which it belongs, and show how it adds to our knowledge and understanding of nations and nationalism. We begin with the influence of the Marxist tradition, which contains within itself some of the stresses and tensions between the classical and post-classical approaches.

CHAPTER 2

The Marxist Tradition

> The bourgeoisie has through its exploitation of the world market given a cosmopolitan character to production and consumption in every country. To the great chagrin of reactionists it has drawn from under the feet of industry the national ground on which it stood. . . . In place of the old local and national seclusion and self-sufficiency, we have intercourse in every direction, universal interdependence of nations. And as in material, so in intellectual production. The intellectual creations of individual nations become common property. National one-sidedness and narrow-mindedness become more and more impossible.
>
> *The Manifesto of the Communist Party,* 1848

The Marxist historian Eric Hobsbawm (1990, p. 105) observes that by the 1870s 'nationalism' had become a factor in the domestic politics of virtually every European state. Throughout the continent there was an interest in recording and celebrating the distinctive characteristics of different nationalities. Nationalist movements were springing up in regions where they had never existed before. The disintegration of the Ottoman and Austro-Hungarian empires was having drastic consequences for central and eastern Europe, especially the Balkans. There were stirrings of xenophobia and rabid anti-Semitism in France, Germany and Italy. The last two states themselves had been newly created by the unifying forces of nationalism, out of a melee of different states, kingdoms and principalities. In Britain, the Irish claim to independence was joined by demands for 'home rule' from Wales. The year 1907 saw Norway secede from Sweden. This phase of heightened sensitivity to national issues culminated in the 'Great War' of 1914–18, the first fought explicitly on grounds of national, rather than dynastic, rivalry and around demands for national self-determination. Hopes that the twentieth century would see a new age of internationalism, and even universal harmony, were shattered as very large numbers of men rallied to their respective 'national' flags. Contrary to many expectations, industrial workers proved as susceptible to such appeals to their loyalty as rural peasants and members of the urban middle classes. This was especially exasperating to adherents of socialism who had put faith in the international brotherhood and solidarity of the working class. In this they had been encouraged by some of the most profound thinkers of their age, including Karl Marx and Friedrich Engels.

Marx, Engels and the national question

For Marx and his followers, as for the major figures in classical 'bourgeois' sociology, the nation and nationalism were not central categories of analysis. Marx did not regard them as offering particularly powerful explanations for the things that really mattered. His major preoccupation was with comprehending the economic forces that he believed gave shape to human history, and in particular with dissecting the political economy of capitalism. As a social revolutionary, he had a secondary and more immediately practical interest in the political development of modern societies, but theoretically he was convinced that political processes were pulled into shape by the economic conditions and forces prevailing at the time. The urgent task therefore was to grasp the characteristics of capitalism as a developing economic system, and determine how this constrained the forms of action and political choices open to individuals and social groups. Consequently the monumental investigation of *Capital* (1961), which seeks to lay bare the 'laws of motion' of modern society, contains only passing remarks about relationships between different countries and national economies, although it makes frequent *ad hoc* use of terminology such as 'home-markets' and the 'domain of national production'. The empirical content was drawn mainly from Marx's deep knowledge of Britain, the most advanced capitalist society, and the work is prefaced by the strongly predictive statement that 'the country that is more developed industrially only shows to the less developed the image of its own future' (1961, p. 9). But the *national* constitution of Britain was unexplored, and therefore the part nationalism could, and would, play in future development is ignored. Marx wrote about British government and politics elsewhere, and he was fond of ascribing particular traits and 'national' attributes to the English, such as a 'sound aesthetical common sense' and 'instinctive hatred against everything motley and ambiguous' (K. Marx, 1953, p. 355). However, such assertions were not given the same careful scrutiny and thought as Marx applied to his economic and historical researches. Britain (or 'England' – terms Marx used interchangeably) was even acknowledged to be exceptional, since Marx believed the transition to socialism might be accomplished there peacefully, yet the implications for the strategy of revolutionary politics were not pursued in any depth. This surprisingly unreflective stance is typical of how Marxism's founders handled national variations and the 'national question'. Consequently they have been criticized for leaving 'nothing that could be called a theory of the nationality question' (Kolakowski, 1978, p. 88).

Indeed, the contribution made to our knowledge of the field by the entire Marxist tradition has been widely dismissed. Giddens (1985) asserts that it does little to illuminate the nature or origins of nationalism. Guibernau (1996) explains why it pays nationalism such scant attention; and Nairn (1977) deems this lack of understanding to be Marxism's greatest historical failure. This marginalization of the issue arose because Marxism sought to oust nations and nationalism from the centre of attention, replacing them with concepts and commitments that had more political significance and explanatory relevance. For Marxists, history is defined by the struggle between social classes, not by national rivalries. Classes are generated by the way in which societies produce their material means of existence. While classes change over time, at their heart there is always a conflict of interests surrounding issues of control of production, the manner in which it is organized, and the distribution of its products. The inequality between the principal social classes, and the possibilities for transforming this, and resolving the underlying conflict, supplies the motive force for social change, bringing about successive phases of social transformation. Beside these fundamental economic and social relationships, other divisions and issues, including those revolving around national differences, are regarded as either secondary and derivative, or insignificant.

Despite losing its influence since the political transformations of 1989, Marxism remains a relevant reference point for discussions of nationalism because it offers an alternative vision of social organization to that proposed by nationalists. The challenge goes further than simply relegating nationalism to a subordinate position, since it proposes grounds on which to expect the decline, and eventual disappearance, of nations and nationalism. The weakness of the theoretical reasoning behind this claim, and the empirical disconfirmation provided by the obvious staying-power of nationalism and nationalist movements, explain why even those sympathetic to Marxism in general find this argument somewhat embarrassing.

Class versus nation

For Marx and Engels, the key social actors are classes, and the organizations and agencies representing them. At numerous points in his works, Marx describes processes through which different social classes are consolidated, and become conscious of their interests. The structural pattern of development which they follow, determined by the changing nature of production, is matched, sooner or later, by a corresponding shift in their loyalties: the objective and subjective dimensions of class come into alignment, as classes 'in themselves' begin to act 'for themselves'. Class becomes the dominant form of self-identification. Within capitalism, the bourgeoisie, the owners of private property, and the propertyless proletariat eventually confront one another. These large classes represent general social interests. In fact, the proletariat, as a class that is 'outside' society, having 'nothing to lose but its chains', represents a *universal* human interest in the abolition of inequality and exploitation. Within the capitalist mode of production, workers become reduced to nothing more than their labour, and accordingly, in the words of the *Manifesto*, they have no country, a view Marx elaborated in his commentary on the ideas of the German economist Friedrich List when he wrote that the 'nationality of the worker is neither French, nor English, nor German, it is labour, free slavery, self-huckstering. His government is neither French, nor English, nor German, it is capital' (Marx and Engels, 1975, p. 280). By overthrowing the power of capital, the proletariat would help eliminate national differences even faster than was happening already, with the spread of commercial and industrial influences that paid no heed to distinctions between countries. Capitalism, with the bourgeoisie as its chief agents, had begun the process of demolishing nationality; the working class would complete it.

The development of 'national' perspectives and organizations represented a step towards this destination. The 'ever expanding union of the workers' that supersedes differences between localities, enabling the formation of a class of self-conscious proletarians, replicates the process undergone by other classes. In the case of the ruling class, Marx noted that by the 'mere fact that it is a class and no longer an estate the bourgeoisie is forced to organize itself no longer locally, but nationally, and to give a general form to its mean average interest' (Marx and Engels, 1970, p. 113). Marx explains in a famous passage how the peasantry could not take the lead in changing society because in 'so far as there is merely a local interconnection among these small-holding peasants, and the identity of their interest begets no community, no national bond and no political organization among them, they do not form a class' (1969, p. 334). Thus the generalization of interests up to and beyond the 'national' level is an important element in class formation. It converts disconnected local conflicts into 'one national struggle between classes', the successful conclusion to which will bring about a 'vast association of the whole nation', free of class divisions. This in turn will lead to the dissolution of the nation into a world society organized according to communist principles.

Marx has been held up to ridicule for insisting on both the international destiny of the working class, but also its ability, and need, to constitute itself first as the 'nation'. The key passage in the *Manifesto* was intended to answer critics who accused the communist movement of being 'unpatriotic', by showing how its aim, to be a world-changing force, far exceeded the limits of particular national aspirations. This utopian suggestion was underpinned by a humanistic vision that saw all people as part of the same universal group, ultimately destined to participate in its development on terms of equality and freedom. Admirable though this may be, ethically and politically, it is deeply incongruous with the rigorous social scientific analysis to which Marx aspired. For workers to see themselves as 'workers of the world', at a time when most had barely come to terms with industrial employment in urban conditions, required an inconceivable leap of faith. Hence critics accuse Marx of being blinded by internationalism in the same way he was blind to other basic social divisions, like gender and 'race'. Arguably, the problem stemmed from the abstraction he employed in his analyses, to get at the underlying and hidden mechanisms of social change. His focus on the economic dimension of social organization, and the single-minded pursuit of class as the key social category, resulted in an under-theorization of people's actual social relationships, and the 'lived experiences' they encountered.

In its actual evolution the reality of class was subject to a myriad of local, regional, sectoral and national variations, and workers were never in a position where a single social identity overrode all others. Unfortunately for Marxism, the identity that came closest to doing so was nationality. As expressed by Hobsbawm, 'for most purposes or at most times class exists effectively within the confines of a community, territory, culture, racial or linguistic group or state' – that is, within a potential or actual 'nation' (1989, p. 128). This inability to transcend national boundaries had decisive importance in accounting for the failures of socialism, and its inability to deliver the concerted class action it promised. National divisions were among the most powerful impediments to the development of a 'proletarian' consciousness of the kind Marx and Engels anticipated, just as they thwarted earlier hopes that the 'revolutionary' bourgeoisie might unite to topple the antiquated remnants of feudal and absolutist empires. The efforts Marx and Engels made to grapple with the combination of national and class issues are evident in the writings that surround the European revolutions of 1848 (see Fernbach, 1973). Their inability to resolve the problem is clear. Thus it can be said that 'the Hapsburg monarchy survived the 1848 revolution precisely because of its skill in playing off its subject nations against one another. Marx and Engels, however, completely failed to formulate a policy designed to counter this' (Fernbach, 1973, p. 52).

The historic role of nations

It would have been strange indeed had Marx and Engels failed to pay attention to nationalism, given its growing significance during their lifetimes, but their attitude to it appeared somewhat equivocal, and their legacy is often described as ambiguous (Spencer and Wollman, 2002). They did not take the nation for granted in any theoretical sense, and it is certainly not correct that they regarded it as 'natural' and given (Özkirimli, 2000). Rather, they could be accused of the opposite failing, a tendency to disregard it as insubstantial, no more than a passing episode in long-term social development (Purvis, 1999). Yet at the level of political analysis, nationalism was an important phenomenon, with definite tactical and strategic relevance. As political activists, Marxists, and the working-class movements they espoused, were compelled to take a position on the national question – that is, to determine whether or not to support nationalist demands and objectives, and what attitude to adopt towards the increasingly national institutionalization of frameworks of government and regulation (Hobsbawm, 1977; Benner, 1995). At this level, it is clear that Marx and Engels themselves did not believe there was a single definitive answer. Quite unlike the question whether or not to mobilize behind the interests of the proletariat, which brooked no debate, decisions about nationalism involved making judgements: whose interests would it serve, and of what value could it be in advancing the working-class cause?

The general answer, which provided coherence to the shifting stands they adopted at different times (Nimni, 1985, 1991) lay with whether or not particular forms of nationalism could be considered to assist economic and social development, by helping capitalism to replace feudalism, to 'mature', and eventually exceed its own limitations. As Nimni puts it, Marxism classically combined economic reductionism with socio-historical evolutionism. Nationalism was measured against the standard of an expected and desired pattern of social change, largely bound up with the fate of capitalism. While Marx recognized the existence of some form of 'nation' or national community before capitalism, he tended to regard the development of nations as running in parallel with capitalism's triumph over earlier forms of economy. What was not adequately considered was how far nations were capable of playing a distinct and separate historical role. For Marx, it was a matter of making short-term alliances and adjustments, since in the long run nations and nationalism would prove dispensable. Where nationalism served no progressive purpose, it was likely to be a force for reaction. Notoriously, this resulted in a distinction being made between so-called 'historic' and unhistoric nations, which tended to coincide, although not perfectly, with differences between big nations and small ones.

Borrowing a distinction from the German philosopher Hegel, Engels developed the thesis that historic nations were those that could prove useful in carrying forward the project of human development. This required that they mobilized sufficient resources, and personnel, from within their own bounds, to undertake significant economic and social progress. In class terms, they ought to be able to produce their 'own' fully fledged bourgeoisie and proletariat. Contenders for nationhood that could not achieve this deserved relegation to the ranks of the also-rans, dismissed rather brutally by Engels as mere 'fragments' or 'residues' of peoples. In the context of most concern at the time – the reshaping of central Europe – Germany, Italy, Poland and Hungary had the wherewithal to play a substantial role, whereas many smaller would-be nations, especially among the Slavs, would not merit serious political support. This argument could be advanced on economic grounds, relating to the size of potential industries and markets. 'National' economies afforded a set of walls behind which capitalist development could take place. Later theorists have identified nation-states as the main building blocks of world capitalism, right through to the mid-twentieth century (Wallerstein, 1974; Brown and Lauder, 2001). Alternatively, or more likely simultaneously, large national units offered important political opportunities, providing scope for representative inclusion of a substantial population, through the development of 'rights' attached to membership of the nation. There were also strong cultural overtones to the thesis, suggesting that 'great' nations were more civilized, with more to offer mankind, than smaller ones. For example, despite the political fragmentation of the German-speaking population into many distinct units (including some 39 separate states) 'German' culture, particularly its contribution to political philosophy, was seen as superior to anything produced by other European peoples. Marx and Engels therefore strongly supported the movement towards German unification, whilst opposing the national aspirations of Czechs, Bulgarians and others.

Such views were far from unusual at the time. According to Hobsbawm (1990) they constituted unspoken assumptions for most nineteenth-century commentators. As an advocate of 'national economies', List stated that 'normal' nationality was conditional upon 'a large population and an extensive territory endowed with manifold national resources' (List, 1885, cited in Hobsbawm, 1990, p. 30). From a different perspective, the English liberal theorist, J. S. Mill, suggested that any member of small national groupings, such as Basques, Bretons, Welsh or Scots, would be better off gaining entry to a large and powerful nation, rather than being left to 'sulk on his own rocks, the half-savage relic of past times' (cited in Hobsbawm, 1990, p. 34). The inspiration for the Italian *risorgimento*, Guiseppe Mazzini, planned for a Europe of the Nations consisting of no more than 11 sizeable units. As Hobsbawm points out, such views implied that 'nations' almost certainly would contain members from more than one identifiable cultural or linguistic grouping. There was no assumption that the political or economic limits of the nation would coincide necessarily with the range of a particular language, culture or 'ethnic' category. Opinions of this sort, usually launched from within one of the 'dominant' cultures, were obviously very wounding to anyone identified with the smaller groups, carrying as they did associations of backwardness, incivility, and eventual disappearance through assimilation or extinction. For 'minority' groups, it hurt to be told that your national destiny was to merge with some other, more viable group, even with a promise to continue to respect your differences.

Eric Hobsbawm and the rise and fall of nationalism

Against the views of 'revisionist' neo-Marxists, and anti-Marxists, Hobsbawm has mounted a robust defence of the main outlines of the classic Marxist position. He stands by the proposition that nationalism has no inherent merit and should not be taken on its own terms. Indeed, he believes it to be 'devoid of any discernible rational theory' (1989, p. 119). Its value must be assessed purely as a means towards other, desirable (by which Hobsbawm means socialist), ends. This does not entail complete hostility towards every brand of nationalist politics, but requires a general attitude of scepticism, and a readiness to engage with specific social and political forces that promote particular nationalist interventions. For a historian, it goes without saying that these conditions change over time. Hobsbawm seeks to correct the common tendency to lump together diverse, often incompatible, forms of nationalism as if they formed part of the same phenomenon. His historical reviews are intended to demonstrate how both the social nature of nationalism and its meaning have been subject to change.

For Hobsbawm, nationalism's origins must be sought in the period of state-building accompanying what he calls 'the Age of Revolution' (Hobsbawm, 1962). During this era there emerged ideas of citizenship extending to entire populations within given geographical spaces. Hobsbawm notes that, at least during its early stages, this did not imply any uniformity of language, descent or historical background. These criteria of belonging gained significance *following* the establishment of the 'modern territorial citizen state' (1990, p. 86). The prime example is the creation of modern France, following the 1789 revolution, which introduced the conception of 'universal' rights available to all who were prepared to affiliate themselves to the state and its system of government. Under Napoleon, as was commensurate with the proclamation of the 'rights of man', this state seemed capable of expanding well beyond the limits of any predetermined French nation. Nationalism was a form of state patriotism.

In many respects the French Republic broke very self-consciously with the past, and sought to shed the baggage of pre-revolutionary society (including even its calendar and weights and measures). The contemporaneous society born during the American Revolution also claimed to have severed its links to the past, and seemed to exist *de novo*, indeed as part of a 'new world'. These examples support Hobsbawm's claim that 'the basic characteristic of the modern nation and everything connected with it is its modernity' (1990, p. 14). They encourage his tendency to scorn attempts to trace the roots of nationality back any further. Before this, he insists, 'nation' was used in a confused way to refer to groups defined by an ambiguous mix of place of birth, common descent, or shared customs. Several such 'nations' could occupy the same territory, or coexist within certain institutions, such as universities and religious foundations, without any expectation of self-government or separateness. Only after the political revolutions of the late eighteenth and nineteenth centuries did it become normal to assimilate the state to a distinctive people, and its entitlement to 'sovereignty'.

Hobsbawm's debt to Marx is evident in three main respects. Firstly, he locates the social origins of the claim to nationhood within particular social strata. Secondly, he regards nationalism as an aspect of ideology, searching out ways in which it has been employed in 'conscious and deliberate ideological engineering' (1990, p. 92). Thirdly, this leads him to highlight the extent to which aspects of nationalism have been 'invented' or manufactured, to serve a purpose. For subsequent commentators, this is the most fascinating feature of Hobsbawm's work (Özkirimli, 2000; Delanty and O'Mahony, 2002). It carries rather obvious echoes of the readiness with which some Marxists dismiss the claims of nationalism as no more than 'false' consciousness. At various points, Hobsbawm is tempted into contrasting the illusions of nationalism with the 'real' situation it obscures.

With regard to the relationship between nationalism and class, the range of examples Hobsbawm adduces in his study of *Nations and Nationalism Since 1780* shows that, when it comes to asserting the need for the state to be enlarged or reconfigured to embrace a 'nation', almost any social group can take the lead, including members of royal households, the nobility (for example, in Poland) and the middle classes. However, certain social layers have a special affinity for nationalist ideas and practices. During the heyday of the development of European nation-states, around 1830–80, the liberal bourgeoisie normally took command. The expansion and consolidation of the state and the territory it governed was important for the growth of national economies. Governments assumed responsibility for securing national currencies, systems of taxation and finance, and rules for the allocation and protection of property, all crucially important for business. In these respects, nationalism served the purposes of a rising ruling class, as 'capitalist industrialization [was] pressed forward by a vigorous bourgeoisie' (1990, p. 30). Yet even if nationalism was seized upon by ruling groups primarily as *their* ideological resource, its very nature as an inclusive philosophy spread its impact far beyond them. Appealing to 'national' allegiances proved an effective way of mobilizing the loyalties of the population in general, although Hobsbawm warns that, in the absence of detailed records, exactly what the 'ordinary' person thought about his or her nation remains obscure. Specific cultural elites were important in developing ideas, values and symbols that unified people across lines of language and ethnicity. In doing so, they helped engender the phenomenon of 'mass' nationalism, which had unintended consequences, such as the fusion of concepts of the nation with elements of popular religiosity and superstition. Thus, although nationalism greatly benefited the ruling classes, it could never be regarded as exclusively their property, a merely bourgeois ideology. Instead, it underwent major alterations in content and effects, as it came under the influence of different social and class interests.

In Hobsbawm's eyes, once the bourgeoisie had released the genie of nationalism, it took on an increasingly negative and divisive aspect. A force for emancipation from the old dynastic empires, and implicitly for democratization and popular inclusion, it came to represent instead retrograde reactions based upon weakness and fear. For example, he believes the links between more recent versions of nationalism and racism are obvious (1990, p. 108), as are connections with other kinds of 'fundamentalism'. In line with Marxist principles, that it is alright to give rising classes a hand to complete their historic tasks, but a failure of vision to do anything which aids the forces of reaction, Hobsbawm draws a sharp distinction between these contrasting modes of nationalism: the unifying, developmental, version which prevailed during the age of revolutions, and the more restrictive, xenophobic version which supplanted it. This transformation reflects a shift in the class basis of nationalism. By the later nineteenth century, he suggests, the running was being made by a new tier of state officials and other professional and lower middle-class types, using nationalism to pursue their own narrow material interests – in jobs, and social influence. They monopolized opportunities associated with the growth of state and public employment, excluding potential competitors; their brand of nationalism was restrictive, anti-change and anti-development. Hobsbawm typifies its proponents as having vested interests in controlling access to jobs, such as station-masters, or schoolteachers, through such means as imposing linguistic or nationality tests. Meanwhile, the capitalist class moved on, to more 'internationalist' perspectives. Squeezed between a confident capitalism and the organized strength of the working classes, sections of the middle classes were insecure and defensive, and various forms of nationalism became linked to such 'socially modest but educated middle strata' as provincial journalists, teachers and lesser officials. As a social force, nationalism transmuted from a movement of 'potential state creation whose logical end is the establishment of territorial states' (1990, p. 153) into its later manifestation, a form of class consciousness typical of the petit bourgeoisie. Although remaining politically influential, and sometimes socially explosive, it ceased to be the central factor in historical change that it had been in the nineteenth century. Like Marx, Hobsbawm looks beyond the era of nationalism, explaining that:

> Urbanization and industrialization, resting as they do on massive and multifarious movements, migrations and transfers of people, undermine the other basic nationalist assumption of a territory inhabited essentially by an ethnically, culturally and linguistically homogeneous population. (1990, p. 157).

In these new, 'plurinational' conditions, groups still make strenuous efforts to control access to positions of reward and to exert influence over state decisions, but, significantly, are as prone to do so in the name of ethnicity and communalism as that of nationality (see also Ignatieff, 1993; Castells, 1997). For Hobsbawm, as Marx predicted, nationalism represents a waning historical force.

The nation: 'invented' or real? Debates within Marxism

Hobsbawm believes nationalism must not be taken at face value, because it is related too closely to the pursuit of particular class interests, and much of what it represents is false or misleading. These reservations bear upon his assertion that a great deal of nationalism has been 'invented'. This does not necessarily mean that those responsible are fully aware of what they are doing, or bent upon manipulation and deception; this would be to adopt too crude a model of ideology. Rather, social invention is a response to changed circumstances, needed especially when change is rapid and extensive. Hobsbawm sees nations and nationalism as products of just such a period of deep social change, and not unexpectedly his thoughts turn to the role of innovation within this process. What particularly interests him are the 'invented traditions' that spring up around nations. Here he includes both 'traditions' which are 'actually invented, constructed and formally instituted and those emerging in a less easily traceable manner within a brief and dateable period' (Hobsbawm and Ranger, 1983, p. 1). This embraces practices with symbolic or ritual meaning, repeated in ways suggesting continuity with the past, which work to inculcate appropriate values and norms of behaviour. Examples central to nationalism include the introduction of flags, anthems and emblems; the development of various ceremonies and recurrent events (we might include coronation ceremonies, national pageants, marches and processions); and the symbolic apparatus of monuments and statues, national spaces and significant historic episodes. Many of these purport to be long established, yet have been introduced and embellished at specific times, often surprisingly recently.

It is important to note that such invented traditions are not peculiar to nations. Hobsbawm's discussion of 'mass-producing traditions' is concerned equally with the way in which social classes gather around them their own set of 'traditions' of a very similar kind (Hobsbawm, 1983). Such practices are designed, or at least operate, to bring together large numbers of people into a new kind of consciousness and collective identity. They are directed towards securing cohesion, legitimizing authority, and enabling successive generations to be socialized into the awareness and norms of the group concerned. According to Hobsbawm, the second half of the nineteenth century, continuing into the twentieth century, was an exceptionally fertile time for the manufacture of such traditions. Often the 'traditions' associated with class and nation overlap. The convergence appears closest among the middle classes, whose size and fragmentation make it difficult otherwise for their members to develop a clear subjective class identification. Compared to the workers, they lack a sufficient sense of common destiny and potential solidarity. Unifying symbols of nationhood fill this gap. Thus nationalism appealed most to that 'large intermediate mass which so signally lacked other forms of cohesion' (Hobsbawm, 1983, pp. 302–3); the new or aspiring middle class recognized itself collectively as the 'quintessential patriotic class'. From this viewpoint, there is a symbiosis between the nation and the middle classes – each helping the other to develop a real social existence. In the final analysis, it appears, nationalism is indeed a form of class ideology, the ideology of the middle classes; essentially it competes with, rather than complementing, the socialism attributed to the working class. Others who approach the issue from a similar position to Hobsbawm's reach a somewhat more flexible conclusion. For example, Miliband suggests that nationalism 'more or less strongly seasoned with various other ideological ingredients is available to, and where suitable seized by, any class or group aspiring to statehood' (1977, p. 102). This suggests that different versions of the 'nation' may emerge, depending on which group happens to be in control, and that classes may struggle over the appropriation and interpretation of national traditions.

Writing as he does about the 'invented' aspects of nationalism lends Hobsbawm to the charge that he attributes to nations and nationalism nothing more than rather grand feats of social engineering (Özkirimli, 2000, p. 116). This verdict would be in line with the general view that Marxists depreciate the significance of nationalism by treating it as ideological. However, his argument is actually more sophisticated. Nations do not consist solely of invented or manufactured elements, and those aspects that are invented have not been conjured out of thin air. Rather, modern capitalist society can be said to operate 'not by the wholesale destruction of all that it had inherited from the old society, but by selectively adapting the heritage of the past for its own sake' (Hobsbawm, 1994, p. 16). A similar emphasis on the 'fabrication' that occurs around nations and national identities is found in other Marxist writers. Thus, Balibar notes how myths of origin, and impressions of national continuity, owe a great deal to the history and ongoing work of social construction (see also Chapter 5). In the formation of nations, he explains, many elements come together, including some that are well established, like language, laws and systems of exchange, but in ways that are new. Only afterwards can the resulting combination be made to look as though it was inevitable, or already there. Contingent outcomes are perceived as if they were predestined (Balibar and Wallerstein, 1991). While this means that in some senses nations are a matter of appearances, this is not altogether to deny them their reality.

Balibar shares Hobsbawm's perception that the modern nation-state assumes such importance in people's lives as to subordinate members of all classes to their status as citizens and as 'nationals'. Hobsbawm refers to the modern state as a 'landscape' of institutions and procedures, providing the setting for lives which it largely determines (1990, p. 86). Balibar notes how extensively the state intervenes in the reproduction of the economy, the formation and education of the individual, the preservation of the family and private life, as well as providing security and protection. This leads people to see the state as 'their own' and to conduct their lives and their struggles within its limits. Yet this is not inevitable. Instead, 'the fundamental problem is ... to produce the people. More exactly, it is to make the people produce itself continually as national community' (Balibar and Wallerstein, 1991, p. 93), with a semblance of unity, despite its class and other divisions. This requires the creation of what Balibar terms a 'fictive ethnicity'. He emphasizes that this does not mean it is 'fictional', or illusory. That 'peoples' conceive of themselves as if they had an identity of origins, culture and interests which transcends differences of individual and social conditions is a real outcome of processes of nation formation, albeit sometimes interpreted wrongly as if it was natural and predestined.

Marxism and national politics

The question of the 'reality' of nations, and its political and organizational expression, has long perplexed Marxists. The problem was at the heart of fierce disputes that arose once efforts were made to put the legacy of Marx and Engels into effect, when the theoretical guidance provided by the classics had to be interpreted in the light of actual political structures and events. This was particularly fraught in the context of the dissolution of the old Tsarist Russian and Hapsburg Austro-Hungarian empires.

Significant contributions towards theorizing nationalism were made in these settings from within the ranks of Marxist activists, and during lively debates in the Communist Second International. Some currents of Marxist thought implacably opposed any socialist *rapprochement* with nationalism. Whereas Marx had supported Polish national aspirations, as a way of weakening the hold of Russia, for example, the leading Polish Marxist Rosa Luxemburg saw them as a pointless distraction from the revolutionary cause. While conceding that national oppression gave rise to genuine injustices, she insisted such issues should be resolved after the revolution, when the main, class, divisions had been tackled. In her opinion, the proposition that nations had a 'right' to self-determination was, like all such universal principles, an 'idle petty-bourgeois phrase and humbug'. A nation's 'right' to exist depended upon an assessment of historical and political conditions, and the part it could play in taking 'history' forward. There was no class for which an independent Poland would serve a clear economic purpose (Luxemburg, 1976; Kolakowski, 1978, p. 91).

Luxemburg claimed it was a fundamental mistake on the part of the Russian Bolsheviks to make concessions on this point, because it allowed all sorts of groups such as Finns, Lithuanians and Ukrainians, some of which she felt had no plausible claim to be regarded as 'nations', to withhold support from the revolution, or to make it conditional upon their national liberation. However, Lenin, the Russian revolutionary leader, was convinced that an independent national state was the 'normal' form of political structure under capitalism, and therefore he advocated the right of nations to determine their own fates (Lenin, 1974; Nimni, 1985). Like Marx, who believed the existence of the 'great' nations enhanced the efficiency of social production, Lenin reasoned that this would help develop society's productive forces. However, 'self-determination' meant no more than an ability to express wishes politically; where a democratic bourgeois state already existed, as Lenin thought it did in most of western Europe by the 1870s, he saw no case for further dismantling of political units. In practice, he was very wary of allowing too much scope for the expression of national viewpoints within the Russian sphere of influence, and keen to ensure that the revolution was not undermined by the break-up of the former empire. He assumed that those who stood to benefit from revolutionary economic and social transformation would not exercise any right to self-determination.

The heated discussion surrounding such questions among

Marxists still left it unclear as to what exactly a 'nation' was. Stalin, whose main contribution to Marxist thought was an essay on *Marxism and the National Question*, formulated an answer. He proposed that 'a nation is an historically evolved, stable community of language, territory, economic life and psychological make-up manifested in a community of culture' (1951, p. 8). This 'solution' has been described variously as doing justice to the 'multi-faceted' nature of nations (Nimni, 1985, p. 73) or as merely additive and empirical. Stalin complicated the issue by stating that if any of these elements were missing, then the claim to nationhood would fall. In practical terms, many nations whose existence is recognized in the world today would fail this test; indeed, once it is looked at closely, few could pass it unequivocally. Stalin's attempt to come up with a definition broad enough to satisfy every competing strand in Marxist analysis failed because it could not overcome the inevitable practical reality, that activists were bound to adopt different positions and interpretations according to their different contexts. Where would-be national groupings were relatively distinct and separated in different territories, then the idea of autonomous 'homelands' or even states, seemed plausible. But in much of central Europe, as would be the case in many later post-colonial, and post-revolutionary, situations, there was such a hotch-potch of linguistic, cultural and family connections that territorial partition was too costly to implement. This was particularly true in the Austro-Hungarian empire, with its cosmopolitan capital, Vienna. At this time, the empire was separated into two distinct monarchies, Austria and Hungary, containing a population of some 53 million divided among 15 nationalities including Germans, Magyars, Poles, Croats, Czechs, Slovenes, Slovaks, Ruthenes, Serbs and Romanians. Of this total, around 24 per cent were Austro-Germans, 20 per cent Magyars and 13 per cent Czechs (Nimni, 1991, p. 120). Territorial boundaries corresponded poorly to these national groupings. Arguments about the fate of nations were especially intense among the 'Austro-Marxists' such as Kautsky, Renner and Bauer. Bauer's work, though 'seldom read nowadays' has been described as the most important and substantial Marxist study of the national question (Kolakowski, 1978, p. 285). There have been recent attempts to revive it (Nimni, 1985; Munck, 1985; Stargardt, 1995).

The central thrust of Bauer's account, owing something to his familiarity with the emerging sociological perspectives of writers like Tonnies and Weber, was that nations are constituted primarily in terms of their shared cultures. For Bauer, the maintenance of nationality was a matter of enabling national cultures to thrive. In his view this was not incompatible with economic development, nor indeed with the pursuit of socialism. In fact, he believed that national differentiation would actually increase following the triumph of socialism, since socialism would let the masses participate in the cultural life of their nations in ways that were impossible under conditions of class domination. Stripped of their class connotations, such national differences need not generate conflict. National cultures could coexist, and mingle, as they did in Vienna, without losing their distinctiveness. As to their origins, Bauer explained them as long-term adaptations to the historical and environmental circumstances in which different groups lived (Nimni, 1991). In his eyes this provided his argument with a materialist framework, compatible with central Marxist tenets.

Bauer defined a nation as 'a totality of human beings bound together through a common destiny into a community of character' (cited in Munck, 1985, p. 88). This focus on the nation as a 'community of fate' and the way he used ideas of 'national character' suggest a greater empathy with nationalist sentiments than is found generally among Marxists. For precisely this reason, Bauer was accused of lapsing into 'idealist' and even 'mystical' conceptions of nations as having some inward 'essence' which marked their development throughout history. Bauer's assertion (cited in Nimni, 1985, p. 76) that any German entering a 'foreign' country would immediately perceive people with 'a different way of thinking, of feeling, people who when confronted with the same external stimuli will react differently from the average German' perhaps confirms this. While supporters may insist this must be understood as the result of historical pressures and experiences which help form such distinct characters over long periods of time, and which therefore are amenable to further change and development, talk of the 'destiny' of nations undoubtedly raises the spectre of a determinism which is not just economic, but also cultural and nationalistic. It suggests that as well as a shared past, there is a goal towards which nations move. There are marked similarities with Weber's definition of a nation as a 'community of sentiment' (Stargardt, 1995), but Weber linked this explicitly to an expectation that such sentiments find adequate expression only within their own state formation. It was a prime concern among Austro-Marxists to keep some distance between the nationality question and the organization of the state. As Renner put it, not very realistically: 'We must separate national and political affairs ... We must organize the population twice; once along lines of nationality, and the second time in relation to the state' (cited in Stargardt, 1995, p. 91). Responsibility for economic, social and military tasks would fall to the state, while nationality would provide the focus for cultural and educational matters. Individuals would be able to decide their national affiliations, making nations into the sum total of all who claimed membership. This attempt to take nationalism out of the realm of politics and economics, thus enabling the resumption of 'normal' class relations, flew in the face of orthodox Marxist expectations that the ideological concerns of nationalists would be grounded in underlying differences of economic interest.

In words that would not be out of place in Durkheim's works, Bauer stated that:

> the nation constitutes a social phenomenon. It is not the sum of individuals, but each individual is the product of the nation; the fact that they are all products of the same society makes them into one community. Those qualities that appear as distinguishing features of individuals are, in reality, a social product – and indeed, for all members of the nation, a product of one and the same society – that is what makes a collection of individuals a nation (cited in Nimni, 1991, p. 157).

By this reasoning, national character is 'not an explanation, but something to be explained' (cited in Nimni, 1985, p. 76). It corresponds to the way in which a particular social reality is represented, as the outcome of the common experiences of a community of people who interact over long stretches of time. Consequently, each nation develops its own peculiar forms of law, aesthetics, morality, religion and even science. What is problematic about this argument, from a Marxist perspective, is how the 'common experiences' and characteristics of nationality relate to divisions and antagonisms between classes. Following Bauer, it seems that classes that grow up, as it were, within the same societal environment will share a national orientation. The fear that national cultures might override class differences made most Marxists into opponents rather than supporters of nationalism. Theoretically, Marxism held that differences between classes, rooted in production, were fundamental and insurmountable; any form of national consciousness 'shared' across class boundaries tended therefore to be dismissed either as 'false' consciousness, or as reflecting some imposed dominant (bourgeois) ideology. Renner points towards a more adequately sociological conception of these matters when he writes that the 'national interest of the worker is entirely different from that of the small businessman, the peasant, the official and the manufacturer. What is at stake is to depict the intersection of a plurality of national and economic interests' (cited in Stargardt, 1995, p. 94).

A related, but independent, effort to come to terms with nationalism emerged from the 'marginal' location of southern Italy, where the Sardinian Antonio Gramsci developed his own version of a non-economistic, non-reductionist, Marxism. Hobsbawm, who has surprisingly little to say about Bauer, regards Gramsci as the only thinker who provides a basis for integrating the nation into Marxist theory as a historical and social reality (1982, p. 29). Like Bauer, Gramsci regarded each national community as a unique synthesis of past experiences and present relationships. He wrote of the 'people-nation' and its 'shared life' (Gramsci, 1971, p. 418), and the possibility of the formation of a 'collective will' capable of representing the aspirations of the community as a whole. Except by force, dominant groups or classes within such a community would not be able simply to impose their own interests upon others; they had to adjust to, and make allowance for, competing interests and perspectives. If successful, they could achieve 'hegemony', or maintain social leadership, but only through some accommodation to the popular will. Through interaction within the framework of the nation, the identities of the various classes could influence and shape one another. Nationalism as such did not 'belong' to any specific class. In this respect, Gramsci moved beyond the instrumental view which orthodox Marxism took of nationalism, and recognized its independent influence upon politics and culture. It could not be 'reduced' merely to the economic, nor manipulated to secure some preconceived version of class interests. In his ability to address 'the specificity of the national phenomenon at its cultural and political levels' (Nimni, 1991, p. 111), as in other aspects of his work, Gramsci escaped the limits of classical Marxism. Even so, because he remained basically a Marxist, Gramsci held to the view that the final determinant of all this lay in production. Despite his sensitivity to the problems of southern Italy and the prejudice shown towards southerners by their northern compatriots, he accepted the necessity for the subordination of minority nationalities within the nation-state, as had happened in France after 1789 with the suppression of Breton, Basque and Occitan minorities. Like other Marxists, Gramsci's primary preoccupation was with the formation and development of states, especially states capable of furthering working-class interests, rather than with the realization of nations. Only national communities able to support a 'proper' state merited attention, and aspects of national identity and nationalism that did not revolve around the state and its activities tended to be overlooked.

Gramsci's ideas had enormous influence on the development of 'Western Marxism' (P. Anderson, 1976), and those following him have tended to reproduce this convergence between nation and state, producing theoretical grounds on which to expect the emergence of the nation-state as the dominant modern political form. A leading exponent of the Marxist theory of the state, Poulantzas, reiterates many Gramscian themes. Like others, he laments the absence of a genuine Marxist theory of the nation, and the damage done by underestimating its importance (Poulantzas, 1978, p. 93). Under capitalism, he suggests, the state 'exhibits a tendency to encompass a single, constant, nation', while social and economic developments tend to be channelled along national lines. This is not because nations exist somehow 'outside' and before capitalism, forcing it to adapt to them. Rather, modern nations, like modern states, develop together with capitalism, with a shape determined by the advancing social division of labour. The nation 'becomes the anchorage of state power in society and maps out its contours. The capitalist state is functional to the nation' (Poulantzas, 1978, p. 99), while at the same time the state fixes the nation's frontiers. The state installs a unified market, and system of government, and renders individuals into 'members' of the nation. Time and space are reorganized into 'national' shape, to form the matrix within which people exist. The past is reinterpreted as a 'national' tradition, and set of 'national' memories, which may involve removing all traces of other possible 'national' pasts. At the extreme, this can take the form of genocide, or expulsion of 'foreign' bodies. As the first modern example, Poulantzas cites the 1915 massacre of Armenians within the new Turkish state.

Conclusion

The theoretical language and approach Poulantzas uses, with its roots in structuralist Marxism, is quite unlike the work of Hobsbawm, and yet it is possible to see many points of correspondence between their analyses of nations and nationalism, exemplifying their common debt to the Marxist tradition, and the founding ideas of Marx and Engels. Both seek to reach an accommodation between a conceptual apparatus that stresses economic relations, and class structures, and the practical political importance of national differences and divisions. For Poulantzas, the formation of both state and nation reflects the balance of forces between conflicting social classes, while class struggles occur within the setting of concrete national configurations. Although working-class practices may presage the eventual passing of the modern nation – and, allegedly, history is always on the side of the working class – even so, they take shape within a national framework. Hence, only national roads to socialism are possible, and there are many of them, rather than the single predestined route laid down by Marxist orthodoxy. This means Marxists must come to terms with the practical influence of nationalism.

Nevertheless, it is not easy to hold the balance. Oftentimes, both practically and theoretically, Marxism seems to have broken on the rock of nationalism, and this has encouraged some prominent theorists to move away from Marxism, on explicitly nationalistic grounds. Attributing the 'conflagration of Marxism as theory and socialism as practice' to this blind-spot about nationhood, Debray (1977) adopted a primordialist view, that nations represent an invariant and primary determinant of history, built almost into the human genetic code. Debray argued that national instincts would always furnish one of the deepest layers in motivation, and so provide an inevitable practical starting-point for political action, even among socialists. In the same year, Nairn (1977) produced his critique of Marxism's failure to address the centrality of nationalism to modern world development, and to recognize as an 'elementary truth' that nation had always triumphed over class. Responding to Nairn, Hobsbawm (1977) warned that what were presented as theoretical advances in this area had a strange knack of underwriting the particular national aspirations and values of the relevant theorist. In Nairn's case, his reading of world history provided justification for Scottish independence. Debray contended that there was little hope for radical transformation of Europe, except under French leadership. For Hobsbawm, such attempts to revise Marxism represented a surrender to nationalism and its political objectives. Others (Blaut, 1982) likewise see such developments from within Marxism as conceding too much ground to the nationalist interpretation of social processes, which treats nationalism as an autonomous force, and the nation as an independent reality. Disagreements as to how far Marxists should go in letting nationalism off the leash of economic determination continue to play their part in efforts to reconstruct Marxism after the demise of communism (Benner, 1995; Makdisi *et al.*, 1996; Nimni, 1991). Unreconstructed Marxists might be forced to conclude that history has settled the argument, since nationalism seems to have demonstrated vastly greater political longevity than Marxism.

CHAPTER 3

Modernity and Modernization

When general social conditions make for standardized, homogeneous, centrally sustained high cultures, pervading entire populations and not just elite minorities, a situation arises in which well-defined, educationally sanctioned and unified cultures constitute very nearly the only kind of unit with which men willingly and often ardently identify.

(Gellner, 1983, p. 53)

The dominant approach to nationalism and the nation coming out of classic sociological theory emphasized the specific conditions of their historical formation, and hence their close association with modernity. Nationalism has been interpreted as assuming importance as a fundamental social feature at a particular time and place, under the influence of a number of special circumstances, and therefore as likely to remain in being only while certain necessary social conditions persist. In other words, although conceding that its role has been of paramount, and even growing, importance in terms of the actual historical development of human society, most sociological opinion treats nationalism as neither 'natural' nor permanent and inevitable. In this respect there has been a notable confrontation between sociological interpretations and nationalist perspectives. Among so-called 'modernists', the central claim is that nationalism, nation-states, and even nations themselves, are products of modern historical developments. Exactly how this has come about, and precisely when it happened are subject to considerable disagreement, so that estimates of the origins of nationalism vary by several centuries.

Among several variants of the modernist position, the work of Ernest Gellner has a particularly emblematic status, due to the clarity and sweep of its broad outlines, and the pugnacious way it was presented. The modern study of nationalism is said to have begun with his contribution (McCrone, 1998, p. 64), which constitutes 'the most important attempt to make sense of nationalism' (Özkirimli, 2000, p. 128), notable still for its complexity and originality (A.D. Smith, 1983, p. 109). At the same time, critics assert that Gellner was captivated by a 'ponderous and static conceptual apparatus' (Kitching, 1985) and that ultimately his work amounted to no more than a series of 'evocative and inspired but unsustained insights' (James, 1997, p. 149). Gellner himself remarked that his position was simple, but distinctively new. His discussions of nations and nationalism formed part of a much larger body of work (1988, 1994b) that sought to formulate a general theoretical outline of the socio-historical development of mankind, compatible with the principles and values of liberal individualism. In doing so, he made a highly influential contribution to what has become a large and mature 'developmentalist' literature, tracing the long-term economic, cultural and political influences leading to the gradual emergence of nations and nationness (Brubaker, 1996, p. 19). Most major works of the closing decades of the twentieth century belong to this tradition (including those of Anderson, Giddens, Hobsbawm and Mann). Writing about the development of British sociology during this period, Perry Anderson (1992b) cites Gellner as one of a number of scholars producing such general socio-historical frameworks, each with something interesting to say about nations and nationalist belief systems.

As with many key figures in this field, there is a direct connection between Gellner's interest in nationalism and his personal biography. By origin, Gellner was Czech and Jewish, raised in a German-speaking household but educated largely in English. His experiences of displacement and forced dislocation from his homeland during the 1930s inevitably coloured his interpretation of nationalism and its consequences. Although written with an air of intellectual detachment and reasonableness, his work is pervaded nonetheless by a horror of nationalist excesses, vividly conveyed by the language he uses to portray nationalist thinking. For Gellner, nationalism is an entirely intelligible, and socially constructive, phenomenon, explainable in wholly rational terms, which all too easily lends itself to abuse and extremism. He felt this particularly likely to occur when people became attached to the ideas, or ideology, of nationalism, for which he had little time or patience. He noted that the intellectual content of nationalism was generally unsophisticated, and prone to error and deceit. As set out by nationalists themselves, nationalism offers a false prospectus. This does not prevent it from exercising a tremendous and usually unhealthy influence over both certain sorts of intellectuals and the general public. Yet Gellner argues its true importance lay elsewhere, as a vital condition for social development and progress. Contrary to appearances, nationalism in Gellner's sense was a civilizing influence, although readily vulnerable to distortion. In his view, nearly all other interpretations had missed this crucial point.

If the 'ideas' of nationalism are misleading or dangerous, then wherein does its efficacy and success lie? For Gellner, understanding nationalism is not primarily about examining the validity of beliefs, but about observing and explaining certain kinds of social practice. As a belief-system, and prevailing mind-set, the dominance of nationalism was tied intimately to the nature and existence of the nation-state, and its role in fostering economic expansion and social development. Since the nation-state took shape in particular historical conditions, the same was true for nationalist practices; they also had to be explained as the product of specific historical forces. The way in which Gellner developed this argument took a strongly functionalist twist. For him, nationalism represented the appearance of a particular style of behaviour and form of relationship with others, which accompanies the transition to modernity. Nationalism was a way of behaving, of *being* national, and of conducting oneself as a member of a nation-state, and nation. These all came into existence together, as part of the development process.

Although Gellner has been hailed as a lonely figure, keeping an interest in nationalism alive when all around took it for granted, his position developed in close conjunction with, and differentiation from, arguments advanced by other academics, including colleagues at the London School of Economics, especially his contemporary Elie Kedourie and one of his doctoral students, Anthony Smith. Gellner disagreed with the former with respect to the weight to be given to nationalism as a set of influential ideas, and with the latter about the extent to which nations had to be seen as deeply rooted forms of social existence. Responding to these positions, he carved out what he regarded as an appropriately materialist argument, which attributed the rise of nations and nationalism to specific economic and social conditions, typical of a given stage of human development. There is common ground here between Gellner and the Marxists, since both seek to explain key political and social changes in terms of their material setting, and the conflicts these generate; but Gellner does not accept Marx's version of social change nor his analysis of the primacy of production and class struggle in driving development forward.

Social change and the birth of nationalism

The main themes of Gellner's approach were assembled in a seminal essay on nationalism that appeared in *Thought and Change* (1964). In this he distances himself both from those who anticipated the imminent disappearance of nationalism as an outdated social and political force, and those who took the opposite stance, attributing nationalism to deep-seated natural or 'dark atavistic forces', bound to shape human societies for an indefinite future. His response is to assert that nationalism is a relatively new force, which would remain powerful and effective just so long as it represented a 'genuine, objective, practical necessity' (1964, p. 160). It was not an aspect of the human condition that would last for ever, nor did it correspond to some inner need of the human psyche. Rather its existence needed to be explained in terms of the circumstances that had called it into being. This implied debunking many of the cherished claims central to nationalist philosophies and historiographies, a task in which Gellner took some pleasure.

According to Gellner, nationalism 'preaches and defends continuity but owes everything to a decisive and unutterably profound break in human history' (1983, p. 125). The historic break in question was the appearance from out of the background of an agrarian setting of a modern society based upon industrialism. The major contrast preoccupying Gellner therefore is that between the characteristics of a 'traditional' social order associated with societies dependent upon agriculture, and the requirements of an industrial society. In his view, nationalism, and the nation-state itself, took shape together during the transition between the two situations, the broad features of which he borrowed from the standard sociological comparisons made by Durkheim, Marx and others, between the relative stability of the agrarian order, and the fluidity and change associated with industrialism. To understand how this generates nationalism and national consciousness involves grasping fundamental differences in the two kinds of social structures, which Gellner spelt out in his concise but closely argued books *Nations and Nationalism* (1983) and *Nationalism* (1997), using a wide range of historical resources. These are handled illustratively, to back up fairly abstract assertions about change, rather than examined in close detail. That Gellner did not look closely at how nationalism took shape in any concrete instance leaves him open to criticism from historians for sometimes misconstruing facts, and generalizing beyond the evidence.

In the agrarian situation, Gellner argues, an immensely solid structural basis of social organization exists, with a high degree of stability, which makes cultural variations and differences among members of the society appear relatively unimportant. The majority of the population are embedded within numerous and varied forms of local cultures, more or less self-contained, and practically taken for granted, while the various elites (military, religious and political) which govern society operate at a level above and removed from these local distinctions. The culture of the ruling groups is distinct from that of the masses, but since they barely interact with one another these differences do not matter greatly – indeed, such marked cultural differences help to reinforce and stabilize fixed social distinctions. Members of the society occupy well-defined social positions and 'know their place', and their values and beliefs correspond closely with their social location – they are particular, rather than universal, in their reach. In such contexts, it is acceptable for those who rule society to speak a different language, adhere to different norms and standards of behaviour and morality, or even follow a different religion, from those whom they govern, without this disturbing the settled order of things, in the same way as different local communities may represent sharply discontinuous social worlds. Either individuals are confined within one such narrow milieu, or they learn to adjust to movement between multiple, but well-defined, social settings, each with a distinct set of social rules and principles. The 'tightness' of the social structure enables them to live with variations in style and codes of conduct. A description of such a society, which fits Gellner's arguments rather well, is given by Giddens (1984, p. 165), discussing fifth-century China.

The rise of modern industry breaks down these compartmentalized structures, both local and hierarchical, and makes similarities and differences of culture far more significant. Indeed, Gellner formulates the shift as one *from* structure *to* culture, making the cultural framework central to an understanding of modernity. He posits an inverse relation between structure and culture as principles of social organization. Gellner's analysis of social change has obvious affinities with Durkheim's account of the transition from mechanical to organic solidarity, or from segmental to integrated social orders, while he also makes ready use of Tonnies' distinctions between *gemeinshaft* (community) and *gesellschaft* (association) (Durkheim, 1964; Tonnies, 1955). His analysis of the agrarian social order tallies with the account Marx provides in the *German Ideology* and the *Grundrisse* (Marx and Engels, 1970; 1973). In other words, there is nothing particularly exceptional in Gellner's approach to the modernization process, nor in the concepts he employs to understand it. What is novel is the connection he makes between these themes and nationalism, and his insistence upon taking nationalism seriously as a key attribute of modern societies.

Likewise, Gellner's description of industrial society has much in common with its depiction by others among his contemporaries who also wished to cast doubt upon the validity of the Marxist analysis of the limits of capitalism, and the implied necessity for socialism. Gellner's conception of industrialism resembles that held by Aron (1967) and Kerr *et al.* (1973), who agreed that industrialization brought about a basic 'convergence' towards certain essential technical and occupational norms, which would prevail in all industrial societies, no matter what their social heritage or political orientation (see Kumar, 1988; Noble, 2000). For Gellner, as for these other writers, industrialism, rather than capitalism, is the fundamental determinant of modern social change, and this directs his attention more towards the characteristics of industrial organization and labour in its abstract 'commodified' form than to the nature of property and its pattern of ownership and distribution. Consequently Gellner is relatively uninterested in the class dimensions of society. Instead, he focuses on the part played by social elites, especially intellectuals and those with high levels of formal education, in establishing the 'cultural' tone and direction of industrialism. They are responsible for developing and upholding the forms of scientific, technical and organizational knowledge that are essential for the proper working of a rational, industrial economy. They also help formulate the 'everyday' rules of conduct and investigation such an order requires. The development of a body of complex, formalized, but practically oriented knowledge leads towards eventual mass participation in educational processes which bring everyone into contact with this version of 'high' culture, enabling it to supersede the 'low' or folk cultures previously associated with narrow local or stratified communities. Hence all members of society come to share certain basic assumptions and premises, or inhabit the same cultural environment.

Nationalism signifies this state of being, and Gellner notes how people come to 'love' their culture, seeing it as an essential condition of their well-being and functioning, because it underpins and makes possible their economic existence. They also see all who share in this culture as people having the same potentiality and fate, a fate denied those who have not gained admission to it (compare B. Anderson, 1983). A sense of solidarity with those who are culturally alike, and of separation from those whose culture is different, typifies the industrial society.

While bearing traces of historical materialism, Gellner's is an essentially liberal view of society, concerned with the way in which individuals locate themselves within social structures. Gellner agrees with Marx that the economy is basic to modern social organization, but rather than the mode of production he puts the labour market at the heart of the modern economy. The effective operation of an industrial economy requires a level of individual and social mobility that is incompatible with the persistence of the extreme differences of belief and conduct that existed in the past. Industrialization therefore has a levelling effect, making all members of society more alike. In particular, labour markets require people to show great adaptability with regard to occupation and skill, and a high level of mobility between jobs. This is possible only given their observance of some general and shared social and technical standards. As the social relationships of the market supersede those of kinship and locality, generic, rather than specific, qualifications and capacities take precedence, and criteria of achievement replace those of ascription. More generally, the extent to which individuals in modern societies are able, and required, to escape the limits of fixed social roles ensures that a large proportion of social interactions take place among relative strangers, and have a transitory, optional, quality. Again this makes it imperative that those concerned should inhabit a shared 'culture', by which Gellner means a style of conduct and expression and body of symbolism, providing a framework of agreed understandings and expectations/meanings. Language plays an important part in this, as the main vehicle of shared norms and understandings, and it is no longer viable for rulers and officials to use a language different from that of the ordinary person. Nor can local communities or other spheres of social interaction shelter behind barriers of non-communication and incommensurable social differences. There is a flattening effect, as the 'great tradition' of society as a whole swamps the 'little traditions' of closed social worlds.

Participation in such 'high' culture, with its standardized and elaborated codes, makes everyone into a 'clerk' (a literate, numerate, socially adept individual), and at the same time into a nationalist. The lines between distinct cultures, which set practical limits to the extent of mobility and mutual understanding, come to define the boundaries of economies, and nations. Successful involvement in contractual relationships among anonymous publics demands that people 'speak the same idiom', understand things in the same way, and share a common conceptual currency. This makes people aware of their nationality, and acutely conscious of their differences from others, with whom they cannot communicate as readily. The limits of the nation are found where the break-lines occur between cultures, or these rather large-scale standardized behavioural 'idioms' of conduct. Meanwhile, mobility weakens the differentiation between social layers typical of traditional societies, and societies take on the shape of 'internally fluid, culturally continuous communities', or nations. Universalism supplants particularism, at least within each such national community, and people become accustomed to moving among a largely anonymous population of individuals who, in this key respect, are like themselves.

So, Gellner posits a series of links between the nation-state and nationalism, centred on an essentially functional relationship between the needs of a modern economy, with its interchangeable units of labour, and the formation of a uniform culture. This makes people aware of their common situation and identity, and stimulates sentiments of loyalty and 'love' for their nation. This is why, famously, he asserts that nationalism does not awaken nations to self-consciousness, but invents them where they did not exist (Gellner, 1964, p. 168). The state plays a key part in defending the emergent 'national' culture, and in providing the educational system that perpetuates it. In fact, Gellner suggests the scale of the educational system sets limits to the size of a viable self-reproducing society, and hence to the feasible range of a national culture. The convergence of these different aspects underpins the core political principle Gellner identifies with nationalism, that of an expected congruence between territory and culture.

Here the 'practical' necessity for nationalism as a mechanism of social integration passes over into a mobilizing sentiment and aspiration. All being well, the boundaries of the national space should correspond to those of the unifying culture, and the individuals who make up the population within that space should participate equally as members of the nation. Once established as a norm, this principle ensures that all individuals will have a unique national identity, and this comes to seem as normal and inevitable as breathing. However, contrary to appearances, this is not given, in the nature of things, but an outcome of these peculiar, industrial, conditions. Nationalism plays a necessary part in enabling the flowering of the industrial economy, and all its benefits. It is characteristic of Gellner's approach that nationalism is treated as something individuals acquire through living within a particular economic and social order, rather than viewed as an expression of the essential nature of a collectivity or some form of 'mass' psychology.

Industrialization, modernization and the formation of nations

Gellner's thesis is worth rehearsing at length, because it contains much that is typical of modernist explanations of nationalism, and also conveys, in exceptionally clear terms, some of the common themes within the theories of industrialization and modernization that were prevalent around the middle of the twentieth century. The emergence of what sociologists consider to be the modern form of society has been so closely interrelated historically with the rise of industry that it is hard not to elide their impact. Many would agree that 'modern society is industrial society; to modernize is to industrialize, and to embrace all of its consequences' (Kumar, 1988). In the theory of 'industrialism', these consequences spill out from the central core of new economic relationships, and new production methods, to bring about a comprehensive social overhaul; all aspects of society are transformed as the systematic effects of change at the centre are assimilated. The sharp dichotomy between 'traditional' and 'modern' (or industrial) societies has been adopted widely by social theorists, and treated as if it involved a definite qualitative rupture in social patterns, rather than a prolonged transition.

Notions of modernization of this kind exercised tremendous influence across an entire intellectual stratum, especially in the United States of America (USA) (for example, Lerner, 1953; Apter, 1965; Levy, 1966; Inkeles and Smith, 1974). They formed an integral part of the framework of Parsonian structural functionalism, where they provided the main interpretation of social change, and were grafted into a strongly evolutionary model of social development

(Craib, 1984; Alexander, 1995). In this approach, basic social issues were analysed in terms of the competing pulls of differentiation and integration. Following Durkheim's lead, modern society was characterized as increasingly specialized, and functionally diverse, but bound together by shared norms and values and common institutional frameworks (Durkheim, 1960; Parsons, 1964, 1966). Nationalism played a positive part in this, as an enabling device for integration. Arguably, nationalism provided the main functional alternative to, and substitute for, religion in doing this at a sufficiently general, 'societal' level. Furthermore, unlike religion, nationalism was a 'secular' framework, which could be construed as promoting a virtuous, 'civic' system of beliefs and values, potentially free of the excesses associated with religiosity. Parsons' notion of the 'polity' as the functional subsystem responsible for government carried this normative sense of the state working for the common good towards the achievement of shared goals. Empirically, polities tended to equate to nation-states. Thus nationalism could be regarded as making a powerful contribution to the management of cultural integration within societies that were highly differentiated socially and institutionally (Delanty and O'Mahony, 2002).

As well as Gellner's focus on coordination of the labour market, other systems of coordination could be invoked in a similar way to explain why the universalization of culture was a functional exigency of modernity. Deutsch's theory of communication (Deutsch, 1966) was one such approach. According to Deutsch, membership in a 'people' consists essentially in the 'ability to communicate more effectively, and over a wide range of subjects, with members of one large group than with outsiders', that is, to share a culture (1966, p. 97). Raising the threshold for effective collaboration among large numbers of people involved enlarging and updating the mechanisms of communication, with the same homogenizing effects as Gellner describes. As well as the economic reasons for this, integration within a more demanding system of political participation, or new forms of administration and supervision of daily life, could also be seen as necessitating more consistent and reliable modes of communication across greater numbers. Numerous specific processes and mechanisms could be nominated as playing a part in this construction of 'national' domains: the transformation of markets; the growth of bureaucratic organizations; the political inclusion of individuals as citizens, or as military conscripts. Armies, bureaucracies, productive and mercantile organizations could all take their place as possible vehicles for nation building. The beauty of the concepts of industrialization and industrial society is that they bundle these processes together in a set of interlocking relationships considered to form part of an overall societal system. It appears to be a matter of choice where one begins and ends the analysis; eventually, everything is connected. In a fully formed nation-state, we are told, 'economic, political, military and ideological power networks tend to be co-extensive and to establish fairly clear boundaries at the national frontiers' (Mouzelis, 1991, p. 70). The corresponding weakness in the approach is a lack of precision in spelling out the causal connections, and an evasive tendency when it comes to putting theory to the test.

The idea of nationalism as a progressive, integrative force, able to smash through barriers of traditionalism and help people along the road towards modernity, led to a preoccupation among modernization theorists with such 'nation building' – helping 'developing' societies to establish themselves as fully fledged, modern, national entities, reaping the benefits already gained by more 'advanced' societies. This project promised to carry many other positive features. Involvement in a nation appeared to imply greater levels of individual participation, autonomy, citizenship and democratization (Bendix, 1965). Such interpretations had obvious affinities with 'liberal' or 'Western' norms, and cultural self-definitions. Modernization was virtually synonymous with Westernization, and with the instillation of the 'civic' virtues that seemed to grow up with the development of the nation-state. Modernization theories and practices had a political, as well as social scientific, momentum – as Alexander contends, they provided a 'metalanguage that instructed people how to live' (1995, p. 13). Kerr *et al.* spoke in glowing terms of how the peoples of the world were everywhere on the march towards industrialism and its fabulous rewards. In the process, they would take on perforce whatever national identities were most fitting to them, not least because 'the industrial society is an open community encouraging occupational and social mobility. In this sense industrialism must be flexible and competitive, it is against tradition and status based on family, class, religion, race or caste' (Kerr *et al.* 1973, p. 35). Implicitly, for all societies, the norm to be achieved was the Western-type nation-state, epitomized by the USA.

In line with Gellner's arguments, for the vast majority of people, nationalism as a modernizing force promised a widening of social

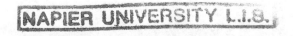

and political horizons, whereas for the minority, who had enjoyed the privileges of ruling and elite positions, it entailed a certain narrowing down from the vastnesses of imperial or dynastic ambition to the humbler limits of the nation and its national culture. The nation constituted a more inclusive grouping than virtually anything most people had experienced before (with the possible exception of the church, or community of religion). For ruling groups, often it became more exclusionary, as nationalism's rise squeezed out the possibility of culturally diverse, compartmentalized, social formations. The emergence of the modern nation-state to dominance has been identified in social theory with the destruction of localism, as societies acquired a more unitary character. People on the national peripheries are drawn increasingly into the centre as 'local segmental organization gives way to the development of structurally and functionally differentiated national arenas' (Mouzelis, 1991, p. 70). This occurs literally, in major movements of human population from rural to urban settings, and from agriculture to industry, as well as intellectually, through a shift in orientations and attachments to the national scale. As Gellner puts it, the emergence of modernity 'hinged on the erosion of the multiple petty binding local organizations and their replacement by mobile, anonymous, literate, identity-conferring cultures' (1983, p. 86). We are left in no doubt as to the progressive value attached to overcoming the limitations of 'parochial', narrow, localized social commitments. Yet, as in many of Gellner's remarks, there is a strong sense of tautology, or at least restatement of the same essential point, since an open, mobile society, more or less, is what Gellner *means* by modernity.

A theory of such proclaimed generality as Gellner's is bound to attract its share of comment and critique (J. Hall, 1998). As indicated already, the telescoping of history into a set of functional linkages of a very general kind makes it relatively easy for Gellner's critics to challenge the time-sequence implied by his account. This has been done on a variety of grounds: that nationalism or the nation-state form existed well before industrialism, perhaps as early as the fourteenth or fifteenth centuries (Greenfeld, 1992; Hastings, 1997); that their progression is not necessarily coordinated with the level of industrial development (Mann, 1995), since some of their strongest manifestations anticipate rather than follow industrialization, for example in Germany and Italy during the nineteenth century, or more recently in many countries of the 'third world'; that the mass educational system supposedly necessary to foster and generalize national sentiments did not come about until long after industrialization – in Britain, for instance, not until the 1870s – whereas early industrialism was compatible with high levels of illiteracy (Guibernau, 1996).

These concrete historical weaknesses can be tied to the flawed logic of functionalism, which reverses the normal direction of explanation by seeing the end state or outcomes of processes as somehow responsible for their occurrence, glossing over the difficulties and contradictions encountered in achieving them. So, the fact that cultural unification can be said to aid the operation and efficiency of modern economies and societies does not *explain* how it has come about, or do justice to the often incredibly painful experiences it entails. To explain this adequately requires an understanding of people's actual motivations and actions, even if the knowledge and ideas that inspire them might seem 'objectively' incorrect, or even foolish. Gellner chooses to portray nationalism in ways that appear almost wilfully remote from how people ordinarily would perceive it. Compared to the passion and dedication it evokes, his vision of an 'ardent' commitment to a 'well-defined, educationally sanctioned and unified culture' with which this chapter opens seems remarkably bloodless. This refusal to engage directly with nationalist beliefs and actions leaves a gap in his explanation, which others have sought to fill by showing how nationalists themselves might construe and act upon the very links he conjectures (Laitin, 1998; O'Leary, 1998).

Gellner's status as a functionalist is contested. He accepted the label for himself, while denying this implied any teleological intent. Supporters suggest he should be interpreted as proposing a looser, 'elective affinity', between nationalism, industrialism and modernity (Mouzelis, 1998). Nevertheless, the arguments are expressed too broadly to cope adequately with the detail and complexity of the very varied relationships that exist between actual versions of nationalism and the relevant features of their social surroundings (Breuilly, 1993). Too many consequences, some of them contradictory, have been attributed to nationalism for them to be rolled up together as meeting the same social needs, or performing the same underlying function. For example, some versions of nationalism strongly favour change, demanding a radical shake-up of the existing social order; others aim to uphold or reassert the values of 'tradition'. Hence nationalism can figure as both progressive and reactionary. Likewise, Gellner's efforts to make sense of the rise of nationalism in industrializing nations fail

to connect with the significance of the later 'separatist' nationalisms which have appeared from within fully industrial nations,
among groups like the Scots, Basques and Québécois (Tyriakin and
Rogowski, 1985; McCrone, 1998). These criticisms point to the need
to differentiate between types of nationalism, rather than looking
for a universal form with a single explanation. However, as we
have seen, Gellner's analysis of nationalism is singularly content-
free. His concern is more with its role in integrating modern societies, than with scrutinizing its precise meaning, or distinguishing
between its many varieties. Other modernists can be criticized on
similar grounds.

State-oriented nationalism

As presented by Gellner, nationalism is oriented towards the state
and its functions, particularly its role in sponsoring mass education
and literacy. Other modernists treat the state similarly, as providing the shell within which nationalist sentiments take shape. This
does not mean that nationalism is explicitly 'about' the state, or
that it worships or celebrates that state, although some versions of
nationalism do so (Mann, 1988). Rather, the nation-state constitutes
a point of reference for action and belief in a way that states in pre-
modern circumstances did not. As we saw with some Marxist
arguments in the preceding chapter, modern states reach much
further into everyday life. However, a recurring problem with
modernism is why, when all is said and done, the units which
come to dominate the political landscape should take the particular form of nations. Why such fusion between the role of the state,
popular sentiment, and a consciousness of nationality? The idea
that sentiments take shape *within* the developing state, as it 'grows'
to attain national dimensions, goes part way to answering this, as
can be seen in the contributions of two leading modernists, whose
work overlaps considerably, Giddens and Mann.

As a leading proponent of the sociological category of modernity (Giddens, 1990), Giddens endorses the view that nations and
nationalisms are distinctive properties of *modern* states, and thus
formed relatively recently (1985, p. 116). He also distinguishes
modern societies from the more traditional social orders that
preceded them, though his primary criterion for this separation is
not the degree of change and stability they exhibit, but the nature
of their class systems. Traditional societies he terms 'class-divided',

because they rely upon political means, including coercion, to ensure that unequal economic relationships between social groups persist, whereas in modern 'class societies', exploitation and inequality are built more directly into economic relationships, through labour contracts and management systems. Structurally separated from the economy, modern states are able to concentrate more exclusively upon 'political' and administrative tasks. This distinction reworks the contrast between feudalism and capitalism, putting the stress on the differing role of the state in the two systems. In Giddens' view, it is also a contrast between 'pre-national' and national state forms. Nationalism grows in association with an increase in the range of the state and its capacity to integrate relationships across space and time, cutting through other forms of interconnection associated with economic, religious and cultural relations. Hence:

> At the same time as they generate and consolidate centralized power, 'drawing in' various aspects of social activity within their scope, states stimulate the development of other ties and interconnections which cut across the social and territorial realms over which they claim sovereignty (1981, p. 196).

In these terms, nationalism is the 'affiliation of individuals to a set of symbols and beliefs emphasizing communality among the members of a political order' (1985, p. 116). As it stands, this definition is too general, since it could apply equally well to the regime of a city-state or even a rural commune. What distinguishes nations from other forms of human grouping is the range and depth of the felt 'communality'. Like other modernists, Giddens sees nationalism as constituting a more inclusive sense of identification, transcending earlier commitments to the smaller groupings associated with 'tribalism', where emphasis is laid upon shared genealogical descent, or other forms of localism, like attachment to particular geographical places or communities. It also implies a heightened orientation towards the state and its activities. Economic developments certainly help bring this about. For instance, the spread of capitalism enables the 'freeing' of peasants from fixed relationships to the land, which also 'frees' them from dispersal in separate, localized communities (1985, p. 145). This links closely with the central role taken by urbanization in such developments, promoting administrative centralization, and fomenting national consciousness. Sentiments of national belonging tend to spread from cities, especially cities that acquire status as national capitals, and centres of political power. These arguments are reminiscent of Marx and Engels' discussions of the rise of the bourgeoisie, and indeed of class consciousness in general, which they regard as similarly transcending narrow exclusivisms, and therefore of the debate as to whether 'class' and 'nation' represent competing or complementary forms of identification. Giddens acknowledges that the development of the modern state is 'intertwined with' that of industrial capitalism, and adds that capitalism provides a much-needed dynamic (profit-driven expansion) lacking from theories of 'industrialism'.

However, in accounting for the rise of nationalism, Giddens places far less stress upon the logic of economic development than he does on the growth of political, and especially administrative, control. Under capitalism, the conceptual and institutional separation of 'politics' from 'economics' (and the related separation of the public from the private sphere) is fundamental. Rather than the mechanisms of the labour market, or even production in general, underpinning national development, it is the means of surveillance and regulation, and the role of the state, which holds the centre of Giddens' analysis, as is clear from his attempt to define the nation-state. He does so in a way that strongly echoes Weber, as:

> a set of institutional forms of governance maintaining an administrative monopoly over a territory with demarcated boundaries (borders), its rule being sanctioned by law and direct control of the means of internal and external violence (1981, p. 190).

This focus on political control and the state is reiterated in Giddens' comment that capitalist 'society' is a society 'only because it is also a nation-state, having delimited borders which mark off its sovereignty from that claimed by other nation-states' (1985, p. 141). In other words, the political, rather than economic, dimensions of social organization define its space. All societies are associated with claims to the legitimate occupation of particular territories or 'locales', and their members have feelings of common identity; but the introduction of precise boundaries around national territories is seen as a specifically European innovation. Modern societies are unlike their predecessors in having such a high degree of territorial integrity. The maintenance and defence of borders therefore assumes exceptional importance, both in terms of the management of their own populations, and in relationships with other states. Hence the development of nations is inseparable from the formation of an international system of nation-states, and from the way in which modern societies are considered to be self-contained, independent entities. The 'nation' itself is constituted as a collectivity of people who occupy a clearly demarcated territory, subject to a single administration, 'reflexively monitored by both the internal state apparatus and those of other states' (1985, p. 116).

Giddens' conclusion that nationalism exists only when states have succeeded in obtaining a unified administrative reach over such sovereign territories means that nationalism for him is 'essentially a phenomenon of the late eighteenth century and after'. Before that, states exercised uneven and discontinuous control over territory; in many ways their influence failed to penetrate into the everyday life of those nominally under their rule. Even the earliest and most continuous of nation-state formations, such as France and England, displayed no more than a 'few core components' of nationhood (1985, p. 119). As late as the seventeenth century, nationalist sentiment in France was 'rudimentary and regionally specific'. However, with the full emergence of modern societies, nation-states became pre-eminent as 'bordered power containers', so that at some level, even if only that of practical consciousness, rather than explicitly articulated discourse, their members were able to share a range of concepts to do with national sovereignty, and with their rights and obligations as citizens. That is, they had taken on board a sense of national, as opposed to local, familial or religious identity. Nationalism is the 'cultural sensibility of sovereignty' (1985, p. 215). Like Gellner, Giddens sees this as providing a surrogate for the 'lost' forms of attachment and belonging which vanished along with traditionalism, and a significant basis for modern individuals' sense of who they are (their 'ontological security'). So 'nationalism engenders a spirit of solidarity and collective commitment which is energetically mobilizing in circumstances of cultural decay' (1985, p. 215). To this extent, nationalism represents and feeds upon an 'attenuated' form of primordial sentiment (as defined by Geertz, 1975). We have a hint here within Giddens' analysis of the potential for return of those 'dark forces' of nationalism that invariably evoke loathing among theorists of modernism.

Mann also regards nationalism primarily as a response to the development of the modern state, with an emphasis on the political and military impulses that this has involved. Only under modern conditions does the state become sufficiently relevant to the social life of the mass of the population for it to 'stably form the focus of many persons' identities or ideologies' (Mann, 1988, p. 45). When this occurs, society becomes capable of being mobilized in the guise of the 'nation'. While this may take many centuries to evolve, the key developments occurred in Europe around the eighteenth century, with the advent of societies organized for systematic large-scale warfare, requiring the gathering, equipping and funding of very substantial forces. This placed enormous pressure on the machinery of the state, which was 'tasked' with securing the necessary means, via taxation and conscription. Hence Mann does not link the expansion in state activities so closely to the economic pressures of capitalism or industrialism, but more to geopolitical rivalry and conflict. In these circumstances, the concept of the 'nation', consisting of all who share a common identity and destiny, serves a purpose both for the state, which invokes such ideas to justify asking people to fight for it, and also for the people, who respond by demanding a say over the aims and performance of the state. As members of 'nations', they possess rights and obligations. Thus nationalism as an ideology, which according to Mann everyone agrees is a modern phenomenon, has an underlying democratic impulse, because notionally everyone who belongs to the nation has these basic qualifications. This is why nationalism asserts the political principle of a correspondence between state and nation (or, the 'people'). In practice, as we will see in later chapters, only certain sections of the population may actively enjoy these entitlements – such as men of a certain age and with certain property qualifications. But where the thrust for 'representation' is thwarted, as it was in the decaying empires of central and eastern Europe, the resentment which builds up can lead to highly aggressive forms of nationalism, including assertions of the need for independence and self-rule.

Mann's conception of nations, and nationalism, summed up in the following passage, brilliantly encapsulates many of the modernist themes:

We cannot define nations ethnically or racially. Nations do not derive from the same 'blood' or 'ethnic stock'; their genealogical histories are myths; they have no 'natural' existence or rights to their own states . . . Indeed, before the nineteenth century there were very few 'nations'. Yet in the nineteenth and twentieth centuries nations were indeed created, and almost all states came to legitimize themselves as 'nation-states'. Wars were fought between these states, often with the enthusiastic support of the 'nation'. So what are nation-states, if they are not ethnic groups? They are *citizen* states, states of mass political membership, the first states in history in which all adult inhabitants have been active participants. (Mann, 1988, pp. 150–1, stress added.)

The forms of nationalism Mann identifies include those devoted very explicitly to the elevation of the state itself, a type he terms 'nation-statist', usually confined to individuals especially closely connected to the state, such as soldiers, officials, and those who have been through institutions of higher education.

Nationalism and uneven development

Modernity has two faces, a face that smiles and a face that frowns. One promises freedom, abundance and fulfilment; the other the pathological dangers of anomie, alienation and isolation (Kumar, 1988; Bauman, 1991). As with modernity, so with nationalism. The image of nationalism as resembling the Roman God Janus, looking forward to the future, and back towards the past, is much utilized (Nairn, 1997; Giddens, 1981, p. 192): for every virtue attributed to it, there is a plausible countervailing vice. Giddens attributes much theoretical confusion to nationalism's dual character, while noting the importance of disentangling various forms of nationalism, and making sure especially that the 'first' nationalism of western Europe is not taken for a model with universal applicability. This has been a problem with modernization approaches, where sometimes nationalism is portrayed as a benign influence, diffusing smoothly outwards from its initial point of origin.

From Gellner's perspective, people are forced into being nationalists by the imperatives of economic development and social change. They do not opt to become nationalists, in some form of willed voluntarism; neither is it an innate response that comes to them automatically. In similar vein, he depicts the spread of nationalism, and the nation-form itself, as pressurized by the massive structural forces unleashed by industrialism. In a striking and much repeated metaphor, Gellner likens its progress to a power of nature, a tidal wave sweeping across the world. Once set in motion, the tide of 'national-ization' seems irresistible, and connected indelibly with modernization. Successive areas coming under its influence are impelled to formulate their own versions of nationality. Thus Gellner explains how nationalism becomes such a powerful necessity throughout the modern world.

It remains to determine why this world has a plurality of nations, and why nationalism is so often divisive. Nothing about the modernist position seems to rule out the possibility that (in the very long run, perhaps) economic expansion and cultural universalization could continue to the point where the entire human population is absorbed into the framework of one vast 'supernation', with its corresponding national identity. Hobsbawm (1990) offers this vision, for example, and theories of globalization, considered later, suggest it is already happening. The main obstacles to achieving this would appear to be limitations set by communication, organization and large-scale administration, including education. Yet, as Gellner concedes (Gellner, 1983, p. 40), the advent of nationalism initiates a period of turbulent readjustment, conflict ridden and prone to violence, which shows little sign of abating. Undoubtedly, modernization carries costs, and a good deal of the negativity surrounding nationalism is linked to the oppositional, and confrontational, manner of its formation. Nations do not simply crystallize spontaneously around the spread of shared cultures: they take up positions against one another. Cultures sometimes have to be inflicted upon people, or forcibly removed from them.

To account for this, Gellner introduced the idea of the uneven diffusion of modernity. The transformations outlined in his sketch of the developmental stages of humanity are positioned in place and time; they cannot happen instantaneously. The rise of nationalism within them parallels the history of industrialization, beginning in the west of Europe, and more narrowly in Britain, and diffusing outwards across Europe and eventually the rest of the world, in a series of waves. The head-start enjoyed by a handful of European nation-states can be put down to a lucky combination of contingent factors, but once encountered they set in motion a determinate process whereby some populations acquire the benefits of progress before others. The gaps that this opens up between populations create new forms of advantage and resentment, amounting almost to a new system of stratification, defined by competing interests in modernization. These differences can be contained within the boundaries of a political unit, as significant regional variations; but in other settings they become grounds for new assertions of national identity, encouraging demands for self-government and separation. The formation of a succession of nation-states is thus precipitated by the phasing of modernization over time. It is, says Gellner, a process in which, at some point or other, almost anyone can feel they have been treated unjustly.

This framework has been employed by Nairn and others (Nairn, 1977, 1997; Hechter, 1975; Orridge, 1981) to make sense of the continuing impact of national interests and rivalries in the contemporary world, and what Nairn refers to as the 'crazy-paving' pattern of national divisions which results. Modernity and its rewards do not diffuse evenly across societies; instead there is competition, and often open conflict, about its control. Peoples and areas that 'lag behind' seek to catch up with, and overtake, those that are ahead in the race. As Nairn puts it, unevenness is the name of the game, and national identities tend to form around the fault lines of modernization; nationalism generates diversity. Gellner himself lived to see his native Czechoslovakia split apart, along lines that divided a more urban/industrial Czech Republic from rural Slovakia. Nairn considers this a rather typical situation, albeit in this case executed relatively peacefully, noting how nationalism is often fuelled by rural–urban tensions, which coincide with relative differences in economic, social and cultural development.

Conclusion

The modernist approach to nationalism favoured by Gellner and his followers has been upbraided for being unduly rationalistic, too wholesome and forward-looking (P. Anderson, 1992b), and for not giving due weight to the emotive forces which nationalism inspires. Critics of the theory of uneven development are not convinced that it explains adequately the occurrence of nationalism, as a specific kind of social and political project, rather than some other form of collective identification. They point to examples where national divisions owe little to differences in development. Orridge (1981) cites the separation of Finland from Russia, Norway from Sweden, and more recent lines of division between many African states whose levels of development appear closely comparable. In other contexts, people seem to be able to live with major differences in economic and social conditions, without mounting any challenge to their shared nationality. Even those who have seized upon the idea of the ongoing thrust of modernization as a major factor driving different sets of people to stake their claims to national recognition have sought to qualify the rather one-sided account associated with the modernists. As noted before, the double-faced image of nationalism reproduces the way in which some nationalists seek to foster a spirit of change and progress, whereas others see it as their mission to preserve, and celebrate, the unique qualities of their past. This means that amongst nationalists themselves, memories and myths of the historic legacy bequeathed by previous generations may be pitted against particular visions of the national future. The history of nationalist movements often consists of struggles around such competing viewpoints. It is not therefore clear that the quest for modernity, and competition for development, suffices by itself to account for nationalism's prominence or durability.

Analysing such nationalist dualities, Nairn (1997) contends that it is the 'raw material' carried from the past, often assuming an 'ethnic' form connected to ideas of the folk traditions of rural, and/or pre-modern times, which lends nationalism its power and passion, fuelling the extremes of behaviour that haunt the exponents of progressive nationalism and expose the limits of modernization theory. Even if the conditions promoting nationalism are new, its contents sometimes appear to be very old. Nairn suggests that it is the combined effect of the uneven impact of change and modernization upon these pre-existing materials and fissures that thrust new nations, and new national identities, into the limelight, and make nationalism such an explosive feature of world history. To explain the continual escalation in the numbers of nations, and would-be nations, vying for position, he says we must look to the continuing impact of deep, communal, structures, and residues of inheritance, blood and belonging. In our next chapter we take up this challenge to the dominance of the modernist perspective.

CHAPTER 4

Against Modernism

The modernist understanding of the rise of the nation, explored in the two preceding chapters, constitutes something of an orthodoxy within the study of nationalism, and yet runs counter to many people's sense of the history of their nation. That there should exist such a divergence in views is unsurprising. Popular narrative accounts commonly portray nations as communities that predate the late eighteenth-century watershed favoured by writers such as Hobsbawm and Gellner. In its account of French history, Microsoft's *Encarta* refers to the 'emergence of France' during the reign of the Merovingian King Clovis in the fifth century AD. Elsewhere, Gutiérrez shows how Mexican schoolchildren are taught that the history of Mexico as a nation dates back to the four-teenth century, and the founding of what today is known as Mexico City, and that the peoples of this region were 'our ances-tors' (1999, p. 74). Consumers of these narratives are encouraged to see the earlier people who inhabited the same physical place as themselves as being Mexican or French, as somehow *like us*. Whether these people were early Mexicans, any more than Clovis was the first Frenchman, is questionable, but in both instances 'France' and 'Mexico' are presented as identifiable entities, the national histories of which stretch back into the distant past.

This discrepancy between the dominant scholarly view and 'common sense' perceptions underlines the significance of the debate about the rise of nations. Modernist approaches provide us with a particular contribution to this debate. The writers explored in this chapter set out alternative perspectives. While equally scep-tical of nationalist historiography, some among these writers are of the opinion that nations, at least *some* nations, really are much older than modernists would have us believe. Further, these theo-rists also maintain that nationalism existed well before its eight-eenth-century manifestations in western Europe, a view that for

63

modernists is tantamount to heresy. Others share the modernist view that both nations and nationalism are, by and large, post-eighteenth-century phenomena, but maintain that the *roots* of modern nations lie outside the modernist historical framework. We begin with the contribution of a pioneering figure in the study of nationalism, Anthony Smith, who belongs to the latter group of theorists.

'The ethnic origins of nations'

Smith's theory of the ethnic origins of nations is one of the most distinctive sociological theories of the development of nations and nationalism. Most extensively set out in *The Ethnic Origins of Nations* (1986) and *National Identity* (1991), and also featuring prominently in other works such as *Nations and Nationalism in a Global Era* (1995a) and *Nationalism and Modernism* (1998), Smith's thesis is central to what writers variously describe as the 'ethno-symbolist' (Özkirimli, 2000), 'ethnicist' (Hutchinson, 1994), or the 'historical ethno-symbolist' approach, as he himself sometimes terms it (A.D. Smith, 1999). As defined by Smith, the ethno-symbolist approach holds that 'most nations, including the earliest, were based on ethnic ties and sentiments and on popular ethnic traditions, which have provided the cultural resources for later nation-formation' (1998, p. 12). In examining this position, we focus on elucidating two core topics of Smith's work since the early 1980s: (1) the historical origins of nations and nationalism; and (2) the processes through which nationalism develops.

The historical origins of nations and nationalism

Smith's thesis has emerged out of an engagement with two alternative accounts of the rise and spread of nationalism. One is the modernist approach that formed the subject of the previous chapter. The other is what Smith himself terms the 'perennialist' position, which holds that nations have existed throughout recorded human history. Smith is dissatisfied with both schools of thought. With regard to perennialism, he argues that while it is possible to point to ethnic communities in antiquity and the Middle Ages that share some features with modern nations, they cannot be classified *as* nations. Among other things, he suggests, these earlier ethnic communities rarely possessed the kind of public culture typical of modern nations. Against modernist approaches, he maintains that national cultures are not simply 'invented' in the modern era, but are based instead on elements drawn from pre-modern ethnic communities.

Smith acknowledges that nations are modern forms of community, dating back not much further than the late eighteenth century, and that nationalism as an ideology and a movement also emerges largely for the first time in this period. However, while he concedes the modernity of nations and nationalism, he holds that they draw sustenance from a 'living', pre-modern ethnic past – with ties to earlier ethnic communities (which Smith refers to as *ethnie*), to their symbols, and to the 'memories' of their values and exploits (A.D. Smith, 1999). Thus, nations and nationalism may be modern, but they are not 'wholly' so. A historic ethnic foundation is necessary to the survival of the nation, defined as a 'named human population sharing an historic territory, common myths and historical memories, a mass, public culture, a common economy and common legal rights and duties for all members' (A.D. Smith, 1991, p. 43). The *ethnie* provides this foundation.

Ethnie are defined as 'named human populations with shared ancestry myths, histories and cultures, having an association with a specific territory and a sense of solidarity' (1986, p. 32). Smith suggests that throughout history we find communities sharing these attributes to varying degrees. In some instances, more powerful communities absorb other *ethnie* as a result, for example, of warfare and religious conversion; though those that survive are transformed in significant ways, such as by changes in the ethnic 'character' of a population due to migration. Smith cites a number of reasons why some *ethnie* are able to survive over centuries. Among the most significant is the existence of a 'myth of ethnic election' that portrays the community as a 'chosen people'; *ethnie* possessing such myths tend to be more resistant to dissolution over time.

Two points can be made here about the significance of ethnic survival. The first is that some *ethnie* survive (albeit transformed in various ways) over long periods, and some do indeed become the cores around which modern nations cohere. We will return to this point below. Secondly, where the ethnic past is chronicled, either by contemporaries or by later generations, it provides 'memories' linking the modern nation back to pivotal national moments or to a 'golden age'. Ethnic survival may also be embodied in the form of some degree of linguistic continuity. In this way, for modern nationalists, the written record is taken as proof of the history of the ethnic culture of the nation. For example, in modern Georgia, especially following independence from the former Soviet Union, the history of the Georgian language has become an important element in nationalist ideology. Whereas history shows the territory to have been part of larger, foreign empires, and therefore its population to have been subjugated by others, Georgian nationalists point to the existence of documents in the Georgian language from the fifth century AD and the language's subsequent survival as testimony to a separate Georgian history and identity (G. Smith *et al.*, 1998). Where the exploits of ethnic 'ancestors' are recorded, they provide a reservoir of 'myths, memories, values and symbols' (A.D. Smith, 1986, p. 15) on which nationalists draw. Modern nationalists can quarry the past to trace the ancient lineage of the nation. Thus, Anthony Smith highlights how 'memories' of the Battle of Kosovo in 1389, which saw the defeat of a Serb-led Christian army by Ottoman forces, 'still evoke powerful attachments' for Serbian nationalists (1999, p. 155). For Smith, the persistence of such ethnic myths and memories is crucial to the popularizing work of nationalists in the modern era since they are used to provide 'lessons' to the nation about its 'golden age' and about the need to defend one's nation (and its homeland) while also instilling a sense of dignity and helping to foster collective identity.

Routes to nationhood: from ethnie to nation

Smith argues that it is possible to identify two broad types of *ethnie* in the pre-modern world that have a bearing on modern nations: 'lateral' and 'vertical' *ethnie*. For Smith these two types form the basis of the principal routes to nationhood in the modern world. In recent writings he has referred to a third path, typical of 'immigrant societies' (A.D. Smith, 2000), such as Australia and the USA. The principal focus of his work, however, has been on what he terms the 'bureaucratic' and 'demotic' paths to nationhood.

In the former case, Smith refers to a community in which the ethnic identity is confined to the upper or noble classes (hence he sometimes terms them 'aristocratic' *ethnie*), and where this group has little in common culturally with those over whom it rules. In the case of lateral *ethnie* that survive over long periods of time, it is the capacity to extend the ethnic culture to other *ethnie*, sometimes even going so far as to adapt its own culture in the process of accommodation, which is crucial to their longevity. In this way some lateral *ethnie* come to form the foundations for modern nations. Thus, he suggests that the roots of the modern French nation lie with the gradual expansion of a kingdom situated in the Île de France under the Capetian kings in the twelfth century and which grew under the later Valois and Bourbon dynasties, until by by the eighteenth century it constituted a territory in which we could recognize much of modern France. The persistence of the symbols and culture of the ruling family and the myths regaling their exploits is important for Smith. The fleur-de-lis flag, for example, which was the flag of the French monarchy until the French Revolution (and was briefly reinstated as the national flag between 1814 and 1830), is associated historically with the Capetian kings. Myth connects the fleur-de-lis to Clovis, fifth-century king of the Franks, who was baptized in the cathedral in Rheims, where kings of France were crowned between the ninth and nineteenth centuries. The significance of such ethnic myths for Smith is that they become carriers of identity and memories over time. 'Vertical' *ethnie*, in contrast, are communities where a strong sense of ethnic kinship, often religious in form, transcends social divisions. Again, many examples of this type of pre-modern ethnic community survive into the modern world. His argument, there-fore, is that sometimes (as in the case of France) *ethnie* can contribute to the development of the political and territorial struc-ture on which the nation later develops and, more broadly, that they leave an important cultural legacy, such as language, myths, symbols and religious practices.

Smith points to different sociological factors that help transform an *ethnie* into a nation and which give rise to two routes to nation-hood. In the case of lateral *ethnie* he argues that in western Europe – the location of the first nations (A.D. Smith, 1991) – from the fifteenth to nineteenth centuries the primary factors are a 'triple Western revolution' of administrative/military, economic and cultural changes (A.D. Smith, 1986). Since these do not occur simultaneously, the process Smith describes is one of gradual transformation. Nevertheless, his thesis is that the state plays an increasingly interventionist role in shaping the development of economic networks within its territory, seeking out new sources of revenue to finance the demands of warfare, and, overall, in estab-lishing a new class of bureaucrats charged with managing the affairs of the state. Accompanying these administrative and economic 'revolutions' is an important cultural change character-ized by the waning power of the church as a result of the ascen-dancy of secular scientific knowledge, and the desire of the state to impose a new secular regime. What Smith is describing, then, is a process of bureaucratic transformation whereby the centralizing state evolves into the ultimate source of power and authority within its territorial domain, and through which, by establishing a common legal framework and (later) a national system of educa-tion, it creates a community of national citizens. It is not, however, a process wherein the state *creates* the nation. Smith stresses that the persistence of myths, memories, symbols and customs associ-ated with the dominant *ethnie* is crucial to the ability of the state to extend its control over the population within its jurisdiction.

The transition to nationhood on the part of historic lateral *ethnie* represents a model of *territorial* nation-building in which the state seeks to transform the population of the territory over which it governs into a national community, often by correspondingly extending the culture of the historically dominant *ethnie* to 'the people'. Smith argues that the territorial model of nation-building has been applied across the world, with varying degrees of success. In post-colonial countries territorial nationalism, centred on the culture of the dominant *ethnie* (as in the cases of Burma, Indonesia, Malaysia and Thailand), became the vehicle for attempting to weld together those living in territories where boundaries had been drawn with little consideration for ethno-geography.

A second path to nationhood emerges from the survival of verti-cal *ethnie*. Vertical *ethnie* have traditionally been subject communi-ties, so the transition to nationhood differs from the route taken by lateral *ethnie* or by movements following the territorial model of nationalism. In the absence of a mobilizing state, nationalist intellec-tuals are the 'motor of transformation' (A.D. Smith, 1988, p. 355) for vertical *ethnie*. Their role is to draw together the various strands of the existing ethnic culture of the subordinate community and trans-form it into a viable, and distinct, national culture. Whereas in the case of lateral *ethnie* internal cohesion arises as a result of the trans-mission of a dominant ethnic culture to the masses, for vertical *ethnie* cross-class unity emerges out of the shared kinship or religious bonds that exist between members. Moreover, while lateral *ethnie* inhabit a strictly defined territorial 'homeland', the boundaries of vertical *ethnie* are not marked by such strict territorial limitations but rather are maintained by a rigid religious/ethnic identity. Nationalist movements arising from vertical *ethnie* may aspire to occupy a territorial homeland, but here the homeland is seen as the sole property of the ethnic community. As with territorial nationalism, which relies on the modern bureaucratic state, ethnic nationalism is also a modern phenomenon, since it is a response to the modernizing policies of a dominant territorial *ethnie*. Since policies intended to promote cultural uniformity within a territory, and to diminish or eradicate the public role of minority ethnic cultures, are confined mainly to the modern period, then *ipso facto* ethnic nationalism is modern.

Although Smith points to differences between lateral and vertical paths to nationhood, he insists both share the necessity of a store of ethnic myths, symbols and assorted 'inherited' cultural practices. As he remarks, without these 'the basis for creating a nation is tenuous and the task herculean' (1996b, p. 386). Throughout his work he maintains that ethno-histories are distributed unevenly: 'those nations with a vivid, widespread sense of an ethnic past, are likely to be more unified and distinctive than those which lack that sense' (1996b, p. 385). Some nations may not have firm roots in pre-modern *ethnie* – as examples he cites Eritrea and Tanzania – but most do. The doctrine of nationalism may be modern, like the forces that contribute to its spread in the nineteenth century and after, but the nations that emerge in this period are not wholly new. Likewise, the enduring significance of historic ethnic myths, symbols and memories ensures that the strength of national attachments is not likely to dissipate in the foreseeable future.

Nations and nationalism before the 'age of nationalism'

Central to Smith's work is his concern to show that the notion of a historical break marked by the transition to the modern industrial society should not be our starting-point for thinking about the origins of nations. The 'battle lines' between modernists and ethno-symbolists are often starkly drawn, sometimes by those writing about them and, on occasion, by representatives of the two approaches. Smith argues that, even for Gellner, the break between the modern and the pre-modern cannot be as total as he is usually understood to have suggested. He cites Gellner's remark that 'nationalism uses the pre-existing, historically inherited proliferation of cultures or cultural wealth', albeit 'selectively' (Gellner, 1983, p. 55) as demonstrating how much nationalists must depend upon the existence of earlier forms of ethnic identity. The nation, then, cannot be simply 'invented' in the nineteenth century as modernists otherwise seem to maintain.

Once it is allowed that nineteenth century nationalism relied on earlier sentiments of ethnic difference, then is it not possible that national identities date back much further than modernists are prepared to concede? Other scholars are ready to go further than Smith in claiming that nations, and even nationalisms, existed well before the late eighteenth-century turning point. One of the most ambitious challenges to mainstream opinion is Armstrong's *Nations Before Nationalism* (1982). Armstrong's objective is to explore the factors that have given rise to varying levels of ethnic identification, and to explain how some polities have been more successful than others in generating a 'national identity' that could be sustained over time. He contends that the 'widespread intense ethnic identification' so often regarded as a novel feature of the modern world has been 'recurrent' throughout Europe and the Middle East for the past thousand years (1982, p. 4). Thus, he highlights how clashes between Christians and Muslims in the Mediterranean by the eighth century AD and, later, in central Europe, sharpened awareness of ethnic boundaries until on both sides 'frontier defense became a major element of the *mytho-moteur*', or the legitimating myth of the polity (1982, p. 91). Developing urban centres also served to heighten awareness of ethnic differences, notably where ethnic segmentation existed within the city, together with separate legal systems for resident ethnic groups. Armstrong also holds that differences between nomadic and sedentary ways of life deeply affected the way groups perceived and marked their boundaries. In the nomadic case, the boundaries of the group are marked by genealogical myths, and group consciousness is sustained by encouragement to know one's clan genealogy. With regard to groups that came to adopt a sedentary way of life, although the genealogical myths associated with ruling families remained significant for the cohesion of the group, over time loyalty shifted from the family as such to the territory it occupied.

Other aspects of his discussion underline that Armstrong is interested as much in the importance of the substance of ethnic identity as in the maintenance of ethnic boundaries. For example, he explores how imperial states sought to generate myths capable of holding together an ethnically heterogeneous population, so that the 'imperial polity constituted the inescapable framework for existence, that its boundaries, physical and mental, constituted the limits of meaningful identity' (1982, p. 131). Elsewhere, examining the growth of the city, he argues that centres where there existed a high degree of civic consciousness became the 'basis for many if not most broader identities', notably identification with the emerging polity (1982, p. 93). Where a city became established as the symbolic centre of a polity, as he suggests Paris had by the thirteenth century, it could become the focus of a 'protonational identity' (1982, p. 170). In such cases, his argument relies on the populations to which he is referring being aware of what it is that makes inhabitants of the city different from those outside, and in the case of capital cities, what it is that the city symbolizes. His focus on the transmission of myth, whether by centralizing political administrations or, more effectively, by religious organizations, highlights how much the maintenance of ethnic boundaries is tied up with the ability to maintain an understanding of what makes 'us' essentially different from 'them'.

Nations Before Nationalism provides an informative account of the social construction of ethnicity, yet it is difficult to see how Armstrong's argument justifies the claim contained within the title. He acknowledges that 'consciousness of ethnic identity became a predominant force for constituting independent political structures' only in the modern era (1982, p. 4), which implies that pre-modern ethnicity generally does not perform the same function. In which case, earlier ethnic communities *are* different from modern nations, and so do not constitute 'nations before nationalism'. Armstrong's discussion of the role of religious organizations in spreading the myth of the ruling elite seems intended to demonstrate that these institutions succeeded in engendering awareness of a national identity, but he does not provide the evidence that would enable us to make a judgement on their impact.

Others are more forthright in claiming the existence of pre-modern nations. In *The English in the Twelfth Century*, Gillingham (2000) examines the evidence for the existence of an English national identity by the middle of that century, less than a century after the Battle of Hastings, in 1066, which marked the beginning of the Norman Conquest of England. Drawing from narrative sources, Gillingham argues that the 'perception of themselves as being English in the sense of being members of a subject population'

(2000, p. 99), evident in accounts produced in the 1120s, is absent from the writings of the same figures a mere twenty years later. What is particularly interesting about Gillingham's work is his argument that the development of Englishness emerges out of perceptions of difference from the 'barbarian' neighbours in Scotland, Wales and Ireland. Indeed, the fact that, by the middle of the twelfth century, writers in England were increasingly using 'Norman' to refer to someone living in Normandy, leads Gillingham to conclude that the English nation was made possible by the demise of the distinction between Norman rulers and English subjects. By the 1140s a 'developing sense of Englishness' (2000, p. 140) had emerged out of interaction with proximate groups. The characterization of the Irish, Scots and Welsh as barbarians also appears to indicate that contemporaries had a sense of the English as superior in culture and values. Gillingham's analysis of the encounters between the English and their neighbours illustrates Eriksen's point that '[l]ike other ethnic identities, national identities are constituted in relation to *others*' (1993, p. 111). The development of a distinct cultural identity is at the heart of Gillingham's claims about the existence of an English national identity in the twelfth century: the English were a nation because they identified themselves as such – *gens Anglorum*, as one contemporary recorded.

The view that the origins of both nations and nationalism predate the advent of the modern era finds support in recent studies by other historians surveying medieval and early modern Europe (Forde, Johnson and Murray, 1995; Bradshaw and Roberts, 1998; Smyth, 1998). Hastings draws on this scholarship to set out what he describes as the 'first half of the story' (1997, p. 11), missing from modernist accounts of when and how nationalism emerges. Among the influences contributing to the development of nationhood, Hastings contends that 'far and away the most important and widely present factor is that of an extensively used vernacular literature' (1997, pp. 2–3). The transition from oral to written language is crucial to the development of a nation, especially where the written language becomes a popular medium for the expression of ideas. The existence of written vernaculars, of varying degrees of scale, meant that by the fifteenth century 'most of the main nations of western Europe' were already in existence, including the English, Danes, Dutch, French and Germans (1997, p. 114). The impetus to move from Latin as the dominant written language to written vernacular languages was the desire among

Christians to reinforce piety among the masses. The solution was to translate the Bible into vernacular languages, and this in turn triggered the development of a vernacular literature. For Hastings, the effect was to 'stabilize' a conscious sense of national identity (1997, p. 193).

The impact of religion on the growth of nationhood in medieval Europe is evident in other ways. Hastings maintains that when religion played an influential role in the construction of nationhood, as it did in western Europe, nationalism was more likely to assume a religious character, most notably where threatening foreign powers adhered to a different faith. While he believes an English nation was already in place before the Reformation, from the early sixteenth century onwards, and especially in view of the perceived threat from its Catholic neighbours, English nationalism became strongly informed by Protestantism. More generally, religion was an important marker of national boundaries and identities in continental Europe during the fifteenth and sixteenth centuries. Whereas divisions between German Catholics and Protestants and 'the country's . . . remoteness from the front line with Islam' militated against the development of German nationhood, the nationhood of Catholic Spain was 'shaped by its position on the frontier with Islam' (Hastings 1997, p. 112).

There are many other factors that encourage the transition from ethnicity to nationhood. Central to Hastings' idea of the nation is that it 'possesses or claims the right to political identity and autonomy as a people, together with the control of a specific territory' (1997, p. 3). Clearly then, the nature of the state is an important force in the formation of nations. For this reason also, England is said to have constituted a nation in a way that France still did not by the mid-eighteenth century, since the former possessed a level of administrative and territorial control, and consequently a 'linguistic unity', the latter lacked. Hastings is concerned to impress, even more firmly than Armstrong or Gillingham, that a developed popular sense of national identity was in existence, most notably in England, long before the conventional modernist starting-point of the late eighteenth century. Moreover, he maintains that nationalism also flourished in Europe from the fourteenth century onwards. Most sociologists, and not just modernists, are none the less of the opinion that 'national' sentiments did not spread widely beyond a small, elite section of pre-modern societies.

Pre-modern *ethnie* and nations considered

Among the core features of nationalist ideology, as defined by Anthony Smith (whose definition is accepted by many other writers), is the proposition that the nation 'is the source of all political and social power, and loyalty to the nation overrides all other allegiances' (1991, p. 74). To what extent was this very powerful, and seemingly very modern, ideology evident in the medieval or early modern period? Writers such as Gillingham, Hastings and Gorski (2002) maintain that nationalism was indeed present prior to the 'age of nationalism'. For both Gillingham and Hastings, nationalism *follows* the development of national identity, rather than preceding it as most social scientists would maintain. As Gillingham puts it in a rebuke to Gellner, nationalism is 'associated more with a threat to a nation than with industrialisation' (2000, p. xx). Both writers also suggest that medieval European nationalism had a political dimension. For Gillingham, the negative characterizations of the Irish and Welsh fuelled nascent English imperialism in the twelfth century. In Hastings' work, the political dimension of pre-modern nationalism is stated explicitly: it is a 'movement which seeks to provide a state for a given "nation" or further to advance the supposed interests of its own "nation-state" regardless of other considerations' (1997, p. 4). In his view, English nationalism, built around the defence of the English nation, emerged in the fourteenth century during the Hundred Years War and grew in the sixteenth century in the face of war with Spain.

Examining the Netherlands, Gorski (2002) argues that a Dutch nation and nationalism existed by the mid-seventeenth century. The idea of a Dutch nation consisted of a number of strands, among them analogies between the Netherlands and ancient Israel portraying the Dutch as a 'chosen people', a myth of ancestry that traced the Dutch back an ancient Germanic people (the Batavians), and, by the closing decades of the seventeenth century, a discourse of popular sovereignty. Thus, for Gorski the Dutch nation was not only a historic ethnic community, understood by its members to be different from other nations, but also possessed within one strand of Dutch nationalism a sense of political community of a kind that most writers argue did not appear until the French Revolution a century later.

A claim that the sense of belonging to a nation was shared by a large cross-section of the population is central to the arguments of this group of writers. Gillingham, for example, states that since it was not just the nobility who stood to gain from pejorative ethnic characterizations of the Irish and Welsh that justified dispossessing them of their lands, but also 'the "ordinary" English-born villagers and townspeople' who moved with the nobles, then it would be 'surprising if there was not considerable agreement' with these characterizations 'across the whole English social spectrum' (2000, p. xxv). Hastings finds evidence of the growth of national identity in the medieval era, especially in England, from the spread of a vernacular literature, notably the use of a vernacular Bible in the conduct of the liturgy. As he maintains, the 'more a vernacular develops a literature with a popular impact . . . the more it seems to push its speakers from the category of an ethnicity towards that of a nation' (1997, p. 20). Gorski similarly emphasizes the role of print culture and public worship in carrying the idea of the Dutch nation to Netherlanders of all classes. Political pamphlets exposed a Dutch population among which literacy was widespread to nationalist myths, symbols and rhetoric. This means there 'cannot have been many Netherlanders who were unfamiliar with the Hebraic and Batavian mythologies, and there were evidently a good many who embraced them as well' (2002, p. 1451).

In a similar fashion, others argue that, as well as the factors already identified, in parts of late medieval and early modern Europe, wars, the threat of invasion, living under foreign rule, and the fusion of religious and national interests, may have conspired to generate some sense of national consciousness among people of all social classes. States also made important contributions towards promoting such nascent national identities. By the sixteenth and seventeenth centuries, thanks to the pioneering efforts of the Kingdom of Castile, there existed in Spain a 'population with a common language, a common faith and a common culture, a people that, with certain exceptions, submitted readily to a ruling house with a modern civil service at its disposal' (Schulze, 1996, p. 126). Hastings would be able to concur with Gelber's assessment that the Reformation, coupled with its struggles with continental European Catholic powers, ensured that by the end of the sixteenth century 'England had a new national identity, conceived as an autonomous community' (2001, p. 57), even if Hastings would see this period as marking more the transformation of English nationhood rather than its creation.

Even so, many critics would consider it improbable that nationalism formed the guiding principle for Tudor kings and queens in their domestic or foreign policy, or for any other medieval

European monarch for that matter. According to Breuilly, the monarchical states of medieval and early modern Europe 'did not . . . justify their actions in nationalist terms and were not so judged by their critics . . . In the political rhetoric of the period the idea of the nation, if it appeared at all, was subordinated to religious and monarchical principles' (1993, p. 76). Even with respect to language policy, which Hastings uses to illustrate the unfolding of English nationalism in relation to Ireland and Wales under the Tudors, arguably the driving forces were monarchical and religious interests, rather than nationalism. As Gillian Brennan (2001) shows, while language policy had been used in the 1530s in an effort to extend the authority of Henry VIII in Ireland and Wales, by restricting the use of the native vernaculars, by the latter half of that century the need to extend the penetration of Protestantism has become paramount, and the use of the local vernacular was now permitted where appropriate. As an ideological movement conforming to Smith's definition, in which the nation 'is the source of all political and social power', nationalism runs counter to the interests of monarchical authority.

Further down the ladder of political authority, it is difficult to comprehend why the nobility and members of the civic elite collectively would support the concept of nationalism, given that very likely it would challenge their influence and status. During the period to which Gorski refers in the Netherlands, Gelber argues that loyalty was 'chiefly to the city or province' while lower down '[m]uch effective power remained with the benevolent dictatorship of town merchants, who set their faces against any notions of sovereignty which might conflict with their commercial interests' (2001, p. 56). Gelber describes a country in which loyalties and identities may have been considerably more parochial than Gorski suggests. Others depict similar circumstances in different countries, even much later. Thus, Junco remarks that in Spain during the first part of the nineteenth century the 'idea of *patria* seemed to be in open conflict with the monarchy' (1996, p. 99). He goes on to argue that until the mid-nineteenth century governments were often 'linked to an oligarchic coalition of landed nobility and newly enriched bourgeoisie, and were utterly afraid of a nationalist idea which meant mass mobilisation and participation, and a new civic education which could detach individuals from tradition, from family, province and religion' (1996, p. 99). In Spain's colonies in South America, similar fears about what the principle of the nation might mean to the masses caused Creole (Americans of Spanish ancestry) elites to be apprehensive about the prospect of national independence (Langley, 1996).

Discerning what concepts of the nation mean to the mass of the population, beyond the opinions of those educated individuals for whom we have records, is fraught with problems. As Hobsbawm remarks, it is difficult to penetrate the 'denseness of the fog which surrounds questions about the national consciousness of common men and women, especially in the period before modern national-ism unquestionably became a mass political force' (1990, p. 79). What is clearer perhaps is the knowledge that it is from the late eighteenth century onwards that the masses become the focus of efforts to *mobilize* them as the nation. The American and French Revolutions, especially the latter, had widespread effects on revo-lutionary leaders elsewhere, including Wolfe Tone, leader of the doomed 1798 United Irishmen's revolt against the British, Simón Bolívar the liberator of Venezuela and agitator of revolution throughout Latin America, and François-Dominique Toussaint-Louverture, the leader of the Haitian Revolution which began in 1791 and which by 1804 had turned the former slave colony into the second independent country in the 'New World'. The impact of the French Revolution also registered among the political authori-ties that opposed it. Colley suggests that the mobilization of civil-ian militia in Britain to counter a possible Napoleonic invasion in the late eighteenth and early nineteenth centuries, a process that involved treating these volunteer soldiers 'indiscriminately as patriots', demonstrated that to 'beat the French, the British had been required to imitate the French' (1996, p. 336).

Again, to what extent the efforts to organize people into nations registered within the consciousness of the masses even in this period is a question that throws up ambiguous findings. In Colley's acclaimed study, which draws on the personal records of ordinary male volunteers to civilian militia in Britain during the Napoleonic Wars, she notes that by 1802 volunteers were required to sign an oath to defend the king, and that 'every volunteer was invited by wartime propaganda to see himself as a guardian of British free-doms and to think in terms of Britain as a whole' (1996, p. 331). She also points out that men volunteered for many reasons – lack of work, exposure to propaganda among those living in urban areas, peer pressure, desire to protect their families, and economic oppor-tunism (for tradesmen, their fellow volunteers were a ready market for their wares). Patriotism, therefore, 'was not the only motive' and 'in some cases it was not a motive at all' (1996, p. 317).

Colley's work underlines the crucially important role of the state in defining the masses as not only members of the nation, but also as its defenders. While the absence of a state machinery may not preclude the development of mass national consciousness, to penetrate the local lives of ordinary people and to encourage them to imagine themselves as belonging to a national community does require an enormous, organized effort. Even where a single political authority existed within a territory, it required considerable motivation and administrative reform to nationalize the masses. From the mid-nineteenth century, states did so with considerable zeal. Weber's classic *Peasants into Frenchmen* (1979) shows how the extension of a French national identity, and the French language, throughout the country was directed in large part by a system of compulsory public education, which although in existence for nearly a century had little impact until the 1880s. Elsewhere, Haas (1997) similarly argues that public education plays a crucial role in taking the idea of the nation to the masses but points out that in many countries, including Britain, Japan and the USA, it was not until the late nineteenth century that public education systems became the carriers of the core values and ideas of the nation. In Japan after 1868, public education became the principal vehicle through which the national values of the Meiji regime were channelled to the wider population, including, by 1890, *The Imperial Rescript on Education* which 'projected the *Volk* view of nation by stating that the emperor presided as the head of the main family, from which all Japanese families subsequently branched out' (Yoshino, 1999, p. 13).

These studies raise some major questions about claims that nations existed outside of the modern era. Where then do they leave Anthony Smith's argument that even if nationalism is a *post-eighteenth-century* phenomenon, nations are built on pre-modern ethnic foundations? Smith's work has attracted similar criticisms. Some argue that he exaggerates the degree of ethnic consciousness and solidarity among pre-modern populations, which did not possess the kinds of institutions that contribute to the growth of national identity in the modern era (Breuilly, 1996). Smith (1998) meets this criticism by arguing that other institutions fulfilled the same role, including popular participation in festivals and rituals, and service in the army. However, what especially bothers Breuilly, like other modernists, is the suggestion that pre-modern ethnic identity necessarily has any bearing on modern nationalism. As he remarks, 'many powerful nationalist movements of modern times have succeeded despite having very little in the way of a rich national history. Can anyone seriously claim that Libyan identity is somehow less well established than Egyptian identity; or that of Slovaks is less strong than of Hungarians?' (Breuilly, 1996, p. 151). Yet, Smith himself accepts that there is no necessary causal relationship between pre-modern *ethnie* and the emergence of modern nations; he is not a perennialist. Moreover, he does not deny that nationalist historiography involves myth-making, for example in the way that earlier historical figures are portrayed as acting out of 'national' interests. Thus, Smith would not take issue with the view that the past needs to be organized and made intelligible as *the nation's* past. Rather, he questions whether it is possible to sustain a common sense of national identity without at least some plausible ethno-history, to which nationalist leaders can appeal, and which is able to provide moral lessons or heroic, motivating tales for those they are addressing. To this end, he argues, nationalists must work with the resources available to them, which are known, even if only to a limited degree, by those whom they seek to mobilize.

There are many examples that support Smith's thesis. Some highlight how the culture of a dominant *ethnie* comes to occupy a significant place in the formation of modern national identities. For example, prior to the Revolution, the French language had been favoured for centuries by what Smith would term a lateral *ethnie*, the kings of France. This royal sponsorship assisted the gradual elevation of French over other 'regional' languages among the nobility and, by the late eighteenth century, throughout many French cities. However, only with the revolution did there emerge a growing concern about the degree of linguistic heterogeneity within France, and a concomitant effort to impose standard French as the national language (Bell, 2001). In this way, the culture of a pre-modern *ethnie* was transformed, by the nineteenth century, into the linguistic medium for the nationalization of public life in France. One might highlight similarly the development of Castilian in Spain as a national language (albeit with less success than in the case of French, given the continuing significance of the Basque and Catalan languages), as a legacy of the historic role of the Kingdom of Castile in the formation of Spain (Mar-Molinero, 1996).

In other instances, the significance of the pre-modern past rests with how aspects of it are used by modern nationalists. Even in France, the 1789 revolution was not the beginning of history. As Bell writes, where the 'radical revolutionaries had briefly envisaged the construction of the nation as an entirely new process . . . nineteenth-century nationalists for the most part preferred the language of "regeneration" and "recovery" ' (2001, p. 200). As he goes on to say:

> Like many of their eighteenth-century predecessors, they envisaged a new structure, but one lovingly put together out of hallowed, ancient material. In keeping with their counterparts across Europe, they engaged in a massive effort of recuperating, preserving, and displaying what now came to be called the nation's heritage of patrimony, including folklore, artworks, music, monuments, costumes, and historical personalities such as Joan of Arc (2001, pp. 200–1).

We see similar processes at work in newly independent countries, where the need is especially pressing to demonstrate the country's legitimacy by underlining its historical pedigree. Where the French case illuminates how the past can be used to establish a national heritage for a new order, in the case of many newly independent countries, the concern is more with mining the past to demonstrate the continuity of the nation. In the Ukraine, following the country's independence from the Soviet Union in 1991, ethno-historiographical work has played an important role in articulating a distinctive Ukrainian identity. This has included studies to support the claim that the history of Ukrainian independent statehood dates back to the ninth century AD, to the medieval Kievan Rus' state, whose culture and language are said to have been Ukrainian rather than Russian (G. Smith *et al.*, 1998).

For Anthony Smith, such examples illustrate that modern national identities are reconstructed around elements of pre-modern ethnic cultures, and that such resources are necessary to maintain national identities over time. It is also possible to show examples to support Smith's argument that where a nationalist movement is not able to draw as effectively as others on pre-modern ethnic resources, because they lack a suitable historical record or where 'evidence' more clearly favours the claims of a rival nation, then it will find difficulty in gaining mass support. Thus, Graham Smith *et al.* (1998) argue that whereas Ukrainian historians have had considerable success in demarcating a Ukrainian national history from pro-Russian or pan-Slavic myths, in the case of neighbouring Belarus, there has been greater difficulty in substantiating a separate Belarusophile mythology capable of challenging the hegemony of Russophile historiography.

Anthony Smith's approach, then, offers a more cautious and qualified treatment of the pre-modern past in relation to modern national identity. In the main, he does not make claims about the existence of nations before the eighteenth century, unlike some of the other scholars discussed in this chapter. Moreover, in demonstrating that the process of creating national cultures in the modern era, whether by states or by nationalist movements, has involved 'reconstructing' elements of pre-modern ethnic cultures, he avoids the difficulties evident in some modernist theories. Whereas one might ask Gellner and Hobsbawm why an 'invented' culture should take root among a population, even if it has the backing of the state, Smith maintains that nationalists commonly build on, and appeal to pre-existing sentiments of ethnic or national difference, which already have popular significance.

Yet, there is something troubling about Smith's argument that at the heart of 'many national communities' is a historic 'ethnic component' (A.D. Smith, 1996b, p. 362). It implies that there is a *real* ethnic core to many nations. This is borne out by his riposte to post-modernists: '[h]istory is no sweetshop in which its children may "pick and mix" (1995b, p. 18). Even if one allows that he is correct in that nationalists will usually make use of recorded history, rather than engage in straightforward historical fabrication, much depends on how history is *interpreted*. Consider, for example, the clashes between Georgians and Abkhazians, who fought a war in 1992–93 over attempts by Abkhazian separatists to declare an independent Abkhazian republic. Both groups lay claim to the medieval kingdom of Abkhazia; Abkhazians argue that the kingdom was founded by their ancestors, and employ this claim to support their quest for independence, whilst Georgians maintain that, in spite of the name of the kingdom, the culture, language and the dominant population was Georgian (G. Smith *et al.*, 1998). In such instances, where rival groups claim the same territory or historic figures as part of their ethno-history, how is it possible to decide who has the most legitimate claim? Even in cases where history is less sharply contested, what does it mean to say that modern national identities are based, as Anthony Smith suggests, on 'antecedent ethnic ties' (1996b, p. 361)? For Smith, the nation – expressed in the singular – is based around *an* ethnic core, but at any one time there will exist numerous, competing national discourses employing contrasting readings of history. Thus, as Bell notes, while for some nineteenth-century French nationalists the importance of 'rediscovering' the pre-revolution past was that it established a national heritage, others – such as those in Action Française, the radical right-wing nationalist movement – 'saw the past not merely as a heritage, but as a literal destination' (2001, p. 202). Today, due to decades of immigration, it is even more difficult to justify claims that national identities are based, in reality, on a core 'ethnic component'. As one reviewer of Smith's *Myths and Memories of the Nation* remarks:

> How many 'Englishmen' of South Asian, Afro-Caribbean or Irish Catholic descent view empire in the same light as their Anglo-Saxon co-nationals? How many French Muslims of Algerian or Senegalese origin regard the Declaration of the Rights of Man as part of their own cultural heritage? How can the *hinomaru* be constitutive of a Japanese national identity that is to include Chinese, Korean and Filipino *zainichi*? (Shani, 2002, p. 400).

Conclusion: 'When is a nation?'

This question, posed by Connor (1994), is central to the work discussed in this chapter and to the writers considered in the preceding one. For the large part, the writers discussed in these chapters are of the view that nationalism necessarily precedes the nation. Some, such as Armstrong, Gillingham and Hastings, dissent from this orthodoxy. There are, however, problems in being a dissenter. Arguably the most important is that the idea of the nation brings to mind not only notions of cultural distinctiveness and the sense of belonging to a community held together by cultural solidarity, but also ideas of shared memories and popular sovereignty. Yet, populations do not just develop an awareness of these ideas as individuals. Rather, people need to be encouraged to think of themselves as a nation, with all the cultural and political implications this concept entails. It is nationalism, as a distinctive form of politics and as a way of thinking about our identity, relations to others and to government, which performs this function. For the reasons outlined in the preceding chapter and also in part in this chapter, the common view is that nationalism is a modern phenomenon. Sociologists such as Greenfeld and Gorski advocate that, as an embryonic ideology, nationalism predates the eighteenth century in countries such as England and the Netherlands, but it is during the latter 1700s that nationalism emerges as one of the constitutive ideologies of the modern era. This is not to deny that national sentiments may have existed in earlier periods – that is, a sense of belonging to a distinctive cultural community – but evidence of national*ism* is much weaker. It is for this reason that Anthony Smith's approach is arguably the most persuasive of the theories examined in this chapter. However, even if one shares his view that modern nationalists typically draw on extant folk myths, memories or symbols associated with pre-modern, sometimes ancient, ethnic 'ancestors' in fashioning their visions of the national community – and many social theorists do not – there are key aspects of Smith's work that are at odds with some of the principal tenets of contemporary social theory. Specifically, the manner in which Smith, in common with Gellner and other classical theorists of nationalism, reifies the nation as a unified and culturally homogenous entity – formed, in Smith's case, around *an* ethnic core – is being subjected to growing criticism by social theorists who stress that 'the nation' is always subject to contestation, especially about who belongs to it. In this way, it is argued that it is impossible to speak, for example, of the development of *the* British nation or the rise of *the* Japanese nation. This does not mean that we should abandon the historical sociology that characterizes Smith's work, and which seeks to identify the consequences of social change; to do so would be to neglect one of the most important tasks of social theory. It does perhaps mean that we need, as Brubaker suggests, to start to think less in terms of how *nations* develop and instead concentrate on the various ways the nation *as a category* is invoked, institutionalized and more generally used as a 'cognitive frame' (1996, p. 16). The following chapter will pursue this understanding of nationalism and the nation.

CHAPTER 5

The Social Construction
of Nations

Nationhood ... cannot be defined objectively, prior to political processes, on either cultural or social structural grounds. This is so, crucially, because nations are in part made by nationalism. They exist only when their members understand themselves through the discursive framework of national identity, and they are commonly forged in the struggle carried out by some members of the nation-in-the-making to get others to recognize its genuine nation-ness and grant it autonomy or other rights. The crucial thing to grasp here is that nations exist only within the context of nationalism.

(Calhoun, 1997, p. 99)

Commenting on Brubaker's study of the eruption of new nationalisms in post-Soviet Eastern Europe, Pierre Bourdieu, the eminent French sociologist, noted it offered 'new terrain for a reflexive sociology of the ongoing fabrication of everything we subsume under the falsely self-evident name of "nation" ' (Brubaker, 1996). This captures rather vividly the tone of hardened scepticism that prevails in much contemporary sociology towards ideas of nations and nationalism. Huge doubt has been cast upon the solidity and permanence of the phenomena of nationhood, from within both mainstream sociology and Marxism. Primordialism, never much more than a straw man, is virtually dead. Beliefs in the historical origins and unique destinies of particular nations which are passionately held among their members have been given short shrift, and often shown to be hollow. With few exceptions, as discussed in the preceding chapter, the general consensus is that sociology should concern itself less with appraising the reality of such claims than with analysing how and why they have been constructed and perpetrated.

Hobsbawm's insistence on the 'invented' character of national traditions can be put alongside Gellner's (1964) thesis that nationalism creates nations where previously they did not exist to convey a strongly debunking style of analysis. A number of influential strands of contemporary social theorizing merge with particular contributions to the analysis of nationalism to encourage this critical, deconstructionist, stance. Brubaker's work on Eastern European nationalism is a good example. In place of a concern with nations as 'real entities and substantial collectivities', which tries to adjudicate between the claims of competing nationalisms, Brubaker advocates an approach which treats them instead as institutionalized forms, practical categories and contingent events – in other words, as social accomplishments. The emphasis is on contingency, and the unintended consequences of human and governmental action, rather than on the determined outcomes of the machinery of social forces and structures.

Constructionist perspectives and the analysis of nationalism

Social constructionism represents a main branch of sociological theorizing, in which human beings are treated as (more-or-less) active, conscious agents engaged in the construction of a shared social reality (Berger and Luckmann, 1967; Alexander, 1982; Waters, 1994). The manner in which they act, individually and collectively, is held to depend ultimately upon the way in which they give meaning to their situation and behaviour. Elements of social constructionism have been present throughout the history of social thought, and kept alive by the impact of distinct approaches such as symbolic interactionism and phenomenology. Recent years have seen the strengthening of this perspective, and a growing attempt to demonstrate how all the key categories of human existence, such as gender, race, class, community and generation, can be shown to be socially constructed. A central topic for investigation, however, is the way these constructs regularly elude the control of those who create them, to take on the appearance of objective, determined, facts. Nation and nationality are no exceptions. Like other products of human activity, they can be objectified, even by the mere act of naming (Mouzelis, 1991, p. 72; Berger and Luckmann, 1967), to appear as entities somehow distinct from the practices of those who create them. From here it is a short step to the perception that they exist entirely independently of human volition. A constructionist interpretation seeks to avert this common intuition, by insisting for example that nationalism is 'all about the construction and contestation of concepts of identity in the social conditions specific to modernity' (Periwal, 1995, p. 229). Such efforts are not always successful: like 'ordinary' members of society, social theorists often struggle to hold on to the perception that society is a human creation, not a given fact.

With regard to theories of nationalism, the origins of a constructivist position have been traced to Bauer (Stargardt, 1995), who recognized the historically contingent element in the creation of nations. In a reversal of conventional nationalistic thinking, Bauer contended that rather than history reflecting the struggles of nations, nations needed to be seen as outcomes of historical struggle. Since they were shaped by various kinds of human activity, including the formation and maintenance of shared cultures, there was no preordained, fixed configuration of nations. Bauer was familiar with contemporary developments in social theory and could have found support for a constructionist view in Weber's insistence on the centrality of meaning to the interpretation of society, the Marxist focus on the role of ideology in creating perceptions which do not match the 'reality' of objective circumstances, and even in the Durkheimian emphasis on the 'collective consciousness' which is integral to the coherence and integration of a social order. Each draws attention to ways in which people, individually and collectively, must make sense of their social location and identity. More recent contributions have accentuated the significance of such processes, undermining naturalizing assumptions that human groups of various sorts are real and enduring, and pointing instead to the extent to which their existence depends upon social practices, discourses and representations (Brubaker, 1996; Calhoun, 1997; Seidman and Alexander, 2001).

This mode of theorizing has important consequences. The rejection of evolutionary developmental models of change that deal with phases of structural transformation is part of a wider scepticism about the relevance of 'grand narratives'. These include narratives of national development and growth, and the social impact of 'modernity'. This implies in turn the abandonment of teleological conceptions of movement towards some final destination, such as 'national' liberation and self-government, or indeed the abolition of nations. Instead, many regard history as basically directionless, shaped by the unpredictable interplay of social pressures and processes whose results are arbitrary and provisional.

These characteristics are seen as typical of post-modernity, in contrast to the well-defined, relatively transparent outlines of the 'modern' era, within which much of the discussion of nationalism has been located. To understand the complexities of the new social contours, there has been some convergence of social theory with philosophy, especially political philosophy, and literary and cultural theory, and this has encouraged a greater readiness to address certain normative questions, of justice, democracy, authenticity, and respect for 'difference' (Best and Kellner, 1997; Seidman and Alexander, 2001). Within the field of nations and nationalism, this has brought about a transfer of attention from the characteristics of nations and nation-states towards a greater emphasis upon national identity and identification – a move from the realm of the object to that of subjective consciousness and perception.

Benedict Anderson and the 'national' imagination

In *Imagined Communities* (1983) Benedict Anderson makes a decisive, if not necessarily fully intended, contribution towards the ascendancy of a constructionist perspective on nationalism. For Anderson, a specialist on the politics of southeast Asia, the wars between ostensibly Marxist states in Indochina during the 1970s tore away the last shreds of hope that socialist internationalism might supersede nationalism. 'Actually existing socialism' in the twentieth century was contained within the framework of nations and nation-states, such as China, Vietnam and Cambodia, whose animosities owed little to Marxist theory or class interests. Anderson shares with Nairn and others the view that nationalism itself has failed to produce anything like an adequate explanation for its extraordinary strength and staying power. His central insight is that nations are artefacts of cultural processes; as Gellner had suggested, their existence is preceded, rather than followed, by the creation of a sense of nationality, and this occurs in people's imaginations, as a cultural construct. Anderson's concept of the nation as an 'imagined community' has become the touchstone for a massive volume of analysis and debate. By the end of the twentieth century, it had become the dominant metaphor for the social scientific study of nationalism.

As with any human community beyond the scale of the 'primordial village', Anderson argues, membership of a nation requires

people to carry out an act of imagination, through which they identify with others whom they will never actually meet or even see.
This is possible only under certain conditions, which did not come
about until relatively recently, with the arrival of a form of communication, the print media, capable of uniting people across large
stretches of time and space. This required both the technological
means (the printing press) and the incentive (the capitalist search
for profits) to expand communication beyond the limits of a small,
educated elite or the confines of a local audience. The vehicle that
allowed access to a mass market was the use of everyday vernacular language. In Europe, this meant the replacement of Latin by
French, German, English, Spanish, Dutch and so on. Religion
helped greatly in this, especially the willingness of Protestant
reformers to adopt the vernacular as the language of worship and
prayer, and to encourage its use among their followers.

Through a selective process, specific vernacular forms were
crystallized and standardized, levelling out the wide variety of
local dialects, to become authoritative versions of national tongues.
Anderson describes how a population able to read the same newspapers, or enjoy the same novels, in the same language, is at the
same time capable of grasping those who appear within them as
inhabiting the same social world, sharing a 'deep horizontal
comradeship' (1983, p. 16). This sense of belonging, comparable in
intensity to membership of a great extended family, explains the
readiness with which people will sacrifice themselves for their
nation, even to the point of death. It creates the 'beauty of *gemeinschaft*' as 'nation-ness is assimilated to skin-colour, gender, parent-
age and birth-era – all those things one can not help' (1983, p. 131).
Membership of the nation becomes intrinsic to the way in which
people see themselves, a fundamental form of self-definition.

Factors other than these linguistic and communicative aspects
also play their part in the process, as shown by Anderson's many
historical examples. He examines especially the formation of nation-
states and nations in the Americas, where it is not the distinctiveness
of language (Spanish or English) which sets boundaries to the different nations, nor even the political participation and consciousness of
the mass of the population, but the establishment of distinctive
apparatuses of administration and territorial government prior to
the breaking of ties with European colonial powers. So nations do
not exist simply in the imagination, but possess tangible underpin-
nings. Yet, for Anderson, what is truly distinctive about them is the
way they are conceptualized, envisaged as solid communities,

which move steadily through history, filled with the simultaneous anonymous activity of vast numbers of like-minded individuals. Their existence as language communities is conjured up largely by the work of modern dictionary writers and literati, who helped create 'official' versions of such languages as modern Greek, Romanian, Russian, Czech, Bulgarian, Serbo-Croat and Finnish; yet still these nations succeed in regarding themselves as somehow ancient (1983, p. 101), and capable of continuing indefinitely along a single historical path.

Marked by their respective, and distinctive, national languages, each nation is known to be limited in its range, occupying a place within a system of many similar entities; but it is also conceptualized as a sovereign power within its particular sphere of influence. Historically, these units replace, and to some extent inherit the qualities of, earlier dynastic and religious social formations. Nations assume the strength and near-sacred character previously attached to ruling households and churches. Again, this quasi-religious status helps explain why nations command such a high level of commitment from their members. Anderson cites memorials to the 'unknown (national) warrior' as exemplifying the anonymous, and sacred, qualities of nationality. Their existence is a reminder that, when necessary, the nation warrants the supreme sacrifice.

Anderson readily accepts that nations are 'invented' features of the modern world. For example, he notes that Indonesia, with which he is particularly familiar, came into existence only during the twentieth century, although its leaders talk with perfect sincerity of a history of colonization going back centuries (1983, p. 19). Time and again, modern nations can be shown to consist of piecemeal reshapings of once distinct territories and societies. In the face of critical assessment, the continuity and unity to which they lay claim can rarely be sustained. This revelation can make them appear spurious and artificial (Miller, 1995); there is a profound gap between the 'reality' and its proclaimed image. Thus, a recent investigation of the national identity of 'Austria' reveals that the name 'the one-thousandth anniversary of which was celebrated in 1996 by numerous ceremonies and a large historical exhibition' actually signifies a variety of different historical entities with a very limited amount in common (Wodak *et al.*, 1999, p. 50). However, where Anderson disagrees with Gellner is in the inference that something 'imagined' is therefore merely fabricated, or false. What is imagined, collectively, takes on a definite social reality. Individuals are subjected to social pressures that can be very hard to resist, as 'imagined' or constructed concepts assume the quality of social facts. Through their circulation within the print media and other forms of communication, terms like 'nation', 'citizenship' and 'sovereignty' gain their resonance and solidity. Coming from a very different intellectual and political direction, Miller acknowledges the power such influences exert: 'How do I know what it means to be British? I find out from newspaper editorials, or history books, or films or songs – and I take it for granted that what I am ingesting is also being ingested by millions of other Britons whom I will never meet' (1995, p. 32). As co-members of a national society, we assume that we inhabit the same world of meanings, information and values. Like much of daily life, our nationality is a 'taken-for-granted affair that assumes that other people think, perceive, and otherwise understand things in pretty much the same terms as we do ourselves' (Layder, 1994, p. 76).

Nations as linguistic constructs

In the examination of processes of social and cultural construction, language holds a position of pre-eminence. The rise of constructionist perspectives reflects a 'turn' towards linguistic analyses among social scientists (Giddens, 1984). The significance of vernacular literature for the development of national consciousness has been highlighted by Hastings, who contends that 'ethnicities ... turn into nations or integral elements within nations at the point where their specific vernacular moves from an oral to a written usage' (1997, p. 12). The centrality of language to the imagined community is a consistent theme of Anderson's discussion. The origins of nations are said to lie with the emergence of 'popular vernacular nationalism' at the point where printed languages replace visual images and symbols as the main means of holding large populations together (1983, p. 29). The pride people take in their nation is, in part, pride in the elevation of 'their' everyday language to official status. Yet it is well established that the gaps between the formation of national boundaries, and the distribution of particular languages, are formidable. By Anderson's own account, national frontiers in the Americas reflect institutional arrangements and political developments that cut across groups speaking the same (official) language. Even though doing so might differentiate them more sharply from one another, no American nation employs a language of state that is 'native' to its territory.

Instead they relegate local languages to minority, often threatened, positions and use languages imported by European colonizers. In the revised edition of *Imagined Communities*, Anderson notes that for American nationalist movements, language was never an issue (1991, p. 197).

Elsewhere, the 'idea' of the nation preceded coherent linguistic foundations. In Hungary, for example, little over half the inhabitants spoke Magyar when it became the state language; for some time the Hungarian nobility carried on speaking Latin, while substantial minorities spoke German, Romanian and Czech. More recently, in former Yugoslavia, a new 'language', Bosnian, has emerged from Serbo-Croat, where previously only a difference of dialect existed. Even discounting the effects of contemporary migrations, few modern nations are without significant linguistic minorities having long-standing connections with the 'national' territory. As with territory, possession of a common language assumes a normative importance within nationalism, as an aspiration to be pursued, rather than a simply factual status. In this respect, it resembles the essential nationalist belief pinpointed by Gellner that 'state' and 'people' should coincide, even though this too is frequently at odds with objective circumstances. Acting upon such beliefs, individuals endeavour to construct the world accordingly, if necessary, and wherever possible, changing objective reality to correspond to their subjective predilections.

The contention that nations grow spontaneously out of a shared language therefore must be heavily qualified. Anderson's thesis can be turned back on him, as it is by Billig, who suggests that 'language does not create nationalism, so much as nationalism creates language' (1995, p. 30). Billig explains that while nations may be imagined communities, 'the patterning of the imaginings cannot be explained in terms of differences of language, for languages themselves may have to be imagined as distinct entities' (1995, p. 36). Once the apparently solid foundations of an 'objective' external reality are chipped away, we are in danger of being sucked into a veritable vortex of imaginings. Furthermore, Anderson's account of print capitalism's role in rationalizing and systematizing vernaculars, and so promulgating new forms of consciousness of belonging, does not always fit well to circumstances in which very large numbers were illiterate. In even the most advanced nations, as late as the mid-nineteenth century, this was true of half or more of the population. The principal impact of the print media therefore was upon the 'reading classes'. Indeed,

Anderson notes that the European bourgeoisie constituted the first significant 'imagined community', capable of assuming that other, unknown, individuals in the same social situation as themselves were alike in motivation and behaviour. Even allowing for language barriers, it is not obvious why the bourgeois imagination should stop short at national frontiers; in economic terms, it was a cross-national class, united (as well as divided) by trade and commercial relations. Trade and industry have a remarkable capacity to transcend linguistic frontiers.

More importantly still, Anderson is singularly quiet on the issue of how the imagined community of the nation extended to include members of different social classes, across the gulf in literacy, standards of life, habits and customs. Even among highly literate contemporary populations, the diversity of published sources and their contents is enough to make us question how far we can be sure that readers do indeed, in Miller's terms, ingest the 'same' conception of their nationhood, or occupy the same social world. Yet in Anderson's account, not only is this essential to the formation of a true national consciousness, but the resulting sense of unity must be strong enough to bond people together in a way which seems 'fateful' and overwhelming. The jump from the conception of a shared intellectual universe to the idea of profound emotional commitment perhaps reflects Anderson's own logocentric universe of meaning. The lack of attention paid to divisions within nascent nations, particularly class divisions, is truly surprising in someone whose intellectual roots lie in Marxism. Conventionally, Marxists have seen the nation and nationalism as part of the 'imagined' universe of ruling groups and classes, who seek to impose their ideology on those below them. Although Anderson refers to the importance of 'popular vernacular nationalism', he pays remarkably little attention to ways in which nationalism might develop from the bottom up. In fact, except in connection to international relations and colonialism, the notion of power is strangely absent from his account.

The production of 'national community'

Anderson describes his approach to nationalism as 'anthropological' in spirit. His interest is not primarily in the doctrinal or ideological content of nationalism, but in its shaping as a particular form of community. However, it is community constructed very largely at the level of language, and in terms of a general conception of writing done *in* one language rather than another. He pays less attention to the writing (and speaking) *of* language, and its impact upon nationalism, while also initially having little to say about any other dimensions of communality. McCrone (1998, p. 6) notes the affinities with Renan's early definition of a nation as a 'large-scale solidarity' which is 'spiritual' in nature, and criticizes Anderson for not developing an account of the ways in which the process of imagining is carried out and sustained. This might require paying greater attention to the 'community' aspect of nationhood than to its 'imagining' alone. Anderson does not dwell on the meaning of 'community', although he implies that it is a unifying framework within which people identify closely with one another; the nation appears to realize Tonnies' conception of *gemeinschaft*. There is a curious debt here to conservative romanticism (Noble, 2000), which afflicts other ostensibly Marxist writers on nationalism as well. Tonnies himself would have doubted that such a degree of organic solidarity could be achieved at the national scale. Anderson's analysis therefore requires some strengthening.

There has been considerable recent interest among social anthropologists in developing an analysis of nationalism and national identity. Eriksen (1993, 2002) discerns remarkable parallels between Anderson's approach and influential anthropological models of culture and symbolic ritual. He too identifies the nation as a cultural community, and describes the processes of reification from which alleged national traditions and identities can emerge. In his own country of Norway, for example, an urban middle class created a 'national' culture out of its reinterpretations of peasant life, inventing costumes, and even a new literary language, along the way. Elements drawn from different sources were synthesized, and solidified, into a coherent construction, which was then presented as 'authentically' Norwegian. In this way, says Eriksen, 'nationalism reifies culture in the sense that it enables people to talk about their culture as though it were a constant' (1993, p. 101). Eriksen's example justifies Gellner's cynicism that 'the cultural shreds and patches used by nationalism are often arbitrary historical inventions. Any old shred and patch would have served as well' (1983, p. 56). History is employed similarly to create a sense of continuity: the first king of Norway, recruited from the Danish royal household early in the twentieth century, took the title Haakon VII, resuming where an earlier dynasty left off – in 1350!

Through such devices, a seemingly solid framework can be built within which the sense of national belonging can be fostered and sustained.

As an anthropologist, Eriksen knows that, beneath the apparent certainty and stability such processes confer, things are far more uncertain and ambiguous. Like all social identities, national identities are constructed in relationship to one another, and the boundaries between them are often ill-defined. As with other forms of social identification, the ideology of nationality offers a theoretical map, and set of conceptual constructs, which does not conform accurately, or even closely, to empirical reality. In Eriksen's words, 'history and social identity are constructed socially, sometimes with a very tenuous relationship with established, or at least, official, facts' (2002, p. 17). Even apparently clear-cut identities, like that of modern Germans, prove difficult to pin down: there are important differences between those who were shaped in the divided East and West ('Ossies' and 'Wessies'), and significant numbers of German-speakers remain 'outside' Germany, in parts of the former Soviet empire. Others, such as Austrians, some Swiss, and Tyroleans, seem extraordinarily close to being German. It is a perennial issue for Austrians to achieve some distance from a German identity. After the debacle of 1945, elements such as Austrian music, films with Austrian settings, and cultural events in Vienna and Salzburg, proved 'very helpful' in the search for things that were 'typically Austrian' (Wodak *et al.* 1999, p. 56), and by implication not German. These examples show how difficult it is to base nationality, let alone nations, upon conceptions of national identity, which on inspection prove to be fragile and open to differing interpretations. Once it is allowed that they are constructed, rather than given, it is unavoidable that more than one construct will be 'plausible', according to the vantage point from which it is produced.

That the criteria for group membership, and therefore who belongs and who does not, are not always obvious creates difficulties for approaches that derive nationality directly from key attributes, such as language or place of residence, or even from a number of them in combination. The space this opens between particular traits and characteristics, and conceptions of national identity, provides the room for processes of social construction. These operate to clarify, question, reinforce or undermine national differences and divisions. Drawing on symbolic interactionism and Chicago School sociology, the anthropological work of Barth (1969) has been especially influential in highlighting such processes with respect to the definition of ethnic boundaries (Jenkins, 1996; Eriksen, 1993, 2002) and, by extension, is extremely relevant for understanding nationality as well. Barth treats such boundaries as outcomes of ongoing interactions through which 'the social construction of external difference generates internal similarity' (Jenkins, 1996, p. 93). This dialectical movement involves the selective use of markers and indicators, which are changeable over time, to bring about social separation, exclusion and inclusion. Definition of membership of national groupings forms a special case of these general processes. In this view, 'nationalism is historically and locally variable and bound up with ethnicity' (Jenkins, 1997, p. 142).

This renders *all* definitions of nation and nationalism subject to contestation and revision. Any approach that takes their meaning for granted is likely to prove vulnerable to subsequent change and negotiation. This includes the idea that some self-evident form of 'imagined' community corresponds to a specific nation. The question instead should be *how* it comes to be imagined and/or constructed in a particular way. Cohen's discussion of the *symbolic* construction of communities sheds light on this. Although he focuses on the smaller, local, community, which he counterposes to national frames of reference, his argument has significance for our understanding of the construction of national identities (Cohen, 1985; Jenkins, 1996). For Cohen, all communities are 'imagined'. They are constructed through the symbolism of 'belonging' and not-belonging, in which distinctions are made between 'us' and 'them'. These are formulated most critically, and carefully, at the margins, in the definition of boundaries. Different characteristics are assigned to those considered to be within the group, from those outside it. Cohen contends that the key point about 'community' is not that everyone within it is really alike, but that (in particular circumstances and situations) people believe in their similarity, and attach priority to it over their differences from others. These are symbolized in various ways, including the use of names, descriptions, images and ideas. Such symbols do not speak for themselves, but must be interpreted, and their meanings unravelled. Attention must be paid to processes through which symbols are created, manipulated and appropriated.

Cohen's view is that the 'reality' and efficacy of a community depends upon its symbolic construction and embellishment (1985, p. 15), while consciousness of community is encapsulated primarily in perception of its boundaries, 'which are in themselves largely constituted by people in interaction'. In words equally well suited to Anderson's imagined community of the nation, Cohen concludes that: 'community is largely in the mind. As a mental construct, it condenses symbolically, and adeptly, its bearers' social theories of similarity and difference. It becomes an eloquent and collective emblem of their social selves' (1985, p. 114).

Cohen (1982) believes that the depth of meaning associated with community and its symbolization increases as one goes down the scale towards smaller and more intimate social settings. Elias (1996) puts a counter-argument, more in keeping with Anderson's thesis, suggesting that symbolization assumes greater importance in a larger collectivity, like a nation, where members do not, and cannot, know one another. The scale and complexity of such a society makes it hard to explain in straightforwardly factual terms what the various members derive from their joint enterprise, and yet they know, in often obscure and incomprehensible ways, that they depend upon each other. Common symbols crystallize this 'we-feeling', providing social expressions of essentially inarticulate feelings. Elias observes how the power of symbolism endows the collectivity with 'a numinous existence of its own outside and above the individuals who formed it – with a kind of holiness formerly associated mainly with superhuman beings' (1996, p. 146). In this way symbols exert a compulsive influence on behaviour and opinion. Uttering the name of the nation may be enough to arouse an almost automatic response of awe and deference.

Elias is interested in the formation of distinct 'national characters', or what, anticipating Bourdieu, he terms the national habitus, the set of dispositions and embodied social learning, which he attributes (like Bauer) to the deposit left by a shared history. The fortunes of a nation become sedimented over centuries into the habitus of its individual members (1996, p. 19; compare Braudel, 1991, on the 'identity' of France). Institutions develop to ensure that the people of a society acquire the same characteristics, and possess the same habitus; this includes speaking a common language. Since it is related to historical events, and processes of state formation, a national habitus is not fixed biologically, but develops and changes over time, albeit gradually and imperceptibly. Elias contends that the German national habitus has been shaped by a location poised between Latin and Slav peoples and cultures; by a sense of 'national' decline since the Middle Ages; by discontinuous development; and by late unification (as we saw earlier, never fully coinciding with the limits of a linguistic or cultural domain). These experiences left their residue, inscribed into national character, and explain a tradition of yearning for strong leadership, exceptional national achievements, and an idealized future recapturing past glories. As Elias observes, having an awareness of the peculiarities of the habitus of one's own nation requires 'a specific effort of self-distancing' (1996, p. 2). Otherwise, like one's compatriots, one tends to be absorbed into its taken-for-granted reality.

As Cohen insists, symbols of community are constructed, and their significance is far from self-evident, or immutable. It is not the mere word 'Deutschland' which triggers a response among Germans (Elias, 1996, p. 324), but the accumulated wealth of meanings and associations it has come to represent. Looking 'behind' the symbols, we invariably find they are more complicated, and ambiguous, than first impressions might suggest. Not only are they understood quite differently by those who belong to the symbolized collective, and those outside it, but they do not necessarily carry the same meanings for all who respond to them from within. Elias may be correct in his analysis of the dominant construct of the Germans, and German-ness, but the history of 'Germany' contains many different possibilities, as demonstrated by the extraordinary transformation from the authoritarianism described by Elias (and many others), to the post-1945 West German model of democratic civility and national economic and political success. This would not have been possible if the German 'character' was innate, or too firmly embedded institutionally and historically. Unless due allowance is made for the varied, and changeable, nature of national character, we will be driven back towards over-deterministic explanations that leave no room for individual or collective freedom of action.

Banal nationalism/everyday national identity

Bourdieu has elaborated the concept of habitus theoretically to refer to 'the basic stock of knowledge that people carry around in their heads as a result of living in particular cultures or subcultures' (Layder, 1994, p. 143; Bourdieu, 1977). It also encompasses the durable dispositions they acquire through their experiences as social actors located in certain kinds of backgrounds and circumstances (such as those of class, gender and generation). Habitus becomes a social second nature, of which people themselves are largely unaware; but by behaving in conformity with it, they help produce and reproduce their social circumstances. In this respect, Bourdieu's habitus occupies a similar theoretical position to Berger and Luckmann's concept of the commonsense knowledge upon which people rely for a sense of the reality and solidity of the world around them (Berger and Luckmann, 1967; Layder, 1994, p. 86). Both approaches have been criticized for failing to transcend the limits of social determination. Bourdieu's concept has been described as a 'Trojan horse for determinism' (Alexander, 1995, p. 137), a view which gets support from Bourdieu's contention that:

> the legitimization of the social order results from the fact that agents apply to the objective structures of the social world structures of perception and appreciation that have emerged from these objective structures and tend therefore to see the world as self-evident (Bourdieu, 1990, p. 135).

If so, what scope is there for actors to see through the 'objective' structures of society and change them? This raises the perennial sociological problem of determinism versus freedom, or structure and agency. Berger and Luckmann's argument resembles that of Elias, in attributing to the sedimentation of tradition as it evolves through time the capacity to endow external realities with an objective quality in people's eyes. This is especially so in generational terms: one generation's 'freely' constructed social relationships and ideas become the socially inherited, constrained, givens of successive social cohorts. Discussing their contribution, Layder notes how the social construction of such external realities is buttressed by the effects of language and other symbolic forms, which allow people to think of them in seemingly detached, 'objective' ways. Flags, emblems, kinship rules, legal and governmental procedures and rituals all become means of expressing the independent reality of such things. Nowhere is this more true than in the sphere of nations and nationhood.

Symbolic marking of nations plays an important part in Billig's (1995) account of 'banal nationalism'. He writes especially of the centrality of the national flag, invariably an object of particular veneration. Billig draws attention to the barely observed use of the flag as part of the background to daily life within a nation. Reproduced as a logo, worn as a badge or fashion item, a national flag repeatedly reminds people of where they are, and to what they belong. In their ubiquity, flags form an elemental support for the everyday constitution of national awareness. Other signifiers of nationality work in the same way: maps, songs and anthems, coins, banknotes and memorials. Above all, linguistic markers are employed continually to indicate the scope and limits of the nation. Billig explains that the unnoticed parts of speech do this most effectively: words like 'we', 'our', 'this' (country, land) and 'the' (people, government) are employed by the media and politicians, and a myriad of other less self-conscious users, to provide a continual reminder and reinforcement of the nation's presence. Because they focus on language, these are examples of the *rhetoric* of national identity, the manner in which we talk (or are talked to) about national belonging. As subjects of this discourse, we are called upon to occupy the national place, to respond as 'insiders'. We learn how to do this until it comes almost naturally, whereas if we are 'outside' our own place, reading a 'foreign' press or watching foreign television, we have a sense of dislocation, unsure quite where the message is coming from or how we should react to it. 'National' news is distinguished from 'local' or 'regional' (let alone foreign) news, and usually accorded more weight. The fate of 'fellow-nationals' is singled out for special attention, whilst sundry traits of nationhood are held up for recognition and approbation. Thus the existence and reality of the nation is embedded into routines of life which operate 'mindlessly' and habitually. This world of mundane nationalism requires the continual reproduction of a complex of beliefs, assumptions, habits, representations and practices, that are diffused as common sense, and taken-for-granted as natural and necessary.

The result is that, while there may be problems about naming or expatiating upon our nationality, we are unlikely to say it has slipped our minds, that we forget what we are. In short, Billig believes we are all 'nationalists', at all times. In his eagerness to correct a misapprehension, that nationalism exists only in exceptional circumstances and 'extreme' forms, this may go too far. We prefer to say that we carry our national identities at all times, reserving the term 'nationalism' for more overt expressions of ideas about national interests and national fortunes. Nevertheless, Billig is surely correct in highlighting the extent to which the existence of nations is presumed, as a feature of the contemporary world, and incorporated into common habits of thought, until it is difficult to find any vantage point that stands altogether 'outside' nationalism. Even denials of nationality or its importance frequently exemplify specific national commitments (1995, p. 161), as Billig shows in examining the extent to which claims about 'globalization' and the weakening of national differences and boundaries often conceal nationalistic assumptions and aspirations emanating from the USA.

We have discussed how language is a crucially important component of nationalist constructs, but there is more to national identity than language, or even discourse, alone. Interestingly, coming from a social psychologist, Billig's book is littered with references to the social nature of national identity as stemming from a particular 'form of life'. National identity is 'more than an inner psychological state or an individual self definition: it is a form of life which is daily lived' (1995, p. 69); identity is to be found in 'the embodied habits of social life'. This includes being 'situated physically, legally, socially' (1995, p. 61). In other words, the positioning which lends a person a national identity is multidimensional, consisting of a great variety of arte-facts, concepts and practices. Following Billig's lead, we could say these features are not necessarily loud and assertive; they provide a background hum within which a particular identity is constituted. As well as grand and universalizing claims about national destiny and ambitions, the difference and specialness around which conceptions of nationhood are built encompasses a host of mundane particularities. Identity-conferring features would include: ways of doing things, forms of landscape, atti-tudes of mind, tastes in popular culture, typical objects, cultural symbols, administrative regulations, and so on. In present-day Scotland, banknotes differ from those of England and Wales, and banks are organized differently; the flag of Scotland (the Saltire) is flown in a way in which the English flag (the Cross of St George) very rarely is; beer is called by different names; kilts are sometimes worn; Burns' night is celebrated; football teams have their own league; and there are distinctive rules for house-buying. These all contribute to the convincingly real distinctive-ness of Scottishness; they make Scotland a palpable and concrete entity. Yet these components can be assembled in varied ways, including 'tartanry', as well as a vehement distaste for all it represents (McCrone, 1992). Merely because a set of routines exists which embody the nation, the work of constructing nationality is not done.

Nation and nationalism as discourse and narration

In line with the direction of much of the preceding discussion, Calhoun proposes we 'treat nationalism first as a discursive formation' (1997, p. 22), meaning it should be examined as a way of talking, thinking and apprehending the world that thereby lends it conceptual form and practical organization. Calhoun contends that the image of a system of nations and national groupings is basic to our mental picture of the contemporary world, as well as to political practice. It is upheld and reinforced not just in words and images, but also through maps, the organization of statistics and census information, systems of communication, and a host of other cultural and political arrangements which depict the surface of the globe as compartmentalized into discrete national societies by a limited number of well-defined boundaries. Benedict Anderson (1991) also considers the constitutive power of maps, censuses and museums, which he analyses in relation to colonial practices of definition, classification and registration of remote populations and geographical terrains. Through such means, colonial powers brought into being distinctions and divisions that did not previously exist, with profound repercussions for later development. Most modern African 'nations' bear little resemblance to population groupings and social structures that existed before colonization. A great deal of post-colonial African politics has revolved around attempts to redraw boundaries imposed by alien powers. Such activities have been a preoccupation of modern states towards 'their own' people, as well as their colonial possessions. National populations are measured and recorded, along with the distributions of services and resources within the national terrain. Few countries are without their 'national' museums and galleries, the contents of which may have been assembled from all over the world, yet which tell some story of national endeavour. At the most basic level, for nearly everyone, membership of a national grouping is a precondition for access to a passport that allows one to leave, and return to, the national territory.

In this way the 'illusion' of a self-evident reality, to which Bourdieu and others refer, is presented as a social and political fact, seen in Calhoun's words as 'always already there, taken as established conditions'. Our understanding begins from an assumption of the given, unavoidable presence of nations, and then operates in ways which bear out and reinforce this expectation. Such a discourse is basic to the shape taken by collective identity in the modern world (Melucci, 1996; Castells, 1997). It works via an 'anonymous, unnoticed permeation of our ways of thinking and talking and making sense of the social world' (Brubaker and Cooper, 2000, p. 16). It is not only nationalism as an explicit political commitment and ideology, but all these everyday practices and assumptions that act to conceal 'the very elusiveness and contingency of the nation's precarious existence' (Bauman, 1992, p. 677).

With respect to the specific discourse of nationhood, Calhoun identifies ten distinctive properties. None of them is indispensable, but together they form a pattern of interrelated concepts and assumptions that confer reality upon nations and peoples. They include: boundaries; indivisibility; sovereignty; legitimacy conferred by conformity with the interests of 'the people'; popular mobilization and participation; direct individual membership; common culture; historic depth; common descent; and territoriality (1997, pp. 4–5). As with efforts from Stalin onwards to formulate definitive criteria of nationhood, their application to actual empirical situations is prone to considerable dispute: where are the boundaries to be drawn? How fully must all members participate? To what extent is there a common culture or heritage? What are the collective national interests? Yet even the very fact of engaging in such debates consolidates the impression that nations really do exist as measurable, observable things, and that such questions have 'proper' answers. As Calhoun says:

> nations are constituted largely by the claims themselves, by the way of talking and thinking and acting that relies on these sorts of claims to produce collective identity, to mobilize people for collective projects, and to evaluate peoples and practices. (1997, p. 5)

From this perspective, the modernist search for a 'general theory' of nations and nationalism seems misguided, because it subsumes too many disparate phenomena. Different varieties of nationalism, different constructs of 'nations', and different evaluations of them seem relevant for different historical epochs, across different parts of the world, and from different perspectives. This supports the conclusion that from the point of view of social theory, there is no systematic way of designating a nation (Zubaida, 1978, p. 53). The task is best left to others, such as nationalists and national politicians. Instead what can be said is that the discourse of nationalism helps determine the *form* in which nations are conceived. For instance, according to Anderson, they are thought of as bounded, sovereign and 'horizontally uniform'. The generality of the discourse allows identical linguistic and rhetorical devices to be employed to argue for a host of different outcomes and possibilities. They enable the construction of a great variety of concrete nations, 'genuine' or potential, competing for space within the conceptual scheme. They can be used with equal effect to make the case for integration, and for secession, to applaud or to condemn national and nationalist aspirations. Parties taking opposite sides in such arguments can do so while talking the same language, and employing the same terms. This renders the various concepts and categories of nationalism 'essentially contested', always open to challenge, negotiation and revision. They are constructed in argument (Reicher and Hopkins, 2001, p. 165). They are also theoretically 'chaotic', without fixed meaning or reference. Yet the very fact of debate, and contention about their application and meaning, buttresses the sense that there is something vitally significant and compelling about them, and something substantial about which to argue.

The burden of social constructionism is that nationalism is not peculiar in this regard; the same analytical approach can be applied to other major frameworks of meaning and categorization, such as class, sexuality, race and ethnicity. An underlying device, common to all of them, is essentialism, which reduces competing interpretations and possibilities to some simple, allegedly decisive, measure or criterion. Nationality can be treated as synonymous with language, with place of birth, or observation of particular cultural mores. In practical terms, such essential traits may be taken to define membership of 'really existing and discretely identifiable collections of people' (Calhoun, 1997, p. 18). With tremendous vigour, the rights and obligations of collectives such as Basques, Québécois, Kashmiris, Tamils and Palestinians can be asserted and disputed. This process itself must be treated as part of the discourse of nationalism, in that 'national identity is always a project, the success of which depends upon being seen as an essence' (Reicher and Hopkins, 2001, p. 222). By identifying the 'core' features of a nation or people, its advocates attempt to exercise control over membership, access and direction. They include some, whilst excluding others. As Calhoun states:

> It has been the tacit assumption of modern social and cultural thought that people are normally members of one and only one nation, that they are members of one and only one race, one gender, and one sexual

orientation, and that each of these memberships describes neatly and concretely some aspect of their being. It has been assumed that people naturally live in one world at a time, that they inhabit one way of life, that they speak one language, and that they themselves, as individuals, are singular, integral beings (1997, p. 18).

Recognizing that they rest upon explicit or implicit social agreements and practices brings all these assumptions into question, and contradicts any idea that they are part of nature. It encourages examination of the multiple realities and alternative constructions hidden behind such rigid, and static, categories.

Amongst cultural theorists, for example, it stimulates investigation of the nation as the product of a form of narrative, written and told in a variety of social and literary modes (Bhabha, 1990; S. Hall, 1995). With their help, a field of meanings and symbols associated with national life can be constructed and disseminated. How this is accomplished is amenable to analysis in terms of the various tricks and stratagems of narration. A key strategy is the steady integration into the ongoing story (or stories) of the nation of a mass of particulars, local details, incidents and events. These display and consolidate both the uniqueness and comprehensive scope of the nation. Echoing Gellner, Bhabha observes how 'the scraps, patches and rags of daily life must be repeatedly turned into the signs of national culture' (1990, p. 297). Almost anything, and everything, is grist to the national mill: landscape, memories, objects and buildings, artistic works. As Benedict Anderson identifies, the modern novel has been especially formative in this regard, although other forms of literary expression (including poetry and song) have also played their part. From this cultural studies perspective, nations can be construed as 'imaginary constructs that depend for their existence on an apparatus of cultural fictions in which imaginative literature plays a decisive role' (T. Brennan, 1990, p. 49). Through the analysis of differing forms of national narration, the impression of the nation as sociologically solid and historically continuous can be scrutinized and thrown open to challenge. Rather than one single 'hegemonic' narrative, which represents the authentic or definitive version of the nation and its meaning, it transpires that there are many voices, telling many 'national' stories. This is particularly evident from the margins of society, and those 'in-between' spaces that surround the national domain. Very different perceptions of the nation's nature and history exist among minorities, and peripheral or subordinate groups, than are found at the centre, among the powerful and assertive. Again this renders the meaning and significance of the nation into highly contested cultural territory.

Upon closer inspection, ideas of progress, shared experience, common objectives, and the 'deep' foundations of the nation, with its long past, so familiar from most national stories, may prove no more than hollow constructions, serving the purposes of particular social groups, whilst relegating others who do not 'fit' the story to positions of subordination, neglect or exclusion. Achieving this requires effort and action, both at the level of discourse and in terms of policy and practice. As Calhoun puts it, 'visions of internally uniform and sharply bounded cultural and political identities often have to be produced or maintained by struggle against a richer, more diverse and more promiscuously cross-cutting play of difference and similarities' (Calhoun, 1997, p. 18). Wodak *et al.* (1999) provide evidence for this, using materials derived from group discussions, individual interviews and political speeches. In the Austrian context, arguments range between conceptions of an inclusive multicultural, multiethnic society that is the 'natural' product of its situation at the crossroads of Europe, to others which verge on the image of a racially 'pure', ethnically distinct, population marked by strictly stereotyped behaviour, mentality and emotions. Austria's national self-perception is worked out in intricate processes of negotiation and joint construction among groups and individuals deploying these varied conceptions. When doing so, many resort to conceptions of homogeneous everyday culture, national mentality and naturalized descent, which blank out variation and disagreement; yet the identities they produce remain highly ambivalent, diverse, dynamic and vulnerable. Similar conclusions are reached in relation to Scotland (Reicher and Hopkins, 2001), where inspection of the debates which raged around issues of independence and devolution in the early 1990s shows that not only were very different ideas of 'Scottishness' in play simultaneously, but also that individuals and organizations were perfectly capable of adopting different definitions according to circumstances, and to suit particular audiences.

The work of constructing national identities goes on at many levels, and crosses many domains. It can be pursued down into the fine detail of situated talk and interaction, to discover exactly how people use everyday ideas of national identity and belonging to make sense of themselves and others. Work exploring such questions is a relatively new departure (Fevre and Thompson, 1999;

Brah *et al.*, 1999; Hester and Housley, 2002). Alternatively, national identities can be seen as being constructed from above, through institutional processes and classifications. Events in the former Union of Soviet Socialist Republics (USSR) exemplify such processes (Suny, 1993; Brubaker, 1996, 1998). Throughout the Soviet era, efforts were made to transcend nationalist ideologies, by propagating concepts of universal Soviet citizenship, and upholding a class-based politics. Yet at the same time the idea of national identity was being thoroughly institutionalized. The USSR was subdivided into 'national' homelands, and internal passports assigned each citizen a particular national/ethnic identification. This categorization of people and the spaces they occupied constituted and reinforced awareness of nationhood, which became a vital mechanism for the distribution of resources and recognition of claims. Hence, beneath the surface, the 'work' of constructing and reconstructing nations continued. The break-up of the USSR after 1989, and the consequent struggles around questions of independence and national frontiers, did not signify therefore the 'return of the repressed', the unlocking of deep and intractable, primordial, identities, but a predictable outcome of the logic of these processes of institutionalization and social construction. Referring to this failure by the Soviet Union to construct a form of identification superseding these narrower national categories, Castells (1997, p. 39) reminds us that although communities may be imagined, this does not necessarily mean that they will be believed.

Conclusion

By now the constructionist standpoint has become something of an orthodoxy among those working on nationalism, even though critics detect more than a trace of old-fashioned essentialism hidden within it (Brubaker and Cooper, 2000; Reicher and Hopkins, 2001). Brubaker has criticized the uneasy combination of analytical constructivism with 'practical' essentialism that pervades many discussions of nationalism, as with other forms of identity politics. Despite its theoretical premises, constructivism does not always escape the dangers of reification. Brubaker insists that whereas reification as a social process is central to the composition of ethnicity and nationhood, so that for example 'the fiction of a nation can crystallize, at certain moments, as a powerful, compelling, reality' (Brubaker and Cooper, 2000, p. 5), as social analysts we must reject the 'realist, reifying conception of nations as real communities'. Although nations and nationhood may appear 'real' to those who live and act within them, the task of the theorist is to see how they come to *seem* like this. Others want to guard against being too radical or one-sided in taking this direction (see Eriksen, 2002, p. 57). Castells, for instance, warns against 'excessive deconstructionism' (1997, p. 29), asserting that in the final analysis national identity is a product of a shared history, and a shared project, and that even if diversified, it is underpinned by experiences common to all the people of a given country. Even so, he accepts the basic tenets of the constructionist approach when he writes that 'nationalism is indeed culturally and politically constructed, but what really matters, both theoretically and practically, is, as for all identities, how, from what, by whom, and for what it is constructed' (1997, p. 32).

CHAPTER 6

Gender and Nation

The notion of what the nation was in its finest hour – when it was most unified, most altruistic – will be of a community in which women sacrificed their desires for the sake of a male-led collective.

(Enloe, 2000, p. 63)

Seen through the eyes of women, or as framed by women's experiences, the world can look very different from how men view it. This is the theme of Cynthia Enloe's feminist work on international relations, which extends beyond the conventional terrain of politics and diplomacy, to consider phenomena like the role of foreign military bases, tourism, the global sex industry, and the international division of labour in agriculture, clothing and banking. In all these, Enloe (2000) shows how women invariably occupy distinctive places, and how ideas about women, and their differences from men, profoundly influence the organization and interpretation of social life. In fact, across the board, women rarely fill the same positions as men, with the same opportunities, capacities and powers. Yet nationalism relies upon asserting and recognizing a past and future that is shared, as a common experience. By demonstrating how relationships within and between nations are constructed around differences between men and women, Enloe puts gender into the picture in a way that suggests it is too important for theorists of nationalism to ignore.

For example, nationalist movements rarely, if ever, take women's situation as their point of departure. On the contrary, nationalism often suppresses women's concerns, or puts them aside until the 'more important' issue of the nation's fate is decided. Hence Enloe contends that nationalism typically springs from 'masculinized memory, masculinized humiliation and masculinized hope' (2000, p. 44). Once one asks where the women are in all this, one sees that they are assigned particular roles in the nationalist drama, usually in support of the leadership and control of men. So, among colonial nations, women were expected to uphold standards of 'civilized' respectability, as teachers, missionaries and wives. 'Third World' women may be required to maintain ethnic or religious cultural standards that have been absorbed into definitions of national identity. Wearing the veil is a contentious example within contemporary Islamic nationalisms.

If existing nationalisms are strongly inflected with masculinity and masculine values, the question arises whether matters would be different if women exerted greater influence. To put it crudely, are international politics violent because men are violent? Would things change if women were in charge? The involvement of women in peace movements across the world, and their readiness to resist and oppose warfare, might suggest so. Enloe goes some way with this argument when she hypothesizes that there might be greater awareness of cross-national identities, helpful in resolving conflicts, if nation-states grew more out of the ideas and experiences of feminist nationalists. Women might have things in common which would defuse national divisions. At the same time, she concedes that the feminist movement is biased towards the standpoint of a rather narrow band of affluent Western women and therefore is not easily absorbed into the politics of societies which are still busy establishing their claims to independent national existence. This makes living as a nationalist feminist one of the most difficult projects in today's world.

One of nationalism's most powerful assertions is that identification with the nation and loyalty to its claims overrides all other commitments on the part of the individual. This contention takes both factual and normative shape, putting the nation before other attachments such as class, region, or religious affiliation. To a perhaps surprising degree, it appears to be endorsed by many social theorists. In their efforts to explain and account for the strength of nationalism, they also convey a sense of its transcendental character. This enables them to discuss national belonging in ways that make it seem uniform and identical for all who share it. Benedict Anderson's conception of the nation as a fraternity (*sic*) bound together in a 'deep horizontal comradeship' (1983, p. 16), like Gellner's image of an 'anonymous impersonal society, with mutually substitutable atomized individuals' (1983, p. 57) suggests that nationalism does away with significant social differences, or subordinates them to its domination. As members of the nation, it appears, all people are alike in the way in which they identify with and respond to its appeal, and participate in its fortunes and cata-strophes. Hence the generality of much of the discussion of national identity, which deals with the relationship between the nation as a collectivity and the individual, without much consider-ation of any intervening factors. Such an approach is deeply at odds with a normal sociological understanding of how people are shaped by their social relationships and group memberships. Recent years have seen a rediscovery of the importance of a range of social 'differences' and a new-found insistence that these cannot be reduced simply to some 'basic' or underlying characteristic, such as nationality. Such arguments are indebted to the inroads made by feminism upon mainstream, or 'malestream' sociology (Abbott and Wallace, 1990).

In common with the bulk of their writings on other topics, clas-sical contributors to the analysis of nations and nationalism seem blind to differences of sex and gender. Up to the 1970s, most soci-ology largely ignored women, except in relation to particular domains, such as family, community, education and religious worship. The majority of social analyses dealt with undifferenti-ated persons and 'individuals', as if it did not matter whether they were male or female. By implication, it could be assumed that effectively they were regarded as male. Men could be taken as representative of the non-gendered subjectivity of human beings, whereas women more often were defined in relation to men, as mothers, wives, sisters and daughters (Allen, 1998, p. 55). The soci-ology of nationalism is no exception. As McCrone notes 'one looks in vain to the works of Gellner, Anderson, Smith and others for a sustained analysis of gender issues' (1998, p. 122). His comment puts a generous gloss on the almost total lack of consideration of the issue in such texts. McCrone's own textbook devotes just four pages to the topic (mostly discussing the work of one feminist theorist); other recent texts do little better (Calhoun, 1997; Özkir-imli, 2000; Delanty and O'Mahony, 2002). Equally, it should be said, many texts about feminism and the sociology of gender say little about the relevance of nationalism and national conscious-ness (Tong, 1989; Abbott and Wallace, 1990).

Does this matter? Clearly there are those, like Enloe, who would say that it does, and not all of them are feminists. Paying attention to the relationship between women, nationalism and gender opens up an important line of critical exploration, to do with the vague-ness and over-generality of many claims made about the nature and relevance of national identities. Most of those who have been active in this field would admit that as yet the study of nationalism and gender remains underdeveloped (Yuval-Davis, 1997, p. 3; Walby, 2000, p. 525; Racioppi and See, 2000); the conversation between the two is fragmented (Ranchod-Nillson and Tetreault, 2000).

Feminists theorize that gender differences are fundamental to the way societies are constituted; generally they result in the skewing of power and control towards the interests of men. If it is true that gender relations are pervasive, and operate at every level of social life (Bradley, 1996, p. 82), then there is no reason to believe the social organization of nations and nationalism is exempt from their influence. We should anticipate key differences in the national involvements of men and women, and expect to find gender differentiation exerting a major influence on the formation and structure of nations. Feminists who have taken up the challenge of understanding these matters would contend that this is not merely a question of adding a missing dimension to existing theories, but requires us to rethink the assumptions and arguments on which they are based (Walby, 1997; Racioppi and See, 2000). This makes the tendency among the authors of many discussions to insert a brief section on the topic, whilst noting that as yet it has not been integrated fully into the mainstream of political and sociological writing (Spencer and Wollman, 2002, p. 51), less than satisfactory.

Ideas of nation and nationhood purport to engage all kinds and conditions of people in the same way, with the same degree of intensity. Appeals are made to the 'national' interest, or to 'patriotic duty' with the expectation that they will elicit the same response, regardless of social positionings, including age and sex. At the level of the banal everyday nationalism analysed by Billig, for example, the national 'we' rarely distinguishes between people on such grounds – to do so would undermine the pretension that it refers to a unified mass of people, thinking and feeling as one. If this impression is to be maintained, there must be no qualification or reservation in its deployment as an expression of a singular sentiment and will. Yet Billig himself notes, almost in passing, that the nationalism which pervades the sports pages of national newspapers is directed very largely towards men, who are more likely to read such reports. Consequently, men's concerns are presented 'as if defining the whole national honour' (1995, p. 123). Thus the issue of gender cannot be ignored. Even so, Billig argues, nationalism is not confined to males; newspapers address both male and female readers as members of the nation, and, he concludes, 'we, the readers, readily accept the deixis of homeland' (1995, p. 126). Maybe so, but do 'we' all accept it in the same way, attaching the same meaning to it? Billig's reference to the differing ways in which the nation might figure in 'the women's pages' and the sports section suggests not, but it is not a theme he pursues in any depth.

Elsewhere, Billig recognizes that possession of a national identity need not mean everyone within the nation-state is identical. He cites Stuart Hall's view that to suppose that identity 'has to do with people that look the same, feel the same, call themselves the same, is nonsense' (1991, p. 49). Like any other identity, a sense of national identity can contain a range of variations and differences, including variations around the axis of gender. This poses a key question: how far can such differences be taken, while remaining within the limits of the 'same' national consciousness? To what extent do men and women perceive their national identity in the same ways, and how far are they similarly embedded within the framework of the nation? Arguments advanced by Enloe and others suggest that the 'gendering' of the nation creates substantial differences in how the sexes relate to it, to the extent that masculine interests and propensities may be upheld at the cost of those of women. The claim that women are less driven by patriotic enthusiasm and nationalistic antagonisms and therefore more active in the cause of peace and internationalism is a prominent example. Some accounts make nationalism appear as an exclusively male preoccupation, whereas women's lives are said to centre elsewhere, in concerns with home, family and community (see Pearce, 2000).

Feminist approaches to nationalism

Feminist critiques of conventional sociology begin from the assertion that

> there is, at best, no recognition that women's structural position and consequent experiences are not the same as men's, and that sex is therefore an important explanatory variable, and, at worst, women's experiences are deliberately ignored or distorted. Furthermore the ways in which men dominate and subordinate women are either ignored or seen as natural (Abbott and Wallace, 1990, p. 5).

Feminist approaches to nationalism presume that these differences of position and experience have implications for how the sexes relate to the nation, its history and characteristics. However, since the critical themes developed by feminists apply to most or all forms of social organization, there is a problem in disentangling those aspects that are specific to nationalism. Since the idea of the nation-state has often been confused with that of 'society', at least in mainstream Western sociology, then the work done by feminists to uncover social differences and inequalities between men and women necessarily applies, by extension, to national formations. All national societies contain unequal relationships and systematic unfairnesses between men and women. For example, there are no labour markets anywhere in which men and women enjoy the same opportunities, or share the same rewards. But this observation adds nothing to our knowledge of nations as such. The fact that in different national societies things are done differently, and therefore show significant variations – for instance, that relations between the sexes tend to be more egalitarian in the Scandinavian than the Mediterranean nations (Walby, 2000) – takes us a little further, by indicating that national frameworks matter, but still tells us nothing specific about the relationship between nationality and gender. This may explain why the feminist contribution has had so little impact so far on the general approach taken to nations and nationalism: it is seen as more pertinent at the level of empirical detail than it is for modifying our overall theoretical grasp. Consequently, awareness of gender, and the lessons of feminism, have yet to be mainstreamed within studies of nationalism. Yet arguments advanced by feminists, and those influenced by them, have been a major factor in the development of new social theory, and this has been conducive in turn to the production of post-classical interpretations of national issues, including those discussed in the previous chapter.

Taking even the most limited view of its relevance, analysis in gender terms can bring things to light that were missing previously from the account. For instance, Sluga's re-reading of peace negotiations following the First World War (Sluga, 2000) reveals how women's efforts to intervene were routinely sidelined by leading male politicians. Attempts to highlight the parallels between arguments being put forward at the time to validate the principle of national self-determination, and those proclaiming the rights of women, were rejected, almost out of hand. Yet there were obvious contradictions in the assertion of the rights of 'peoples' to determine their own futures, at a time when at least half of those people were excluded from taking part in any such process by virtue of their sex. Whenever it came to choosing, the national principle was put ahead of the aspirations of women, and it was left to nations (that is, to men) to determine how far women should be given rights to vote, and to participate in political life. That it was commonplace for women who married foreigners to have to forfeit their entitlement to nationality shows how uncertain women's attachment to the nation was during this period. Nationhood appeared a specifically male prerogative.

Elsewhere Sluga (1998) traces this distortion in the connection between gender and nationhood back to the origins of modern nationalism. The declaration of the 'Rights of Man' that underpinned the French Revolution of 1789 inevitably raised the issue of whether such rights were gender-specific. Despite their active role in events surrounding the revolution itself, women quickly found themselves excluded from the political arena; it was not until 1944 that French women got the vote. Through such processes, gender became a significant site of national identification. Nations were not only constituted from ethnic and 'racial' materials, as emphasized by writers like Smith and Hutchinson, but were also gendered in their composition. The differing relationships of men and women to their nations were not incidental features, but represented a systematic bias, with far-reaching consequences for conceptions of gender, as well as those of nation. As Sluga puts it, 'by the late nineteenth century, representations of women's difference legitimated masculine agency and subjectivity, and designated the capacity for self-determination as contrary to women's feminine nature' (2000, p. 502). Like most other major social undertakings, the making of nations was men's work. Benedict Anderson's reference to the nation's imagined community as a fraternity reflects this bias, an impression sustained by the total absence of discussion of women from his account of the making of the prototypical nations of Latin America.

What Sluga refers to, in an understated fashion, as the 'difficult relationship of feminism to nationalism' springs from the way each veers towards a universalizing discourse, giving primacy to one particular distinction as the overwhelming force that binds people together into a collectivity. Whether it be gender or nationhood, this force is seen as taking precedence over any other 'internal' difference, unifying those who share it, and opposing them to all who do not. Thus, for Anthony Smith (1991) national identity is the most powerful and durable form of collective consciousness in the modern world. Given this assertion of an essential homogeneity, anyone seeking to stress some alternative distinction poses a threat to such unity (Davies, 1999). So nationalists and feminists seem to be drawn into unavoidable opposition: claims for the emancipation of women threaten to undermine the avowed unity of the nation, whereas national differences weaken the proclaimed commonality of condition among women across the world. Both sets of claims have what Calhoun would call a 'totalitarian potential', capable of being used to 'trump' other values and identities (1994, p. 326). The history of nationalist and women's movements is riven with examples of debates about how the realization of one set of interests should wait upon the achievement of the interests of the other (Enloe, 2000, p. 62).

Faced with the challenge posed by alternative systems of membership and classification, such as those put forward by feminists, nationalism can respond in two ways. It can deny their significance, treating them as relatively superficial or trivial, as it does usually with differences of class, region and status. Or it can make use of them, as differences which support and buttress, rather than denying, its own importance. This is how most writers see the relationship between nations and gender: nationalism utilizes assumptions about gender differences, and in doing so, underwrites and consolidates them. Nationalism becomes a key enforcer of gender relationships and the accompanying inequalities. Writing about the Yugoslavian context, for example, one observer notes how deeply nationalism and sexism are interwoven, one nourishing the other. Thus

> women often embody the nation, they are bearers of its honour and love. In nationalist discourse woman is either the mother of the nation or the sex object. She is either a protector and regenerator of the collective or a possession of that collective. These symbolic images have been used by the media [in] getting the nation ready to face the enemy (Morokvasic, 1998, p. 75).

Here women have a definite place in the nation, perceived as vital to its value and survival; but it is a place set apart from that of men. The nation is gendered at its very core.

Feminists who assign a primordial significance to gender differences (Firestone, 1971; Daly, 1978) would hardly expect things to be different. In a world essentially constructed around gender, nations are no more exempt from its influence than any other set of social arrangements. In the light of the universal suffering of women, national variations, like those of ethnicity and 'race', seem a matter of indifference. Yet how gender is conceived has important consequences for the fabric of nations, since they must absorb those gender distinctions that already exist, perhaps as a permanent part of the human condition thus far. Like all other social formations, nations will rest upon a foundation of absolute gender difference. Theories of 'patriarchy' can operate in this way. The concept of patriarchy has been a highly contentious part of the feminist lexicon (Crompton and Mann, 1986; Walby, 1990). For some, it signifies a system of male domination reaching into every aspect of the lives of women and men. From this viewpoint, the treatment accorded to women within Yugoslav nationalism is no more than a straightforward expression of patriarchal ideology, which justifies and legitimizes a structure of social relations in which men are privileged, and women disprivileged. We could expect to find similar attitudes displayed towards women in all national discourses, since they form a deeply ingrained part of a patriarchal world-view; there is nothing special to explain, except perhaps some particular details. Others might view this as an over-generalized approach, sacrificing historical and empirical grasp through its emphasis on the invariant properties of gender relationships. Critics of the concept of patriarchy see it as encouraging a reductionist, essentialist approach to explanation, in which everything comes down to a rather predictable reassertion of the power exerted by men over women. As in debates surrounding the nature of nationalism, the battle over essentialism has been central to the development of feminist theorizing, as well as directly relevant to various kinds of feminist political practice (Anthias and Yuval-Davis, 1992; Cockburn, 2000).

Radical feminists believe that gender is too basic to be affected by national variations. Walby (1992) identifies a number of alternative general approaches to understanding the links between 'woman' and 'nation'. A number of commentators, perhaps the majority, and predominantly male (though an exception is Greenfeld, 1992), espouse an opposite view, that gender really makes no significant difference to our understanding of national issues. Others treat gender and nation as distinct considerations, which may combine to produce particular effects: for example, a 'double burden' for women who occupy positions in oppressed national groupings. This implies that there can be significant differences among women, some of whom might enjoy the benefits of an advantageous nationality. This argument has led many feminists to move away from the essentialism which treats all women alike, as members of a single category, to insist on the need to consider how different groups of women – such as white and black, Muslim and Christian – may meet with contrasting experiences. Some would take this further, seeing the situation of women as varying substantially according to their particular national location. It was suggested above that Scandinavian women might experience very different patterns of inequality to women belonging to nations in other parts of the world. Finally, some theories work from the premise that gender and nationality are interrelated in complex and dynamic ways, a position exemplified in Walby's own conclusion, that 'gender cannot be analyzed outside of ethnic, national and "race" relations, but neither can these latter phenomena be analysed without gender' (1997, p. 195).

The patriarchal nation?

Despite these varying angles of approach, there is common ground across much of this writing. Not least, in most discussions one can detect the outlines of the unequal relationships between men and women associated with patriarchy. Some theorists (Mann, 1986; Stacey, 1986; Pateman, 1988) prefer to confine this concept to a particular set of attributes that are pre-modern, and to that extent, prevalent before the rise of the modern nation and nation-state. Mann describes a patriarchal social order as one where power is held by male heads of households over all junior males, females and children; there is a clear separation between public and private spheres of life; and power in the public sphere is shared among male patriarchs, to the complete exclusion of women. He mentions that this is an ideal type description, but not far removed from the reality of social organization for many hundreds of years (Mann, 1986), and still recognizable in societies of Africa, Asia and the Middle East. Close connections between family, kinship, household and lineage are important here (Stacey, 1986). According to Stacey, as a separate public realm grew beyond the limits of the family and home, men capitalized on their patriarchal power from within the family, to secure control over new areas of political and economic life. Women became 'domesticated' (more confined to the household and family) and where they did enter public life, and employment, did so under the domination of men. As Mann notes, these arrangements became institutionalized, and persisted for nearly a century and a half. The nation-state and nationalism took form within these parameters. Hence, doctrines of nationhood and citizenship,

> when elaborated, made clear that the person and the nation were not universal: servants, almost always, and usually labourers and those without property were not to be an active part of the political community . . . Women got similar treatment. Despite the rhetoric of liberalism women were not included in the nation (Mann, 1986, p. 49).

Here the 'nation' is synonymous with the public sphere, the political world of citizenship, civic responsibility and privilege.

As Walby points out, so far as the timing of nationhood is concerned, if political participation and access to public life is the measure, then women gained membership of the nation in different ways, and at different times, from men. Mann's comment that 'full legal and political citizenship in the nation-state were achieved and then maintained comparatively easily by women' is not likely to command much support among feminists! Indeed, in many contemporary nations, women are still excluded from much of public life.

The relevance of all this for understanding the connections between gender and nation is that this complex of links between family structures, the private/public spheres, and the relationships of men to women carried over into the structure of the nation-state in ways which continue to be determinative. In some respects, nationalism actually foregrounded them. Mosse (1985) describes how the emergence of modern bourgeois society, especially in German-speaking countries, sharpened distinctions between the 'proper' realms of male and female activity, linking them to notions of respectability; women were seen as belonging in the home, while men were expected to engage in business and political affairs. The growth of strongly masculine fraternity groups, hotbeds of nationalistic sentiment, added to the close alignment between ideas of sexuality and nationhood. While masculinity was the foundation of the nation, women were accorded primacy as custodians of social tradition (Mosse, 1985, p. 17; Pryke, 1998). In such ways, the social changes associated with the formation of modern nations stimulated a 'firmer delineation of gender boundaries, which coincided with the simultaneous rise of the bourgeois public sphere and the privileging of the patriarchal household as a microcosm of the social, economic and political order' (Sluga, 1998, p. 92).

Within this microcosm there figured strong images of the roles and duties of mothers and fathers, which were transferred symbolically to the macro domain of the nation. Men and women were expected to fulfil national obligations in the same way as they conducted their household duties: by carrying out distinct and complementary functions. At its crudest, women should produce babies for the nation, whilst men trained themselves in readiness to fight, to protect the 'womenandchildren' (Enloe, 1990). This was conducive to a view of the national community as a 'natural' extension of family and kinship relations, which harmonized well with interpretations of the nation that stressed its organic, biological foundations. Definitions of gender could thus be made to appear natural and fixed, given in the way in which the family and kinship structures of society were organized. Most obviously, they could be underwritten by ideas about the fixed biological or sexual nature bestowed upon men and women, inherent 'in the blood' in much the same way as national and ethnic identities. Benedict Anderson notes how this enables the nation to take on the same air of disinterested solidarity as the family: 'In everything "natural" there is always something unchosen . . . precisely because such ties are not chosen, they have about them a halo of disinterestedness' (1983, p. 131). According to Anthony Smith, the metaphor of the family is indispensable to nationalism; both evoke 'strong loyalties and vivid attachments' (1991, p. 79).

Balibar (1991) examines these connections more fully, pointing to ways in which notions of nation, 'race', family and gender work together to produce particular results. Along with the relationships of marriage and descent that operate through the family, the criteria of genealogy assume a central importance for placing people into their various ethnic, national and racial groups. Conceptions of human 'nature' are accompanied by a whole system of allegedly natural differences, including sexual schemas to do with issues like heredity and interbreeding. The various acts of classification and hierarchy this entails 'are operations of naturalization *par excellence* or, more accurately, of projections of historical and social difference into the realm of an imaginary nature' (Balibar and Wallerstein, 1991, p. 56). Thus Balibar contends that 'racial' characteristics are always interpretable as metaphors for differences between the sexes. Normally, marriage and sexual relationships form within the national population, and the nation embraces the individual within a large extended family or kinship network, from the cradle to the grave. The family is 'nationalized', and, along with it, relationships between men and women. Despite the emergence of the 'private life' of the family, the state always shows a great deal of interest in its regulation and management. With the rise of the nation-state, to a great extent, this involves a transfer of control from religious agencies to governments. For instance, the state assumes responsibility for maintaining records of family connections and alliance. Emphasis on connections of family, blood and sexuality draws ideas of nation and race close together: hence 'every discourse on the "fatherland" or nation which associates these with defence of the family and birth rate is already ensconced in the universe of racism' (Balibar and Wallerstein, 1991, p. 106). We can add that it is embedded likewise in a framework of sexism. Indeed, as one commentator puts it, 'nationalism is a system of values and a code of honour that defines who is and is not a *real* American or German or Korean . . . The moral economy of nationalism is gendered, sexualized and racialized' (Nagel, 2003, p. 146).

Women and the nation

The kinds of connections we have been exploring enter into the most ambitious attempt so far to explicate the relationships between gender and nation: the work of Nira Yuval-Davis and her collaborator Floya Anthias (Anthias and Yuval-Davis, 1989, 1992; Yuval-Davis, 1997). Peterson (1994, 2000) offers a somewhat similar framework. Yuval-Davis presents an account of what she regards as the main 'intersections' between the two phenomena, making it evident that women's real and imagined position within the family exerts an extensive influence over them. This is apparent from the primary emphasis placed upon women's reproductive role within the formation of the nation and national consciousness. On the one hand, this is a biological contribution: women are the mothers of the nation, who produce its next generation. But, as mothers, they also play a major part in socializing this successor generation, passing on the nation's distinctive culture and value-system, together with a sense of national membership. Biologically and culturally, therefore, women have a particular obligation towards the nation's future, but, in line with assumptions conventionally made about gender differences, this is treated as being more about the maintenance of existing

patterns and values than about their creation. Thirdly, in performing these functions, women are also instrumental in reproducing
the boundaries around their ethnic or national groups.
Furthermore, society uses women, and their gender characteristics,
to symbolize and signify the nature of the nation and ethnicity.
Finally, women participate directly in a variety of national struggles, including political, economic and military processes (Anthias
and Yuval-Davis, 1992, p. 115; Anthias and Yuval-Davis, 1989).
The last of the above-mentioned forms of involvement is intended
to register explicitly the fact that women do engage actively in
national processes, and cannot be treated merely as passive participants whose part is defined by others. Otherwise, the focus on
symbolic and reproductive roles might encourage the view that
woman only sustain what men create.

The gender agenda sketched out in the preceding paragraph has
far-reaching consequences for nations. Despite the impression
created by nationalist ideology, women cannot be treated as
peripheral to, or somehow 'outside', the national framework – far
from it, since according to Yuval-Davis it is women who reproduce
nations, biologically, culturally and symbolically. As one of her
chapter headings has it, we are confronted by 'nationed gender
and gendered nations' (Yuval-Davis, 1997, p. 21). With regard to
the biological function, for example, as Balibar's remarks already
hinted, while women are defined as the primary reproducers of the
nation's members, then issues concerning the rate and quality of
reproduction bear down especially heavily upon them. Although,
obviously enough, both sexes are involved, national strategies to
do with the birth-rate, or differential rates of reproduction between
groups, are directed mainly at women. When the Palestinian
leader Yasar Arafat said that the principal duty of Palestinian
women was to breed faster than their Israeli enemies (Yuval-Davis,
1997, p. 36), the sentiment could have been replicated in many
national situations. A leading concern of national governments has
been with maintaining their birth-rates, partly to ensure sufficient
human resources for internal purposes, but also to keep pace with
the growth of other nations. At times, anxieties are reversed, and
controls are placed upon excessive numbers of births, as in India
and China, and almost always it falls to women to take primary
responsibility for birth control measures. Meanwhile, particular
groups may come under pressure to have more or fewer children
– especially where ideas are abroad about the relative calibre of the
parental stock, such as those put forward by eugenicists, or those

with a horror of the breeding potential of an 'underclass', or some other national minority. Given these quantitative and qualitative concerns, we find a range of interventions into the life of families and couples, including policies relating to contraception, abortion, pre-marital sex, child-care and so on. Invariably, women are prime targets for such actions, while arguably they are designed and carried out, frequently by men, on behalf of what could be construed as male interests. Certainly feminists would make this case, and in many societies it would be difficult to deny its truth. In general, nations exercise considerable control over the area of sexual reproduction, and associated patterns of conduct, and in doing so they enforce expectations about behaviour appropriate to the sexes, as well as to the national grouping (Nagel, 2003).

Even with respect to these aspects of the interface between nationality and gender issues, it is hard to distinguish the 'biological' from the 'cultural'. Since birth is the main route to eligibility for membership of the nation, the national interest in reproduction extends to the area of 'legitimate' birth, with concern to regulate sexual liaisons and forms of marriage, and to eliminate 'improper' forms of sexuality, which might include homosexuality, prostitution and 'miscegenation', all of which at different times have been defined as crimes against the nation. How this is done clearly varies between nations and different periods of history. Nevertheless, the ubiquity of the cultural channelling of biology and sexuality is evident, and again, the links between gender, race and nation are all too apparent. By comparison, the intersection between gender and the wider 'cultural' sphere of reproduction is vast, as the opening words of Yuval-Davis' discussion (1997, p. 1) betray: 'constructions of nationhood usually involve specific notions of both "manhood" and "womanhood" '. Here gender is embedded in the very meaning of nation, what it is to be national, and how members of the nation should behave. As the editors of a collection of papers on the theme put it:

> Nationalism defines who belongs and who does not belong to the national collectivity and prescribes appropriate gender and sexual identities by which genuine members of the nation may be recognized. National identities are also associated with specific forms of sexuality and particular ethnicities. (Charles and Hintjens, 1998, p. 6)

Yuval-Davis ranges widely in examining the myriad ways in which gender and sexuality become part of the cultural resources of society, and its various collectivities. In effect, their use as aspects of nations and nationalism forms no more than a sub-category of a much wider deployment in the construction of all sorts of communal, ethnic and racial boundaries, and types of social identity and difference. With regard to many sorts of collec-tivity, women find themselves constructed as symbolic custodians of its boundaries, carriers of its honour, and vehicles for the repro-duction of its particular culture across the generations (1997, p. 67). Expectations placed upon them are not shared by their fathers, sons, husbands and partners. For instance, their 'virtue', or lack of it, as individuals and sexual beings may be taken to reflect back upon the nation, in a way that male virtue does not. Conversely, men may be judged in terms of other supposedly national traits, such as valour or determination.

In the case of the imagined community of the nation, particular gender characteristics and roles may be attributed to the nation itself – such as 'Mother India' or 'Mother Ireland'. It falls then to women to uphold the associated virtues and strengths. The nation may be held to possess an idealized femininity, or masculinity (as a 'warrior' nation), and be represented in male or female form, as with Britannia, Germania, the French revolutionary symbol Marianne, Uncle Sam or John Bull, or the numerous figures and statues of national heroes and martyrs that cover the land. National myths of origin and foundation often contain references to sexual acts and roles, and to the part played in national devel-opment by real or fantasized male and female figures (Benton, 1998). Nations are commonly spoken of as the fatherland or mother-land. The national territory is also the 'homeland', which shares the intimacies and warmth of the family home. The national language is the mother tongue, learned at the mother's knee, close to the family hearth. In these and many other ways, ideas of nation and gender blend into one another until they become indistin-guishable, and often unnoticed.

The interplay between notions of 'manhood' and 'womanhood', and processes of national construction, goes beyond these symbolic and representational forms. We have touched already upon the question of citizenship, and access to the public realm where key decisions are made and national projects defined. Yuval-Davis suggests that for women, citizenship is always struc-tured dualistically (1998, p. 178), since they participate in its general characteristics, and yet are subjected to specific laws and regulations that pertain to them as wives, mothers and females.

These include definitions of rights with regard to ownership of property, voting, access to employment, welfare and control over children, as well as formal recognition of nationality and ability to hold a passport. In some countries, women cannot drive cars or attend school. Recognition of citizens' rights, and 'full' membership of the nation, has been linked closely to distinctions between public and private domains, and active and passive involvement (Yuval-Davis, 1997). These distinctions are not hard-and-fast, but politically constructed, so that there is often considerable negotiation and struggle around their limits. The battle for women's suffrage is well known, but forms only part of the effort devoted to expanding, and equalizing, the citizenship rights and duties available to women and men. Given what has been described already, it is understandable that issues to do with reproductive rights, including birth-control and abortion, and more general questions of women's rights to control their own bodies, assume such importance in the arena of national politics. As Yuval-Davis emphasizes, this does not mean that with respect to any of these issues all women occupy a single position. There are women who are vehemently 'pro-choice' and 'pro-life'; in favour of, as well as opposed to, female circumcision; keen to open up the military to female involvement, or to demonstrate against it on pacifist grounds.

Since some definitions of citizenship extend it well beyond the sphere of politics and public life, to encompass economic, social and communal rights (Marshall, 1950), including those vested in the 'private' areas of family and civil society, it is unlikely that these distinctive gender features will ever vanish altogether from the national scene. In Israel, for example, a society where considerable steps have been taken to equalize citizenship entitlements between the sexes, women still experience great disadvantages within the family, and a very limited role in political life. The public/private divide is institutionalized so that whereas the state regulates the public sphere, religious authorities maintain control over personal life; and, of course, the rights available to Arab women living in Israel are radically inferior to those possessed by Jews (Bryson, 1998). As ever, gender divisions are cut across by other national, religious and ethnic differences, which confound any simplistic generalizations about the advantages and disadvantages various groups enjoy. As with other groups, the social reality women encounter remains varied and complex, and no simple statement of a feminist agenda will do justice to it (Yuval-Davis, 1998, p. 179).

This does not prevent reality itself undergoing 'simplification' in certain extreme situations. Given the essentializing possibilities contained within the construction of both nationalism and gender differences, their combination produces an awesome potential logic of simplification. We see this in the heightened relevance of gender in conditions of national warfare. Conventionally, possession of full national citizenship has been tied to readiness to make the ultimate sacrifice, to die for one's country, which has been seen as something men must do. In an age of military professionalism, and total war, differences between civilians and armed combatants have eroded, and this equation perhaps has lost its meaning. But even where women do put on military uniforms, they tend not to be seen as part of the front-line forces (Enloe, 1988; Bryson, 1989; Sparks, 2000). It is men who are expected to put their lives at risk in the name of the nation. However, this does not exempt women from the ravages of war and national conflict. Instead, their symbolic and material importance to the nation exposes them to retribution from the nation's enemies; the violation of the nation can be achieved through the violation of women. Recent national and ethnic struggles in the former Yugoslavia, and in Rwanda, have brought this to world attention. Several contributors to the collection edited by Charles and Hintjens (Allen, 1998; Benton, 1998; Morokvasic, 1998) deal with the significance of threats, fears and rumours, as well as the reality, of rape as a weapon in national struggles (see also Peterson, 2000).

Used against the women of another nation, rape constitutes the ultimate transgression of national boundaries, challenging just about every connection we have made between gender and national identity. In war situations, and when countries are invaded, frequently they are described as having been 'raped', as with Kuwait in 1990. According to Morokvasic, rape in Yugoslavia was condemned not for what it did to women, but as an attack on the nation. All women became vulnerable, because each in their own person represented the hostile nation, its honour and its future potential. In such situations nations can be driven back towards those essentializing conceptions that insist upon the biological, and ethnic, foundations of nationhood and identity. In the Yugoslav context, women found themselves compelled to adapt to ideas of themselves as Serbs, Croats or Bosnians, often against their own inclinations and resistance. Yet, even here, not everyone succumbed; there were those who continued to identify themselves as Yugoslavs, or, still more inclusively, simply as women (Allen, 1998; Morokvasic, 1998; Cockburn, 2000). Even *in extremis*, choices could be made, confirming that it is impossible to define a single female perspective on the nation, or an unambiguous stance for women to adopt towards national conflicts (Ranchod-Nilsson and Tetreault, 2000, p. 7).

Conclusion

For reasons that should be perfectly obvious, feminists prioritize gender and its social significance over other issues. Intentionally or not, their contributions bring its varied effects together so as to highlight its importance, and perhaps endorse its nature as a fundamental determinant of social life. Others do the same for ethnicity, 'race', class and religion. However, it is important to remember that these, and numerous other factors and dimensions, tend to be in play at the same time. Gender always works as one among many influences and determinants, including those that are 'national', shaping them, but also shaped by them. This point is made even by those who are not much concerned to assess the part gender plays in national developments (Hobsbawm, 1990; A.D. Smith, 1991). Individual and collective identities have many components, and it is far from easy to decide which, if any, of these forces deserves to be treated as primary. The hope or expectation that one dimension holds the key to ultimate understanding is futile. The project in which Yuval-Davis and other contemporary feminists are involved seeks to move away from this kind of reductionist, hierarchical analysis, to make greater allowance for variability and contingency among the manifold combinations of factors that occur in real social relations. A characteristic feature of Yuval-Davis' work is that she seeks to deconstruct each of the conceptual items she employs, insisting that they have no predetermined meaning or content, but need to be understood situationally, in the light of particular contexts and circumstances. There is no single set of relationships, or causalities, which tie nations and genders together; instead, they work as a part of a network of dynamic interrelationships and interactions.

This position owes much to post-modernism and the analysis of discourse. According to Seidman, the post-modern conceptual reorientation in sociology has led to a stress on the fluid, multiple character of social reality; the local or situationally produced nature of social institutions; the interpretive efforts of individuals; and the social production of identity (Seidman, 1998, p. 319; Calhoun, 1994). At the same time, Yuval-Davis is keen to deny that 'anything goes'. Real material considerations and consequences must be taken into account, including relationships of power, which rule out the 'free-floating' nature of some post-modernist positions. Among the lineaments of power is a general tendency for women to be oppressed by, and subordinated to, men. Yet even this does not hold true universally. Some women exercise power over men, and the relative oppression experienced by different sorts of women varies greatly. Yuval-Davis is fiercely antagonistic to any attempt to assign an essential homogeneity to social categories, whether these be women, 'communities' of the oppressed, ethnic groups, or nations.

Many of the approaches we have been considering consciously resist the temptation to revert towards a homogenizing view, of the kind often associated with 'identity politics', which constructs groups as if all members share identical interests and viewpoints, within boundaries which are fixed – whether these are women of a particular nationality, ethnicity, religion or colour (Yuval-Davis, 1997, p. 86; Anthias and Yuval-Davis, 1992). In terms of nationalism, a simple refutation of this assertion would be that not only are women active in a variety of national movements, but they can be found almost always on either side of national arguments. It is no more true of women than it has been of the 'international' working class that they have 'no country' (Pearce, 2000, p. 17). For these reasons, more recent discussions have tended to locate the analysis of gender within the context of a series of other difficult, and frequently overlapping, concepts: ethnicity, 'race', nation, class (Anthias and Yuval-Davis, 1992; Charles and Hintjens, 1998; Ranchod-Nilsson and Tetreault, 2000; Nagel, 2003). Much of this work has been accomplished at a theoretical level, on the basis of conceptual analysis and critical reflection. Yuval-Davis' own writings are highly theoretical, and only sparsely informed by examination of empirical evidence. Consequently, elaborate claims are built sometimes upon evidence that is little more than anecdotal, or highly case-specific, and the particular nature of nations and nationalism is frequently overwhelmed by the mass of material relating to race and ethnicity. Feminist contributions have succeeded in shifting the focus away from the previously relentless neglect of women in the literature, but there is still a need for a great deal of empirical work to tell us more about how women, and girls, actually relate to their national contexts and national identities.

CHAPTER 7

Nationalism and Racism

Above all, white nationalists are driven by a sense of urgency. America, they believe, is fast becoming a nation dominated by non-white people. Since they believe that it is the white blood and white genes – and the white culture these have created – that are responsible for America's past greatness and success as a nation, this development can have only catastrophic consequences, according to their reckoning.

(Swain, 2002, p. 17)

Swain's *The New White Nationalism in America* (2002) focuses on the symbiotic relationship between nationalism and racism in the USA. It is concerned with the activities of white nationalist movements and organizations like the European-American Unity and Rights Organization (EURO) and the National Association for the Advancement of White People (NAAWP), and their ability to appeal to white American voters. According to Swain, such organizations differ from both older white supremacist groups and more radical movements that espouse the inevitability of race war. The challenge of the new white nationalism lies in its potential to attract support from millions of disaffected white Americans who 'do not consider themselves racists and who would never dream of joining an organization like the Klu Klux Klan but are nevertheless upset over current government policies, angry with minorities, and worried about the future' (2002, p. 34). The new white nationalists have an undeniably racist and radical nationalist agenda. Rather than white supremacy, the leaders of EURO and the NAAWP, David Duke and Reno Wolfe, have committed their organizations to separatist white nationalism and the ideal of a 'Euro-American' nation-state. Although they tend to box clever publicly when referring to notions of racial inferiority/superiority, the new white nationalists do not shy away from describing races as possessing innate racial traits, such as differences in intelligence.

Their ideology is founded on a belief in a distinct white, Euro-American, racial identity.

For Swain, part of the threat posed by the new white nationalism lies in its efforts to disassociate itself from redneck racism. She points out that the titles and rhetoric of new white nationalist organizations are intended to distance them from older racist movements, and position them instead as credible alternatives to mainstream political parties. To legitimate their defence of white identity, the new white nationalists adopt the language of identity politics and multiculturalism, in keeping with similar actions by African-Americans, for example. Swain argues that though their solutions may be radical, the new white nationalists address matters of concern to many white Americans, such as affirmative action, immigration and the fear of (black) crime. The views they express resonate with more mainstream conservative opinion in the USA, such as the ideas of former Republican Senator Pat Buchanan, even if they are prepared to take them much further in both rhetoric and policy. Perhaps the most important factor contributing to the potential impact of the new white nationalists is that 'they address many pressing issues of race and nationality that are usually ignored in more mainstream discourse' (Swain, 2002, p. 6). In the face of 'norms of political correctness and racial taboos' that limit the possibility of the 'honest dialogue' Swain believes to be needed, the new white nationalist groups 'may offer the only forum for candid discussions of race' (2002, p. 6). Swain herself concludes that there is a need to tackle the perceived grievances, otherwise more white Americans will be pushed towards racial nationalism, and she advocates measures to 'refashion a collective identity that can transcend race' (2002, p. 252).

Of course, these issues are not limited to the USA. As a category for classifying human beings, and as a social issue, 'race' transcends national boundaries. For Winant (2001) the development of concepts of race is bound up inextricably with historical 'global racial dynamics', beginning with European transatlantic conquests and slavery. Nevertheless, the meaning of race, the form that racism assumes and indeed the *making* of races, are deeply rooted in the local circumstances in which they become manifest. As Holt puts it (2000, p. 21), 'neither race nor racism can live independently of its social environments, the times and spaces it inhabits'. Since the late eighteenth and early nineteenth centuries, racism and 'racial formation' (Omi and Winant, 1994) have been profoundly shaped by the political and social peculiarities of their national settings, and by the politics of nationalism. Consideration of this relationship is a principal concern of this chapter. We begin by examining the theorization of nation and race.

Nation and 'race'

There is an idea abroad, accepted as much by cloistered intellectuals as by ordinary people going about their daily business, that everybody knows what race is. The idea of race is a self-evident 'fact', requiring no protracted thought. (Hannaford, 1996, p. 3)

In contrast to Swain, some social theorists insist on keeping nationalism and racism apart, claiming that they are exercised by quite different concerns. Writing in the 1940s, Arendt deplored what she saw as the 'old misconception of racism as a kind of exaggerated nationalism' (1973, pp. 160–1). On the other hand, Nairn (1977) makes precisely this connection. In a frequently cited observation, Benedict Anderson remarks that the 'fact of the matter is that nationalism thinks in terms of historical destinies, while racism dreams of eternal contaminations, transmitted from the origins of time through an endless sequence of loathsome copulations outside history' (1983, p. 136). However strident its adherence to the nation, he argues, nationalism will permit 'foreigners' to become members of the nation. The ability of immigrants to become 'nationals' illustrates how 'from the start the nation was conceived in language, not in blood, and that one could be "invited into" the imagined community' (1983, p. 133). In contrast, racism is pathologically preoccupied with preserving the purity of the 'blood'. With racism, the primary source of identity is inscribed on or within the body of the individual: 'Niggers are, thanks to the invisible tar-brush, forever niggers: Jews, the seed of Abraham, forever Jews, no matter what passports they carry or what languages they speak and read' (1983, p. 136). In short, culture and nationalism are flexible in ways that biology and racism simply are not.

In some respects, Anderson's reading of nationalism and racism is a truism. Studies of racism commonly state that 'races' are represented typically as distinguished by physical or biological characteristics. Thus, Omi and Winant define race as a 'concept which signifies and symbolizes social conflicts and interests by referring to different types of human bodies' (1994, p. 55). Elsewhere, Marx writes of 'racial domination' as resting on a 'distinction of peoples according to categories of physical difference' (1998, p. 3). It is almost unnecessary to add that, for most social theorists, 'race' does not in itself have explanatory value. As Winant comments, although the 'concept of race appeals to biologically based human characteristics (so-called phenotypes), selection of these particular human features for purposes of racial signification is always and necessarily a social and historical process' (2001, p. 317). As Winant's remarks indicate, contemporary social theorists are concerned with how races are 'made' or how humans are *racialized* according (usually) to physical differences. Writers such as Miles (1989) and Winant (1994) explain that racialization need not always be *racist*. For example, Winant (1994) describes how in the USA in the late 1960s, following the civil rights movement, Chinese, Filipino, Korean and Japanese Americans began increasingly to define themselves as Asian-Americans, in response to their common experiences of racism. On the other hand, racialization may indeed be racist. The general point is that racism and racialization are taken to refer to processes whereby meaning is attributed to biological or physical difference. Miles insists as a principle that racial differentiation should be understood as referring to underlying biological traits, otherwise there is a danger that the concept of racism may suffer from 'conceptual inflation' (1989, pp. 41–68).

Nationalism, in contrast, is frequently defined as being first and foremost concerned with advancing and defending the interests of the nation as a *cultural* community. As Anthony Smith observes, it is 'primarily a cultural doctrine' (1991, p. 40), and writers have consistently cautioned against the view that a 'national character' somehow indelibly marks each member of a nation. Thus, the eighteenth-century philosopher David Hume remarked that while 'they allow that each nation has a peculiar set of manners, and that some particular qualities are more frequently to be met with among one people than among their neighbours', 'men of sense condemn' the view that every member of a nation displays the same qualities (cited in Eze, 1997, pp. 30–1). With racism, however, as Anderson says, the divisions between races are taken to lie *outside* history, as a natural condition of particular 'races', and therefore inherent in every member. Furthermore, some would maintain that nationalism and racism have markedly different political objectives. For instance, Guibernau argues that where nationalism 'wants to regenerate the nation, make its culture flourish and its people feel engaged in a common project that transcends their own life-spans', racism is a 'doctrine of denial of political, civic and social rights' (1996, p. 90). Smith spells out the differences more explicitly in one of his earlier studies of nationalism: 'ideals of citizenship and independence, of fraternity and the homeland, and of an historic identity, which are of such concern to nationalists, play only a minor role in racist thinking' (A.D. Smith, 1979, p. 87).

For the purpose of analysis, nationalism and racism can be distinguished as different types of ideologies. Racism is marked by notions of inherent and hierarchically organized difference that are not *generally* constitutive of nationalism. Nevertheless, in practice there are many instances where the boundaries between the two blur. This is possible because both ideologies organize individuals into groups by invoking notions of cultural similarity or difference. Taking up Smith's claims, ideals of citizenship, fraternity and homeland are not absent altogether from racism. There are countless illustrations of racialization working to deny the claims of certain groups to belong in a homeland, because their members are understood to be culturally, and irreconcilably, different and which are intended, in turn, to strengthen the bonds between 'us' at the expense of 'them'. In this regard, we would follow the argument of Jenkins (1997) that both nationalism and racism are ideologies of ethnic identification, where ethnicity itself is understood, after Barth, as 'the social organization of cultural difference' (Barth 1969). Doing so alerts us to the cultural dimensions of 'race' and racism, explored more fully below, and to the place of ethnicity within nationalism. Seeing nationalism and racism as 'historically specific allotropes or versions of the wider principle of ethnic affiliation and classification', as Jenkins (1997, p. 74) suggests, moves us away from the view that culture is the sole preserve of nationalism, whereas the concern of racism proper is with biology.

As in the work of Armstrong (1982) and Anthony Smith (1986), a good deal of the discussion of nationalism centres on issues of ethnicity. The practice of distinguishing between 'ethnic' and 'civic' forms of nationalism is widespread (Ignatieff, 1993); in the former, membership is conferred through ancestry or 'blood', whereas membership of the latter is gained through birth or residence in the national territory. The two are usually taken to refer to different types of community, one cultural (ethnic nationalism) and the other political (civic nationalism). Clearly it is important to make such distinctions, for there are very obvious differences between a nationalism that resorts to strict definitions of community membership, such as through a combination of religion and ancestry, and one that is looser and more inclusive, like the 'official' nationalism of the USA. Moreover, the categories of 'nation' and 'ethnic group' do not overlap neatly. The claim to a national homeland is not a necessary feature of ethnic identification, where the principal concern is with the culture of the group, but it is central to the idea of the nation. However, to think that nationalism could be completely devoid of a cultural commitment is misleading. A notable contribution by Kymlicka (1999), on whom we focus in our discussion of liberal nationalism, is that he illustrates that 'civic' visions of the nation are committed to the protection of the culture of the dominant ethnic group within a national territory.

Making the connection between nationalism and racism via ethnicity calls into question Anderson's sharp differentiation between the two. From the middle of the nineteenth century, if not earlier, nations came to be conceived increasingly *as* races, or as emerging *out of* races. In this intellectual environment, the articulation of visions of racially bounded nations contributed to the racialization of groups such as Jews in Europe, and black and native Americans in the USA. However, there are serious difficulties in understanding nationalism as *causing* racism. Many scholars share the view that racism should not be seen as an effect or consequence of underlying phenomena such as capitalism, the rise of the nation-state or, indeed, nationalism. According to Miles (1989), though racism as a concept dates to the early twentieth century, and what we refer to today as scientific racism – that is, the attempt to classify 'races' hierarchically – dates to the late eighteenth century, both build on an earlier history in which groups were distinguished and ranked according to physical and cultural characteristics.

While social theorists may reject the notion that one can be reduced to an effect of the other, there is undoubtedly some form of relationship between nationalism and racism. An alternative perspective has been to think of the two as being brought together at key national moments, typically in periods of domestic political crisis or transformation. In this way, in his now classic study of racial politics in 1980s Britain, *There Ain't No Black in the Union Jack*, Paul Gilroy remarked, in response to Anderson, that the 'politics of "race" . . . is fired by conceptions of national belonging which not only blur the distinction between "race" and nation, but rely on that very ambiguity for their effect' (1987, p. 45). Reflecting on terms such as 'the Island race' and 'the Bulldog Breed' he added that the British nation is 'represented in terms which are simultaneously biological and cultural' (1987, p. 45). In more general theoretical terms, again prompted by reading Benedict Anderson, Goldberg holds that 'as *concepts*, race and nation are largely empty receptacles through and in the names of which population groups may be invented, interpreted, and imagined as communities or societies' (1993, p. 79). These criticisms challenge any straightforward differentiation between biology and culture and, therefore, between racism and nationalism. The key issue they raise is the ambiguity of the boundaries between them.

Benedict Anderson contends that nationalism is always less prescriptive than racism about the criteria determining membership of the collective: people may become part of a national community, in a way that they cannot swap 'races'. However, there are times when the boundaries between nationalism and racism collapse. Balibar makes the point effectively: 'the connection between nationalism and racism is neither a matter of perversion (for there is no "pure" essence of nationalism) nor a question of formal similarity, but a question of historical articulation' (1991, p. 50). As articulated within nationalist discourse, the nation is a remarkably elastic entity, whose parameters can contract or expand depending on how it is defined. For Balibar, racism can assist nationalism in its efforts to give a sense of the nation as a bounded entity; it does so by highlighting the unity of the nation in contrast to racialized outsiders. As he remarks: the 'racial-cultural identity of "true nationals" remains invisible, but it can be inferred (and is ensured)' by contrast with 'false nationals' (1991, p. 60). National elites may prefer to remain largely quiet about the nation's particular racial characteristics, because specificity runs counter to the populist objective of nationalism. Thus, if whiteness *per se* had not provided the symbolic foundation of the American nation, as Lind (1995) suggests, but instead the more specific notion of an Anglo-Saxon race, then effectively this would have excluded large numbers of the white European immigrants who arrived in the country in the late nineteenth century. More generally, if nationalism relies on a progressively more exacting search for *the* defining racial features of the nation, then it throws up questions about previous generations of migrants who, over time, have become 'naturalized' into the nation (such as Irish and German immigrants to the USA). In the end, it renders problematic the idea that there is any natural foundation to the nation. For Balibar, if followed to its inherent excess, racism is counter-productive for nationalism. None the less, racism continues to have a significant constitutive role in the articulation of the nation. In his words:

> Racism is not an 'expression' of nationalism, but *a supplement of nationalism* or more precisely *a supplement internal to nationalism*, always in excess of it, but always indispensable to its constitution and yet always still insufficient to achieve its project, just as nationalism is both indispensable and always insufficient to achieve the formation of the *nation* or the project of the 'nationalization' of society (1991, p. 54).

For this reason, it is necessary to consider further the way in which culture can be racialized and how, in turn, biological features can be nationalized, or taken as visible markers of the nation's boundaries.

As to the relationship between racism and culture, although there are some significant theoretical differences, most contemporary theorists accept that racism does impinge upon culture. Miles, for example, opposes broadening the idea of 'racism' to include beliefs or practices that express hostility towards 'strangers' (xenophobia) or even cultural prejudice (ethnocentrism), if there is no biological referent. Even so, he acknowledges that racism can involve attributing negatively evaluated cultural characteristics to people, but maintains that these ascribed cultural differences can be traced to prior signification processes, through which meanings are attached to selected phenotypic differences (1989, pp. 70–1). Others question the explanatory power of biological racism in accounting for the treatment of certain groups within national societies – such as, historically, Jews and Muslims in Europe – arguing instead that while such groups *are* subject to biological racism, the hostility or unequal treatment they receive is explained better by evaluations of their ascribed cultural difference. Thus, Modood suggests that non-white populations in Britain are subject to a 'cultural racism' that 'evokes cultural differences from an alleged British or "civilised" norm to vilify, marginalise or demand cultural assimilation from groups who also suffer from biological racism' (1997, p. 155).

Modood's analysis contributes to a wider argument, concerning the extent to which a discredited biological racism has come to be displaced gradually by a more culturalist form of racism, evoking notions of innate cultural difference. Much attention has been paid to the 'new racism', said to have emerged first in the United Kingdom (UK) and USA in the late 1970s, which is distinctive in downplaying 'old' hierarchical notions of biological inferiority and superiority, instead stressing cultural difference (Barker, 1981; CCCS, 1981; Gilroy, 1987; Omi and Winant, 1994; Ansell, 1997). The work of writers as different as Miles and Modood calls into question the view that nationalism and racism work towards radically different objectives. With the partial exception of Miles, these contributions highlight the *mixture* of nationalism and racism, underlining Omi and Winant's assertion that 'racism, like race, has changed over time' (1994, p. 71), and confirming Balibar's point that nationalism has no 'pure essence'. For this group of theorists, it is important to explore the historical circumstances in which nationalism and racism become fused.

Racialization, imperialism and 'nation building'

> Racism is always nationally specific. It invariably becomes enmeshed with searches for national identity and cohesion that vary with the historical experience of each country. (Fredrickson, 2002, p. 75)

During the nineteenth century it became increasingly commonplace to speak of nations in racial, if not racist terms. Although Shafer (1968) notes that frequently 'nation' and 'race' were used interchangeably, suggesting a lack of clarity, or absence of reflection on their meaning, a remarkable degree of intellectual energy was expended trying to identify scientifically the underlying characteristics of nations. John Stuart Mill was among the more prominent figures consumed by this pursuit, considering it sufficiently weighty to form part of a new branch of science: 'political ethology' (Varouxakis, 1998). Given the growing importance of nationalism, it is not surprising it attracted so much attention, which can be understood as a continuation of the Enlightenment concern to render the social world an object of scientific endeavour, as much as the natural world, and to reveal its underlying laws. In this context, nations and 'national character' were portrayed in terms that depicted them as marked by objective differences, and as displaying superior or inferior qualities. As the scientific study of the 'races' gained momentum, 'race' and racism came to inform these 'scientific' classifications.

Thus, regardless of the naturalistic language in which their observations were couched, European philosophers and scientists did not usually make racial distinctions between European nations. But often they saw *Europeans* as constituting a distinctive race, a view held by leading Enlightenment luminaries such as Hume and Kant (Eze, 1997). Ernest Renan, often cited for his view that the nation is a 'spiritual principle', expressed in his famous essay *What is a Nation?* (Renan, 1990), was firmly committed to the notion of humanity as structured hierarchically along racial lines. Only when referring to the 'European race' did he challenge the idea that biological, and thus racial, differences, existed among Europeans (Todorov, 1993). Others saw nations in exactly these terms. Writing as late as the 1930s, a distinguished British anatomist and anthropologist, Arthur Keith, thought nations and races were synonymous (Barot and Bird, 2001). It is instructive that the leading British sociologist of the period, Ginsberg (1962), thought the question worthy of a critical response. Nor was this belief confined to Europe. In Japan, where Spencer's Social Darwinism was embraced during the early years of the Meiji Restoration (Kurauchi, 1960), a racial mythology developed as part of a larger nationalist ideology, representing the Japanese as a nation united by 'blood', a bond that, in turn, linked the nation to its emperor (Yoshino, 1997).

These intellectual reflections on nations and 'races' cannot be separated from wider processes of political and social change. Imperial expansion in the late nineteenth and early twentieth centuries made an important contribution to the growing self-definition, and more especially the self-racialization, of European nations. In some respects expansion illustrated how racialization could surpass national boundaries, even, as Benedict Anderson suggests, *erasing* national difference. Fanon, the celebrated critic of colonialism and racism, remarked that in Africa the colonizers encountered not people of other nations but 'the Negro': 'this vast continent was the haunt of savages, a country weighed down by the curse of God, a country of cannibals – in short, the Negro's country' (1965, p. 171). Fanon himself often chose not to identify the colonizers as 'British' or 'French', referring instead to them as 'Europeans'; he also alluded to how, in addition to racializing whiteness, colonialism served to elevate the values of the colonizing nation through its encounter with the 'colonised race' (1965, p. 34). For Hannah Arendt, imperial expansion created a unity that held together European societies strained by growing individualism and class divisions. The racism that accompanied expansion of the British empire became, she claims, the 'very backbone of British nationalism'. To illustrate this, she quotes Lord Curzon, one-time

British Foreign Secretary and Viceroy of India, saying that 'the peculiar genius of each nation shows itself nowhere more clearly than in their system of dealing with subject races' (1973, p. 154). Imperialism, then, involved not only the racialization of the colonized, but also, simultaneously, of the colonizing nation. Its general effect was that the 'nation's virtues were heralded as the antithesis of the vices of the racialized subject. The nation idealized itself in the process' (Nicholson, 1999, p. 178). Todorov provides an interesting example in his study of nineteenth-century French thought, observing that one of the principal ways of defending French colonialism was the doctrine of *assimilation*, which sought to 'make over the indigenous "races" in the image of France, out of a belief that France is the perfect embodiment of universal values' (1993, p. 259). Similar phenomena are evident elsewhere. Japanese expansionism in the late nineteenth century was justified by arguments much like those employed by European imperialists: the civilization of inferior 'races'. As Weiner suggests, for the Japanese the 'existence of empire confirmed not only Japan's status as a truly civilised nation but their own manifest superiority *vis-à-vis* the peoples of East Asia' (1997, p. 112). The 1898 Spanish–American War, which involved fighting in Cuba, the Philippines and Puerto Rico, contributed to the racialization of the American nation. Theodore Roosevelt, who led his 'Rough Riders' regiment in the war in Cuba and became US President in 1901, believed war could reinvigorate both race and nation by unifying (white) Euro-Americans, just as the earlier conflict between 'white' and 'red' men in the American West first forged the 'American race'. As Gerstle says of Roosevelt's vision, the 'greatness of America ... could only lie in the exploits of Euro-Americans forged by battle into a single and superior race. Out of such convictions was the twentieth-century nation born' (2002, p. 17).

Perhaps the most fundamental consequence of imperialism and colonialism is its contribution to 'nation building'. These processes unfolded at a time when states across the world were becoming increasingly conscious of the importance of fostering mass patriotism, to give national societies a much needed social glue to further economic and social modernization. In this regard the effectiveness of imperialism can be overstated. As Cannadine shows, by the closing stages of the nineteenth century, concerns about the 'dangerous classes' in Britain, especially in London, led them to be compared 'in their character and their conduct – to the "negroes" of empire' (2001, p. 6). Yet, imperialism undoubtedly helped to define the racialized boundaries of the nation and, by confronting 'subject races', projected a sense of imagined internal national unity. In the same way, in late nineteenth and early twentieth-century Japan, society was marked by severe tensions wrought by the onset of a process of socio-economic transformation, yet the 'mission' of imperial expansion 'reaffirmed a sense of national solidarity and "racial" superiority among the Japanese people, regardless of what class they occupied at home' (Weiner, 1997, p. 113). Imperialism facilitated the creation of a privileged national community that stood above class interests, because its members were made aware that, through their place in the heart of the empire, they belonged to a superior race. Travel and migration to, as well as service in, the colonial territories accentuated this sense of superiority. Imperialism also stimulated competition between imperial nations. The scramble for territory by European states at the close of the nineteenth century was commonly articulated not only as a natural aspiration on their part – an 'irresistible movement' that 'carries the great European nations along toward the conquest of new lands' as French Prime Minister Jules Ferry saw it (Todorov, 1993, p. 261) – but as a duty *because* of their 'race'. Not to live up to this 'duty' would mean falling behind other European nations. It would also allow other nations of the 'superior race' to dominate markets and, as Ferry adamantly believed, relegate France from the 'first rank to the third and fourth'. In effect, this was a merger of Spencerian 'survival of the fittest' with nationalism.

While Arendt credits the 'transformation of nations into races' to imperial expansion (1973, p. 157), we should not neglect the significance of racial boundaries drawn closer to home during the same period. What Arendt sees as the upshot of colonial racism, Balibar attributes to the racialization of European nations in opposition to Jews: the concealment of tensions – including class and ethnic differences – within the majority population. Other writers detect similar processes at work in the USA (Goldfield, 1997; A. Marx, 1998; Nelson, 1998). Anthony Marx argues that anxiety about divisions among whites in the USA, and their consequences for the Union, led political elites to favour white unity at the expense of the rights of black Americans. As he comments, the 'state instantiated "white nationalism", with the torque of this enforced racial identity proving powerful enough to integrate populations otherwise at war and engaged in ongoing competition' (1998, p. 2). When a programme of legislative change introduced by the Federal government in the wake of the Civil War strengthened and extended the rights of black Americans, sparking a hostile reaction in the South (including the formation in 1866 of the Klu Klux Klan), the response from Washington was to apply the 'salve of racial domination' (1998, p. 131). As Marx adds, the 'nation had to be united, at least for whites, to make a modicum of centralized state rule workable' (1998, p. 131).

Latin American societies present a different set of experiences. Here, social stratification is informed by a complex system of racial classification. By the end of the nineteenth century, miscegenation between the descendants of white Europeans, black Africans and indigenous Americans had created societies that while headed by a white elite were none the less increasingly racially mixed, certainly much more so than the USA. Wade (1993) points out that political elites in Latin American countries recognized the necessity of formulating a concept of national identity that acknowledged the heterogeneous racial structure of their societies, in which the overwhelming majority of the population was non-white (see also Wright, 1990; Hanchard, 1994; Radcliffe and Westwood, 1996). The celebration of the *mestizo* – a person with European and indigenous ancestry – and 'race mixture' more generally, as the basis of national identity suggested that the nation was founded on racial equality and hybridity. However, for Wade this was only one aspect of the position assumed by political elites: the 'mestizo was idealized as of bi-ethnic or tri-ethnic origin, but the image held up was always at the lighter end of the mestizo spectrum' (1993, p. 11). In practice, the nation's future lay with a process of *blanqueamiento* ('whitening'), to be achieved through European immigration and by fostering the values inherited from European ancestors, thus negating the influences – biological and cultural – of the inferior Indian and African 'races'. Thus, Wright (1990) shows how the Venezuelan government was authorized to subsidize the immigration of European agricultural workers in 1831, 1837 and 1840, while in 1891 a new immigration law prohibited the movement of blacks and Asians into the country. In spite of the myth of racial equality, racism, particularly towards blacks, was pervasive, while for all the complex manner in which it was articulated by nationalist elites, the boundary of the nation was no less racialized.

The comparative sociological experiences of Europe, Latin America and the USA underline Fredrickson's point about the national specificity of racism. Nevertheless there are interesting parallels across national boundaries. For example, as with imperialism, processes of 'internal colonialism' (Hechter, 1975) harnessed racist theories to the project of nation-state building and justified the negative treatment of particular racial groups and their exclusion from the national community. More generally, there is common ground in the way that the fusion of nation and race with regard to the domestic population was intensified through the efforts of political elites to nationalize their societies. Many Latin American countries had emerged only recently as independent states from under the shadow of the Portuguese and Spanish empires. What is striking about the combination of nationalism and racism in the fifty years or so from the late nineteenth century is its centrality to the management of political and social development, and to the efforts of elites to *control* the substance and boundaries of the nation, whether through the inculcation of the correct values, restrictions on immigration and miscegenation, or indeed through racial alchemy. In many respects, the advocacy of miscegenation in Latin America, even if intended to 'whiten' 'blacks', could not be further from Roosevelt's expressed desire for such mixing to occur in the USA only among white Europeans and their descendants. Even so, they were directed towards the same objective: the forging of a nation.

Beyond racism?

As the twenty-first century dawns, the world racial situation is quite distinct from its antecedents, from the old world racial system of more-or-less explicit white supremacy. Sure, there were early parallels, rehearsals, and prefigurations of the racial break that occurred around the end of World War II. But the world was racially organized in a quite different way during the imperial epoch that ended with World War II, than it was – and is – in the post-war break (Winant, 2001, p. 290).

By this point, two related issues should be clear. Firstly, racism is not anathema to nationalism. The incipient phase of 'nation building' beginning in the late nineteenth century was characterized by explicitly racist discourses and practices across the world, a phenomenon made possible by the degree to which racist theories became accepted among elites and other members of the privileged 'races'. Second, the fusion of nationalism and racism was far from a marginal alliance confined to the activities of 'extremists'. What is remarkable about the coming together of nation and race in the late nineteenth and early twentieth centuries was its *normality*, not its irregularity. In Brazil and the USA, for example, for a number of reasons, race was *central* to the processes of trying to transform these societies into nation-states. Though in distinctive ways, racism was inextricable from influential forms of nationalism in each of them.

Some regimes stand apart in raising the fusion of nationalism and racism into systems of legalized racial segregation. Jim Crow in the southern USA between the 1890s and the 1960s, Nazi Germany between 1933 and 1945, and apartheid South Africa between 1948 and 1991 are rightly classified as the 'overtly racist regimes' of the twentieth century (Fredrickson, 2002). Jim Crow was the system of segregation in the southern states of the USA (the name refers to an early nineteenth-century minstrel show character) usually taken as commencing in the 1890s with legislation that, among other things, led to the disenfranchisement of blacks and prohibited inter-racial marriages. Legal segregation ended formally in the 1960s, but many commentators argue that racial segregation persists in the USA today. Though Jim Crow emerged only in certain states of the USA, nevertheless it links with nationalism in a number of ways. With regard to the southern states themselves, Fredrickson argues that although there were numerous grounds on which whites had a vested interest in maintaining a system of racial domination over blacks, by enlisting *en masse* in the Union army during the Civil War the latter ensured that they were 'complicit in thwarting southern hopes for independent nationhood' (2002, p. 106). Anthony Marx (1998) maintains that Jim Crow owed much to the hands-off policy of Federal government and, in particular, its desire to prevent divisions occurring among whites that would threaten the unity of the nation-state.

In South Africa, apartheid (meaning 'separateness') was the formal policy of central government. Under the half-century rule of the Afrikaans-dominated National Party a regime emerged that became representative of the white minority population, and created a deeply racially segregated society, institutionalizing differences between its four so-called 'races': whites, coloureds, Asians and blacks. Nationalism may not have caused racial apartheid in South Africa – as with Jim Crow, economic reasons concerned with the protection of white material privileges are more usually cited here (Winant, 2001) – but it provided part of its justification; through the disenfranchisement of non-whites, South Africa became a white nation-state. For Afrikaners the existence of their nation depended on maintaining its 'purity', and apartheid served this purpose by keeping the nation white. Laws banning inter-racial marriages and indeed legislating against all sexual relations between members of different 'races' – such as the 1950 Immorality Act – imposed a rigid racial framework on South African society, as did those intended to ensure physical and cultural segregation, including the imposition of racially differentiated educational curricula.

There are parallels with both Jim Crow and anti-Semitism in Nazi Germany, although the latter exceeded the other regimes in its systematic annihilation of those designated as racially 'inferior'. Nationalism and racism mixed seamlessly in the pervasive anti-Semitism of Nazi ideology, in the expressed view (not least in Hitler's *Mein Kampf*) that Jews were contributing in various ways to the degeneration of the German race and in the subsequent concern with maintaining the purity of that race by any means (McMaster, 2001). The 1935 Nuremberg Laws demonstrated the Nazi obsession with the relationship between blood and nation. The Reich Citizenship Law declared that only those of German 'blood' were citizens of Germany, and stripped German Jews of their citizenship. The Law for the Protection of German Blood and German Honour also underlined the significance of blood bonds for the nation, prohibiting marriage or sexual relations between the newly defined 'Germans' and Jews, and forbidding Jews from displaying the national flag or colours.

The brutality and *official* racism of these three regimes represent the extreme manifestations of the fusion between racism and nationalism. Indeed, for Hitler the primary job of the state was to be the 'maintainer of a nation's blood. Other than this, the state has no purpose in the long run' (cited in Linke, 1999, p. 209). However, these regimes were not the only ones formally to practise anti-Semitic or white racist policies. During the 1930s, numerous continental European countries passed laws that meted out negative treatment to Jews, identifying them as different from members of the nation, even if not to the same extent as Nazi Germany. Equally, white racist policies were not restricted to apartheid or Jim Crow. From the 1901 Immigration Restriction Act through to the early 1970s, successive Australian governments restricted immigration of non-whites – a practice known as the 'White Australia' policy. Many white Australians, including the most senior political figures in the country, saw controls on immigration as essential for maintaining the racial unity of the Australian nation.

The far-reaching revulsion against the Holocaust exposed policies informed by racism to wilting criticism. Anti-colonial revolts,
and widespread decolonization from the late 1940s onwards, also
shook the foundations of white supremacy and provided stimula-
tion to oppressed groups in the imperial heartlands. The Cold War
gave added impetus for the US government in particular to
address the racism endemic within its own society; a state that
tolerated the oppression of its own people would hardly be the ally
of choice for governments emerging from the imperialist yoke. In
the period after 1945, racism came under growing pressure.
Apartheid alone grew in strength in the second half of the twentieth century, though it too became increasingly isolated until it fell
apart in 1991.

Yet, racism as such has not retreated to the sidelines. Discussing
the USA, Winant (1994) argues that the meaning of racism today
has become unstable; for example, white politicians of the right
complain about the 'racism' experienced *by* whites as a consequence of policies that accommodate the demands of racial minorities. Where once the meaning of racism in the USA was
comparatively unambiguous – it was the ideology and practice of
white supremacy – today what racism means has become subject
to considerable contestation. Winant's analysis nevertheless illustrates, like Swain's very different approach, that the importance of
race in the USA has not diminished. Nor, in general, has it become
divorced from mainstream nationalism and from the politics of
national identity and belonging. The ambiguity about the concept
of the nation, or more precisely who *belongs* to it, means that it is
always hostage to conflicting interpretations, some more illiberal
and restrictive than others. As Bauman observes, assimilation and
racism 'seem to be radically opposed. And yet they stem from the
same source – the *boundary-building* concerns inherent in the
nationalist tendency' (1990, p. 176). Just as the meaning of racism
changes, so too the fusion of nationalism and racism has evolved,
adapting to changing cultural and political circumstances.

Brazil is an especially interesting case. Though Brazil was the
last republic in Latin America to abolish slavery (in 1888), it did not
witness either the *de jure* apartheid of South Africa or the Jim Crow
of the USA. On the contrary, from the 1930s there developed a
view that miscegenation had produced a 'new Brazilian', so that
the racial divisions that scarred other societies, such as the USA,
were absent. Like other Latin American countries, the first stage of
nation-state formation in Brazil was informed by the ideology of

branqueamento (in Spanish, *blanqueamiento*). The next stage of development, during the 1930s, was underpinned by an ideology of racial tolerance. Rather than viewing blackness as something to be overcome, this stressed instead the positive dimension of hybridity. Freyre, the anthropologist who did much to establish this view in works such as *The Masters and the Slaves*, believed racial coexistence on the plantations and widespread interbreeding had helped ensure Brazilian society was 'of all those in the Americas, the one most harmoniously constituted so far as racial relations are concerned' (1986, p. 83). Freyre upheld the contributions made by native Americans and Afro-Brazilians respectively to the cultural development of Brazilian society, celebrating the role of racial mixing in forming the Brazilian national identity. His account became central to the populist nationalism that developed during the 1930s, as the regime of Gétulio Vargas (which came into power in 1937) sought to win popular support, including among Afro-Brazilians.

The notion of racial democracy continues to be viewed with national pride in Brazil. In an inaugural address in January 2003, President da Silva, while recognizing that racial discrimination is a problem in Brazil, remarked that it was a 'nation where miscegenation and syncretism imposed their own original contribution to the world' (da Silva, 2003). Some analysts argue that a nationalism based around racial tolerance, and celebrating hybridity, is preferable to the experiences of racism and nationalism elsewhere (Cleary, 1999). However, many more observers have been critical of this notion of racial democracy, highlighting evidence of deep racial inequalities in Brazil, and arguing that this account of a racially tolerant society is largely mythical (Hanchard, 1994; Radcliffe and Westwood, 1996; A. Marx, 1998; Winddance Twine, 1998). Some explore how this myth has embedded itself within Brazilian society. Hanchard remarks that in the 'process of nation-state and industrial development, the ideology of racial democracy has become national common sense that has informed both popular folklore and social scientific research' (1994, p. 74). Though successive Brazilian governments espoused the idea of racial democracy up to the 1980s, still they sought to limit non-white immigration.

For critics of Brazilian 'racial democracy', a principal issue is the way its suggestion of unity and equality serves to deflect attention away from widespread societal racism. In Europe and North America since the early 1980s a growing number of commentators have turned attention towards what they see as a 'new racism'. While eschewing notions of racial hierarchy, this none the less represents humanity as divided into groups marked by immutable, natural differences. Contributors to this debate hold that the novelty of the 'new racism' is the manner in which it codes cultural differences as being based in biology (Gilroy, 2001). Thus, Barker, author of a seminal study of the 'new racism', underlines that at its core lies a view that it is 'in our biology, our instincts, to defend our way of life, traditions and customs against outsiders – not because they are inferior, but because they are part of different cultures' (1981, pp. 23–4). A more recent addition to this debate has been Taguieff's concept of 'differentialist' racism (2001, pp. 200–8), which takes further the argument that racism exists even where there is no reference to biology *or* to hierarchical differences of any kind. Differentialist racism champions cultural pluralism. Its exponents hold that 'universalist antiracism' – which stresses a *common* humanity – constitutes the 'true racism, the only racism' since it seeks to undo the natural cultural diversity of humanity (2001, p. 27). White nationalists in the USA, much like the British National Party or the French Front National, portray whites as victims of a multiculturalist racism that protects minority cultures, but does not afford them the same recognition. Others have argued that racism employs ethnic signifiers, such as culture, religion and language, to construct racialized boundaries; as Anthias and Yuval-Davis comment, 'anti-Muslim racism in Britain relies on notions of the "non-civilized" and supposedly inferior and undesirable character of Islamic religion and way of life, rather than an explicit notion of biological inferiority' (1992, p. 12).

There has been some controversy about the newness of the culturalist or 'new' racism (Hickman, 1998; A. Brown, 1999; Mac an Ghaill, 1999). Modood argues that 'Europe's oldest racisms' (1997, p. 155), anti-Semitism and Islamophobia, are similarly culturalist (see also Silverman and Yuval-Davis, 1999), and we have pointed already to the significance of culturalist racism for late nineteenth-century nation-building. The significance of the 'new racism', for Barker (2002) and others, is that its exponents seek explicitly to distance themselves from old-style racial supremacists. The Chairman of the British National Party distinguishes his organization from the 'crude racism' of some other far-right groups, arguing that his 'racial realist' ideology is founded on the view that 'we believe not just that our people are different from others, but that such genuine diversity is worth preserving. It is not a matter of "superiority" or "inferiority" ' (Griffin, 2003). People are therefore understood as belonging *naturally* to different cultural groups or nations. The 'new' or 'differentialist' racisms in Europe are inextricable from debates about immigration and the putative consequences for the national 'way of life'. European exponents of 'new racism' claim to address a novel phenomenon: the problem of integrating 'alien' cultural practices, and the inability to assimilate 'mass immigration'. The distinction between natives and immigrants highlights the racialization of the nation, since it implies that somehow it is pure, untainted by 'foreign' influences or blood. Returning to an earlier point, it illustrates the difficulty of drawing clear boundaries between biology and culture within the new racism.

The 'new racism' runs counter to Brazil's 'myth of racial democracy' in many respects, not least in that the latter portrays the nation as racially hybrid whereas the former sees nations *as* races. Yet, as in Brazil, the fusion of race and nation within the 'new racism' forms part of the mainstream political culture. Parties such as the Front National (France), the National Alliance (Italy), and the Freedom Party (Austria) in Europe are among a number of far-right parties that have seen considerable success in national elections in the late twentieth and early twenty-first centuries. It is not only that these parties have been able to move in from the margins that has brought issues of race and nation more prominently under the political spotlight. These matters have also been fanned by more conventionally mainstream political parties, and by sections of the press and media. This illustrates the durability of the relationship between nationalism and racism.

Conclusion

Whether 'blow-dried, grammatically correct, coat-and-tie race-baiters' (Dolman, 2002, p. 24), such as David Duke, will be able to mobilize the level of popular support feared by Swain (2002) is hard to tell, though Duke has enjoyed some electoral success (serving as an elected Member of the Louisiana House of Representatives between 1989 and 1991). Swain's argument rests more on concerns about *future* developments, and what *might* come about. There is no doubting that the complex politics of nation and race continue to coalesce in the USA. It has been argued that the significance of this relationship may be greater, due to the changing demographics of American society: 'America is shifting from a predominantly white country to one where people of colour are increasingly numerous and consequently becoming more visible. As a result, race affects the lives of more Americans than ever before' (Pulera, 2002, p. 9).

We should not be surprised about how 'race' and racist thinking inform debates about national identity and citizenship. In the making of the nation, racial dynamics play an important role in the constitution of 'its culture' and 'its people', not just on the political fringes, but in the heart of mainstream political culture. As Anthony Marx puts it, surveying the interaction between racial politics and nation-state building, 'nations have all too often been built through purposeful racial, ethnic, religious, class, or other internal exclusions . . . Such exclusion of specified others has been central to nation-state building, rather than tangential' (1998, pp. 275–6). Racism may not regain the kind of widespread acceptability it enjoyed within government and society up to the mid-twentieth century, but neither should we expect to see racism – however it is coded – retreat to the shadows of social and political life.

CHAPTER 8

Liberal Nationalism?

For those who profess the complete autonomy of the individual, man's dignity is diminished whenever he is made to feel that he is not completely self-determinant. It is generally accepted today, however, that most of our ideas and tendencies are not developed by ourselves but come to us from without. How can they become a part of us except by imposing themselves upon us? This is the whole meaning of our definition. And it is generally accepted, moreover, that social constraint is not necessarily incompatible with the individual personality.

(Durkheim, 1964, p. 4)

For its critics, nationalism is beyond reason. For Dunn, nationalism is the 'most unthinking and the most immediate political disposition of all' (1993, p. 57). In contrast to liberal thought, which prizes the autonomy of the individual, nationalist ideology routinely presents our attachments to the nation as beyond deliberation. National identities are conferred, not chosen, while the nation is a community of fate and destiny. As Miščević remarks, for the nationalist the nation is a 'non-voluntary community to which one belongs by birth and early nurture' (2001, p. 21). Critics object to the insistence that we have commitments to the nation and to our fellows that are as 'non-voluntary' as the demand that, when 'your country needs you', you must be ready to defend it and, if necessary, die for it. They are concerned that national partiality means that intolerance of the stranger is never far away. Thus, Lichtenberg suggests, 'many people ... suspect that violence, hatred, and distrust of the Other, embodied in a sharply divided world of "us" and "them", always lurk within the nationalist's heart' (1997, p. 158). In short, with its appeals to myth, tradition and nature, nationalism remains rudely resistant to the idea that the 'choosing, deciding, shaping human being ... is the central character of our time' (Beck and Beck-Gernsheim, 2002, pp. 22–3).

Over the last decade or so one of the most interesting developments in the study of nationalism has emerged in direct response to exactly these kind of criticisms by articulating, in various ways, a liberal defence of nationalism. This chapter will explore this body of writings, and some of the critical replies to it. As will become apparent, almost exclusively this work has involved political philosophers. To date there has been relatively little discussion of this debate in sociological studies of nationalism (though see Spencer and Wollman, 2002), although at its core stands an issue that Emile Durkheim and generations of thinkers since have recognized as central to social theory: the relationship between the individual and the social. Durkheim understood well the power of 'patriotism' (he does not refer to nationalism). In *The Rules of Sociological Method* he writes of how the 'pressure' of the social fact of 'nationality' bore down in his time upon the individual: '[f]or the present . . . in the vast majority of cases it is materially and morally impossible for us to strip off our nationality; such a change is generally considered apostasy' (1964, p. 105).

The writers we explore below also hold that nationalism deeply colours our personal values, but argue with Durkheim, though maybe with greater force, that social influences do not necessarily negate personal freedom and liberty nor predispose us to national chauvinism and xenophobia. It is difficult to reduce liberal nationalism to a set of core beliefs, since not all those grouped as 'liberal nationalists' hold identical views. However, a prominent theme among them is the argument that nationalism (the social) is compatible with personal autonomy (the individual). These theorists seek to build a defence of nationalism that reconciles the 'nationalist belief that individuals are the inevitable product of their culture' and the 'liberal conviction that individuals can be the authors of their own lives' (Tamir, 1993, p. 13). The following discussion appraises the extent to which these writers can realize this objective. The first part explores the liberal defence of nationalism in the writings of three writers, beginning with one of the earliest significant contributors to this debate, Yael Tamir.

Liberalism and nationalism: Yael Tamir

Tamir's *Liberal Nationalism* (1993) is a philosophical argument for what she terms an 'alternative national view' (1993, p. 167). This 'alternative national view' begins from the position that however much nationalism may have contributed to terrible human tragedies, there is nothing inherently wicked about it. For Tamir, there is much to be valued in the sense of community that nationalism engenders: membership of a nation provides us with the beliefs and values necessary to make judgements *as an individual*. In identifying with the nation, we become members of a fraternal community whose members share mutual obligations and a feeling of 'togetherness'. While defending the idea that people are embedded within cultural communities, nevertheless she maintains that the extent to which cultural and national affiliations are constitutive of our identity depends upon personal reflection. People should be able to decide what, if anything, their national affiliation means to them. As she comments, a 'national culture is not a prison and cultural ties are not shackles' (1993, p. 37). If people wish to preserve the national culture of their choice, and seek public expression of this culture, it should be their right to do so. The claim that individuals have a 'right to culture' runs throughout *Liberal Nationalism*. Tamir argues that liberals and nationalists both have tended to misinterpret people's values as being respectively the outcome of choice, or shaped by membership of a cultural community. Liberal nationalism, in contrast, recognizes that individuals acquire certain values through socialization within their national community, but holds that people always have the *potential* to make cultural choices. By virtue of living in a culturally pluralist society they will be exposed to different ways of life that may lead them to question the values they acquire from their own nation. In this way, nationalism and liberalism can be reconciled.

This argument has two notable implications. The first concerns the question of obligations. As Mason (1997) comments, many political philosophers argue that people have special obligations to compatriots, as members of the same political community, such as the obligation to participate in civic life. Tamir maintains that we owe these obligations not through bonds of citizenship, but through our membership of nations. If individuals consider their membership of a nation to be a constitutive element of who they are, then 'their self-esteem and well-being' will be 'affected by the successes and failures of their individual fellow members and of the group as a whole' (1993, p. 96).

Furthermore, if individuals care about the general well-being of the community and its members, then they have an obligation to it. Conscious that such an argument could be interpreted as suggesting that we need not care about those who are not members of our nation, Tamir stresses that is unlikely that people will develop associations only with fellow members. Through various associations, such as work relationships, people will develop ties with non-members and come to care for these individuals. Moreover, she argues that a commitment to the nation does not override our personal autonomy. People should feel comfortable in not supporting an action with which they disagree, even if ultimately it would benefit the nation. In general, Tamir's discussion is intended to justify the 'right of individual members of every nation to give preference to the shared pursuit of common interests' (1993, p. 115).

The second implication is that people should be able to express their identity publicly as well as privately. Since individuals can only fully express their attachment to national community in conjunction with others, this necessitates a 'communal domain . . . where one's communal identity finds expression' (1993, p. 74). This may sound like the traditional nationalist call for nations to have their own state, but Tamir maintains that preserving the autonomy of one's national culture – for her, the core of nationalism – does not require a nation-state. Nevertheless, her notion of a 'communal domain' indicates that while nations need not be fully independent they will usually have territorial control over some policy areas, such as education.

Tamir's understanding of self-determination has two serious consequences. Firstly, while the rights of minorities within a 'liberal national entity' (1993, p. 163) will be protected, its unity will be underpinned by a 'distinct cultural foundation' (1993, p. 163). Tamir acknowledges this means that '[m]embership in this entity will be more accessible to certain individuals, capable of identifying the political entity as their own, than to others' (1993, p. 163). In effect, then, the culture of the dominant group will permeate areas of public life within these territories. Though Tamir is careful to stress that acknowledging the 'right to culture' does not have to lead to the creation of independent nation-states, Lichtenberg (1999) argues with good reason that for 'domestic purposes, there is little to distinguish Tamir's national communities from traditional states' (1999, p. 175). For some critics, this raises doubts about whether in practice the idea of liberal nationalism is fully consistent with personal autonomy.

A second corollary of Tamir's thesis is that the nation-state as we conventionally understand that entity will cease to exist. While territorial boundaries may not change significantly because the rights of national groups can be accommodated by devolving control over sub-territories, the national (or federal) government will 'surrender' decision-making powers in relation to 'economic, strategic and ecological issues' (Tamir, 1993, p. 151) to supranational bodies, such as the European Union (EU). What Tamir is proposing is nothing less than a wholesale revision of the concept of national sovereignty. Tamir sees the movement towards supranational bodies as needed in a world where there is growing realization that states can address certain issues, such as the environment, better if they pool their resources. From the perspective of national minorities, such entities offer the advantage that because they are avowedly multinational they will not seek to impose cultural uniformity and, indeed, in the case of the EU there have been policies actively to support minority national cultures. Nationalist parties in the EU, such as the Scottish National Party and the Convergence and Unity Party in Catalonia, support the EU for exactly this reason.

As these thoughts illustrate, Tamir is conscious of the need to balance the scales. Ensuring national minorities a form of self-determination is balanced on the other side by a wider process whereby sovereignty is redefined within the framework of supranational entities. This balancing act cuts through *Liberal Nationalism*: the rights of minorities within devolved territories balance the right of a nation to self-determination, while elsewhere the right of a nation to self-determination is checked by the principle that this is a *universal* right. The latter point in particular highlights Tamir's desire to locate nationalism within a liberal framework by arguing that the right to self-determination is shared by *all* nations, not just by some. Tamir's experiences as an Israeli citizen, peace campaigner and liberal intellectual inform her desire to find reasonable solutions to the problems that plague her country and others across the world. In practice, however, her argument requires other nationalists to display the same degree of reason and liberalism. Even critics who judge that Tamir presents a reasoned intellectual case remark that the litmus test is whether it is realizable in practice. Levinson, for one, doubts that Tamir 'offers much real guidance as to how to respond to the actual nationalists who are most often found on the front pages of our newspapers and in the forefront of our consciousness' (1995, p. 645). Ultimately, this constitutes the test of *all* liberal defences of nationalism.

Neither civic nor ethnic: liberal defences of nationalism

In a sense there is nothing new about academics defending the virtues of a species of nationalism. Though many oppose nationalism *tout court*, some discriminate between types of nationalism. There is a well-established precedent for differentiating between 'civic' and 'ethnic' nationalisms, and for preferring the former to the latter (see Ignatieff, 1993). This civic/ethnic dichotomy retains a good degree of analytical purchase within the study of nationalism, but it is a distinction towards which many of the writers discussed below exercise some caution. Specifically, they reject the proposition that membership in a civic nation is not a cultural matter. The point is made by Kymlicka (1995) who maintains that even in the USA, often seen as a classic example of a civic nation, membership involves integration into a cultural community distinguished by a common language and shared historical memories and values. Those who advocate civic nationalism as the preferred form of nationalism tend to base it upon membership of a political community, rather than a shared common culture. Unlike the defenders of civic nationalism, liberal nationalists accept the idea that people can be bound by a common culture, from which they draw inspiration.

The rights of minority cultures: Will Kymlicka

A central move made by liberal defenders of nationalism is to recognize that individuals value their cultural membership of nations. While many scholars might wish these attachments to subside, writers such as Tamir argue this is unlikely to happen. Indeed, the argument that people should not be expected to give up what they hold dear is central to Tamir's work; hence the final chapter of *Liberal Nationalism* is entitled 'Making Virtue out of Necessity'. Other writers take a similar line, among them Kymlicka (1991, 1995, 2001), who maintains that addressing conflicts of interest between majority and minority nations in established societies involves recognizing the importance of cultural memberships for self-identity. Kymlicka and Tamir share much common ground. Both assert that liberal democratic states are not culturally neutral, since they have a vested interest in promoting a common culture. This calls into question the idea of purely 'civic' nationalism. Perhaps most significantly, both make claims about the fundamental importance of national cultures for individual identities. Where Tamir refers to the 'contextual individual', Kymlicka underlines the significance of 'societal culture'. Kymlicka defines 'societal culture' as follows:

> A culture which provides its members with meaningful ways of life across the full range of human activities, including social, educational, religious, recreational, and economic life, encompassing both public and private spheres. These cultures tend to be territorially concentrated, and based on a shared language. (Kymlicka, 1995, p. 76)

This approximates closely to what we might think of conventionally as a national culture. We have already noted how Tamir regards the values and beliefs we derive from our national culture as essential for making sense of our social experiences. Kymlicka also insists that the capacity to make choices presupposes individuals to have acquired a set of values on which they base their deliberations: 'freedom involves making choices amongst various options, and our societal culture not only provides these options, but also makes them meaningful to us' (Kymlicka, 1995, p. 83). Hence for both Tamir and Kymlicka, nationalism is to be defended on the grounds that it ensures people can continue to make cultural choices. If the culture of a minority nation suffers at the hands of a majority nation, then its members lose a vital element of their personal freedom.

There are also some key differences between the two writers. Whereas Tamir is concerned with cultural membership of nations in general, Kymlicka focuses on the rights of minority cultures, whether those of national minorities or of immigrant groups. The former category refers to groups that have been incorporated into a multinational state, either voluntarily or involuntarily. Kymlicka has in mind the Québécois and Aboriginal populations in Canada, both national minorities by virtue of having been incorporated involuntarily into Canada when it became an independent country. Kymlicka points out that, with very few exceptions, most countries in the world are multinational. It is even more difficult to think of any country that has not experienced some immigration, and thereby become, to varying degrees, 'polyethnic'. While Tamir stresses that preserving one's culture is a matter of individual choice, for Kymlicka, national identity is an identification that generally we do *not* choose. The distinction is important, because Kymlicka's defence of nationalism stems from a belief that people have deep ties to their nation, and so cannot be expected to make the 'sacrifice' of giving up this attachment. Rather, people should be entitled to preserve their culture as a right. Tamir sees the right to culture as an individual right; for Kymlicka, it is a group right, because its necessity stems from the power differential between majority and minority groups. Group-differentiated rights are intended to protect minority cultures from political actions taken by dominant groups.

To summarize, Kymlicka argues that individuals require access to their societal culture as a basic element of their freedom and that group-differentiated rights designed to protect this freedom are therefore perfectly compatible with liberal theories of rights. Nationalism, conceived as the desire to preserve one's societal culture, is both legitimate and understandable. On the basis of this argument Kymlicka sets out three types of group-differentiated rights: 'self-government rights' for national minorities; 'polyethnic rights' for immigrant groups; and 'special representation rights' that may be exercized by both national minorities and immigrant groups. The reason for Kymlicka's distinction between the rights of national minorities and those of immigrants is that the former are incorporated into a new society *as a group*, whereas, by virtue of leaving their national society, immigrants 'voluntarily relinquish some of the rights that go along with their original national membership' (1995, p. 96). The distinction has attracted some criticism. If access to their culture is important to individuals' self-identity, then critics wonder why immigrants and their descendants should have any lesser entitlement than 'native' national minorities (Parekh, 2000).

Nevertheless it is the rights of minority nations that most preoccupy Kymlicka in *Multicultural Citizenship* (1995). Since these are groups having a fair degree of institutional autonomy, often territorially concentrated and with a strong sense of cultural difference from the rest of the population, their relationship with the wider society appears more problematic. Most of the time, according to Kymlicka, the rights of national minorities can be accommodated within existing, though modified, national frameworks. Many multinational societies, to use his terminology, permit minority nations a degree of self-government, in an effort to maintain territorial unity. France, despite strong resistance to recognizing the cultural autonomy of minority nations such as the Basques and Bretons, allows Corsica powers of self-government exceeding those of the mainland regions. The official language of the largest Canadian province, Quebec, is French, reflecting the fact that over 80 per cent of its population is French-speaking. A resolution passed by Canada's House of Commons and Senate in 1995 recognized Quebec as a distinct society within Canada. In Spain, although the 1978 constitution declared the 'indissoluble unity of the Spanish nation', it allowed for the establishment of 'autonomous communities' with differing degrees of political autonomy, including the power to promote languages such as Basque and Catalan which had been suppressed for much of the twentieth century.

Enabling national minorities to exercise rights to self-government is defensible for Kymlicka on the grounds of both the importance of access to their societal culture, and because it ensures their 'long term viability' (Kymlicka, 1999, p. 140). Recognizing that these rights may not prevent further challenges to the authority of national (or federal) governments, he maintains that denying them will only fuel resentment. Given the weight that attaches to existing within one's own territorial national culture, what holds a multinational society together? Doubting that common values or a shared culture will bind any multinational society, Kymlicka confesses he has no clear answer to this question. Because there is such a threat to the unity of multinational society, others seek an alternative conception of liberal nationalism, which resolutely opposes group-differentiated rights. Thus Miller (1995) makes the case for a rejuvenated, overarching national identity, capable of uniting polyethnic and multinational societies.

The nation as an 'obligation-generating' community: David Miller

At first glance, there appears to be a degree of agreement amongst liberal defenders of nationalism concerning the virtue of the nation as a moral community. Writers as different in their approaches as Kymlicka and Miller concur that participation in a common culture furnishes individuals with an important source of identity and a vital moral resource in making sense of the social world. More broadly, a surprising number of scholars defend the national community on the grounds that feelings of membership provide a key source of social cohesion. Certainly Tamir appreciates the nation's value as an ethical community, which inspires us to develop a duty of care for fellow members. Elsewhere, Anthony Smith writes of how nationalism helps with the recreation of 'feelings of fraternity and kinship and the mobilization of citizens for common goals' (1995a, p. 155). Even writers who are openly critical of nationalism nevertheless defend the virtue of belonging to the national community. For example, Viroli champions the 'love of country' embodied in patriotism, on the grounds that it has the capacity to generate solidarity, but (unlike nationalism) without 'fomenting exclusion or aggression' (1995, p. 8). Among a fairly diverse bunch of writers, we can point to a similar tendency to justify national membership because it encourages us to have a commitment to others, and to work towards a common good, rather than our individual self-interest. This limited agreement, however, masks often-marked underlying differences. As we have noted, Viroli defends patriotism rather than nationalism, maintaining that people feel close to representative institutions because they preserve common liberty and enable them to take part in public life. By contrast, liberal defenders of nationalism tend to argue that people identify with political institutions because they embody important ethno-cultural values.

There is also a difference in motivation. Kymlicka's concern is with strengthening the position of minority national communities *vis-à-vis* the majority. Others such as Miller, and Lind in *The Next American Nation* (1995), advocate strengthening an all-embracing national culture within a national territory. Lind argues for a liberal nationalism centred on a 'common language, common folk-ways, and a common vernacular culture' partly to combat the divisions he perceives in 'multicultural America'. Lind's opposition to affirmative action policies and his rejection of the notion of the USA as a multinational society contrast sharply with Kymlicka's defence of minority rights.

As we have seen, Kymlicka's essential defence of nationalism is that access to our 'societal culture' is basic to individual freedom, as it provides us with the information and values needed to make our way through life. Preventing individuals from accessing this culture is to deny them a foundational component of their liberty. Miller's defence of nationalism also recognizes people's deep attachment to their 'inherited national identities' (Miller, 1995, p. 184), but is more grounded in the ethical significance of national-ism. Miller is an arch-exponent of the argument that nationalism is defensible because belief in the existence of a common bond between members of a nation encourages people to show 'special obligations' towards fellows (Miller, 1995). Kymlicka's defence of nationalism, like Tamir's, is based on ideas of personal freedom; Miller's relies more on nationalism's capacity to generate unity and obligation amongst members.

Miller's argument is intriguing. Like other liberal exponents of nationalism, he wishes to demonstrate that nationalism can be defended. In part, he does so by showing that nationalism is not necessarily *un*reasonable; arguing indeed 'simply that identifying with a nation . . . is a legitimate way of understanding your place in the world' (1995, p. 11). In addition, he sets out to provide an ethically grounded defence of nationalism which treats the nation as an 'obligation-generating community' (1995, p. 82). He maintains, for example, that a sense of obligation to one's fellows is necessary to sustain a welfare state. He is sceptical that people pay taxes to help support welfare only because they might require support one day; rather, he holds that they do so because they feel an *obligation* towards fellow members of a community they value. For Miller therefore it is necessary that state and nation, as near as possible, should be congruent (a reminder of Gellner's definition of nationalism). Indeed, he makes the bold suggestion that where differences are wholly irreconcilable it may be necessary to consider moving members of minorities to be with their compatriots so that 'two more or less nationally homogenous entities can be created' (Miller, 1998, p. 276). Recourse to such a policy is justifiable on the grounds that where people believe others to be not just citizens of the same state, but *compatriots*, then it is 'more likely that they will be able to solve collective action problems, to support redistributive principles of justice, and to practise deliberative forms of democracy' (1995, p. 98).

On such grounds, Miller is convinced that it is possible to justify a national community bound by a public culture, by which he means a 'set of understandings about how a group of people is to conduct its life together' (1995, p. 26). He admits that it is difficult to specify what the content of this public culture may be, though he does say that it will comprise 'political principles' as well as possibly 'cultural ideals' (1995, p. 26). He insists that this common culture is not static and should be the product of, and subject to, public debate. It is desirable, therefore, to enable people to develop relations of trust and fellowship, irrespective of their particular ethnocultural identity. Of course, this claim rests on the assumption that people *do* share a common culture, that doing so makes them feel obligated towards other members of what is, after all, an 'imagined community'. Perhaps even more significantly, Miller's argument hinges on people taking their national identity as seriously as he suggests they do. In fact, we might say that all the writers who defend the idea of national community on the grounds

that it sustains social cohesion are taking nationalism very seriously. To what extent is this sentiment shared by the mass of the
population?

Defending the indefensible? Responses to Tamir, Kymlicka and Miller

Liberal defenders of nationalism have come in for some sharp criticism. Opponents have described the idea of liberal nationalism
variously as 'oxymoronic' (Levinson, 1995), 'irresponsible'
(Vincent, 1997) and, ultimately, 'immoral' (Miščević, 2001). There
is no space here to enter into detailed consideration of the arguments we have presented so far. Miščević provides an engaging
and extensive analysis in *Nationalism and Beyond* (2001). Below we
examine what from a sociological perspective we take to be the
core issues for critics: (*a*) that nationalism can be defended because
of its significance for our self-identity and because it generates
obligations to fellow members; (*b*) that nationalism creates unnecessary boundaries between people.

What is so special about nations?

Central to the work of Tamir, Kymlicka and Miller is the view that
membership of a nation provides an important source of personal
identity. Kymlicka and Tamir state that it is uncontroversial even
among more conventional liberal theorists that people's identities
are informed by their membership of human communities, such as
the nation (see especially Kymlicka, 1997). The emphasis placed on
the personal significance of national identity troubles critics in two
main respects. They question the assertion that nationalism is
defensible because an individual's national culture is constitutive
of their self-identity. They also query claims made about the capacity of nationalism to generate a sense of fraternity and mutual
obligation among members of a nation.

Let us turn to the first of these criticisms. Without doubt, our
sense of who we are, and how we make sense of our world is
informed by the cultural knowledge we acquire in the course of
social life. Does this mean we must agree with Kymlicka (1991) that
our 'cultural membership affects our very sense of personal identity and capacity' (1991, p. 175)? What exactly is meant by the

suggestion that a national culture deeply shapes our world-view by conveying to us a distinctive set of beliefs? Most significantly, perhaps, it implies that a national culture will remain a *national* culture irrespective of social change. Yet, as we will argue in our later discussion of globalization, it is difficult to sustain a view that human communities today are bounded entities, if they ever have been. Walker stresses this point when arguing that people make decisions on the basis of values shaped by their relationship to institutions such as the media, work and religious organizations which, in turn, are governed by norms that 'hold true across many different territories and ethnic communities' (1999, p. 149). Walker maintains that these transnational norms often override the values we acquire via our national culture.

A related line of criticism suggests that humans have a wide array of social attachments, each of which will influence in different ways the decisions they make. Vincent underlines this, when he remarks that nations have 'little everyday significance for most individuals – at least for most of the time – whereas groups like families, religious affiliations, occupations and the multiple associations of everyday life press upon us all with depressing (and often joyful) regularity' (1997, p. 286). Elsewhere, Walker (1999) argues that membership of a farming community or urban neighbourhood could act as resources of meaning for some, in the same way that membership of ethnic communities does for others. While Miller recognizes that our membership of nations will 'tell us, *in part*, who we are' (Miller, 1997, p. 74, emphasis added), a great many other aspects of 'who we are' could prove to be of greater routine significance in determining how we make sense of the social world. The policies advocated by liberal defenders of nationalism can entail major changes, on the basis of what is, by Miller's admission, just one aspect of our self-identity.

Some commentators therefore question the extent to which national cultural values can be said actually to underpin our self-identity, as well as the treatment of national identity as if it outweighed other possibilities. The significance of national identity is further challenged in terms of whether or not it does generate obligations towards our fellow members. To assume so presupposes that people share broadly similar (and distinctive) values and cherish membership enough to feel a 'duty of care' to their fellows (Tamir, 1993). The first of these presuppositions is highly problematic. For example, Miller suggests that the character of American national identity is 'unusually individualistic' (1995,

p. 94). However, individualism is not a value peculiar to Americans. In many countries with more extensive systems of public welfare, sections of the population would support a more individualistic culture, and a reduction in public welfare provision. Nor is it obvious that American culture is 'unusually individualistic'. In 2002, George W. Bush launched the 'USA Freedom Corps', an initiative invoking the idea that 'patriotism is proven in our concern for others – a willingness to sacrifice for people we may never have met or seen' (Bush, 2002). National political leaders are often vague about what 'our' specific national values are. Thus, Tony Blair (1999) claims that what marks the British as 'different' is the fact that they are 'hard working, tolerant, understated, creative, courageous, generous'; the American President says one of the 'essential American values is compassion' (Bush, 2001a), and the Prime Minister of New Zealand speaks of the 'timeless New Zealand values of fairness, opportunity, and security' (Clark, 2000). What is striking about these statements is the *non-national* quality of the 'national' values. They indicate some substantial difficulties in attempting to pin down the constituent elements of a national culture.

Even liberal defenders of nationalism struggle with defining the parameters of a shared national culture. Miller begins by describing a public culture that binds members of a nation so deeply that they feel obligations towards each other, yet by the end of *On Nationality* he refers to values that are as 'far as possible independent of group-specific cultural values' (1995, p. 137). How can cultural values be non group-specific, and yet still sufficiently 'national' to enable a group to feel different from another nation *and* to feel bonds of obligation? Arblaster (1995) conveys the suggestion that the idea of a national culture need not mean that *everyone* adheres to the same view of that culture, but merely that there are various cultural traditions or phenomena that we might say are distinctive of a particular nation. In Britain, he suggests, the tradition of choral singing is uniquely Welsh and is therefore 'one of the things that gives Wales its distinctive individual identity' (1995, p. 198). However, while many people in Wales (and outside) may very well associate choral singing with Wales, this does not mean it has significance for their personal sense of national identity. Indeed, even where certain cultural markers might be regarded as truly distinctive of a nation, they can be the source of division, rather than obligation, among people who claim the same national identity. The Welsh language, for example, might be even more readily identified as uniquely Welsh, but linguistic politics in Wales can create deep rifts between sections of the Welsh population (Day, 2002, p. 229). Thus the claim that people share a distinctly national culture is enormously problematic.

Of course, this does not preclude the possibility that, despite different interpretations of what it means to be Italian or Canadian, the people of these countries nevertheless feel some sense of mutual obligation. What is difficult to ascertain is how far these are obligations towards fellow members, rather than just feelings of attachment to the nation in a more abstract sense. Miller contends that our willingness to contribute financially to the maintenance of systems of welfare derives from 'prior obligations of nationality' (1995, p. 72). Yet, people may pay for other reasons, such as out of 'social conscience than a sense of national solidarity' (Parekh, 1999, p. 315), or simply because they are legally obliged to do so. In the Nordic countries, it is widely accepted that the commitment to paying for public services through income tax remains strong. Yet across a number of EU countries (such as Germany, Sweden and the UK), Taylor-Gooby (2001) finds that people are less willing to pay personally for public services. In the UK in particular, he argues, people are willing to pay for services from which they will directly benefit (Taylor-Gooby, 1998).

Caney (1999) identifies a further problem with Miller's argument, commenting that even if people are 'motivated to promote the well-being of those with whom they identify, it does not follow that they have an obligation to do so' (1999, p. 126). A poll conducted by a South Korean newspaper in September 2002 found that 53 per cent of South Koreans would be willing to pay higher taxes to support reunification with North Korea. While people may feel 'motivated' to support this development through a sense of shared Korean identity, it does not follow that they are *obligated* to do so (*Financial Times*, 21–22 September 2002).

Some people may feel obligations towards fellow nationals, just as some may view their national identity as a constitutive element of their self-identity. The liberal defence of nationalism, however, assumes that people set *significant* store by their national identity and (at least in Miller's case), that this attachment *generally* induces obligations to fellows. Brighouse (1997) says of Miller that he 'treats it as a given that people *will* feel national attachments' (1997, p. 384). As we have seen, there are good reasons to doubt that national identity is always as salient for people as liberal defenders of nationalism suggest it is.

Can nationalism be liberal?

As yet we have not examined what is the most fundamental objection to nationalism for many commentators: that it is inherently illiberal. The writers we have been discussing all acknowledge that nationalism can lead to excesses. As advocates of liberal nationalism, it is vital for them that diversity within the national group should not be repressed. Miller argues for an 'ongoing collective debate about what it means to be a member of this nation' (1995, p. 153) and stresses that nationalism is consonant with cultural diversity. Yet, as noted before, the crucial test is whether nationalism can be liberal *in practice*.

It is easy to point to instances where nationalism fosters unease about 'foreigners' living within the national territory. Even countries frequently characterized as 'civic nations', such as Britain and France, experience a 'recurring anxiety' (Spencer and Wollman, 2002, p. 113) about outsiders. Anxiety is especially marked in media debates over migration, and is highlighted by periodic surges in support for political parties prepared to take a 'tough line' on immigration. In the Netherlands, a country broadly known for its social liberalism, the Lijst Pim Fortuyn, committed to a restrictive immigration policy and openly anti-Islamic, became the second largest party in the country's parliament following the 2002 elections. Around the same time, other European countries experienced a growth in support for parties with similarly strong anti-immigration policies. In Norway, the Progress Party won 26 of the country's 165 parliamentary seats in 2001, while in France the former leader of the National Front, Jean Marie Le Pen, secured nearly 17 per cent of the vote in the 2002 presidential elections. These parties regard immigration as a threat to the essence of national culture. For liberal defenders of nationalism, such situations merely point to the need for a more liberal nationalism; they do not undermine it in principle. How then might one challenge the *idea* of a liberal nationalism? Critics would answer in terms of the tensions between 'insiders' and 'outsiders' that they see as an unavoidable element of the politics of nationalism.

Nationalism displays an interminable preoccupation with difference, which manifests itself in two ways. On the one hand, of necessity it strives to maintain the cultural boundaries *between* nations. For nationalists, concentric cultures need to be separated because they challenge the very foundations of nationalism: the belief that nations are culturally unique entities. Hence neighbouring nations are presented as fundamentally different, bound by a culture and values distinct from, if not at odds with, 'ours'. On the other hand, nationalism is intolerant of difference *within* the national territory and *within* the nation. In its extreme form, this can lead to efforts to 'cleanse' the national territory of foreigners or foreign influences. More routinely, intolerance of outsiders is evident in the unease felt towards immigrants and their descendants, towards the presence within the national territory of those who do not speak the national language, or who retain an attachment to an 'alien' culture and values. Whether with regard to neighbours or minorities residing within the national territory, the inherent concern with difference means that nationalists, of whatever shade, will endeavour to preserve whatever it is that they believe makes their nation unique. At best, this means that outsiders will be viewed as requiring some degree of cultural transformation or control, rather than as individuals to be valued in their own right. At worst, they are seen as indelibly marked by their own national culture and therefore bound to remain irrevocably different.

Liberal nationalists like Miller and Tamir seek to evade the criticism levelled at more radical nationalists by arguing that immigrants can learn to embrace the national culture of the society to which they have moved. As liberals, neither believes that the act of immigration implies people must give up their ethnic identity. However, as nationalists, they maintain that immigrants should be prepared to integrate themselves into the national culture of their new home. Critics would question the extent to which migrants should be asked to take on an adopted national character. Indeed, Freeman (1994) asks how it is possible for immigrants to take this step, if the culture has been forged, as Miller suggests, by 'forebears' who have 'toiled and spilt blood to build and defend the nation' (1995, p. 23). How can an immigrant whose own 'forebears' were connected to another territory, and nation, possibly be expected to feel the 'obligation' to carry on this memory, as Miller asserts all the nation's members should? As Freeman says, if 'such memory is an *essential* part of national identity, then immigrants are required to do what is impossible: to share historical memories with the descent-majority' (1994, p. 84).

Looking at the issue from a different direction, when it comes to a question of necessity, why would the state admit only those who have a 'shared culture and identity – the competence to act as a member of *this* particular society', as Tamir proposes? To take but two examples, it is difficult to imagine the position Australia or the d be in today, had they imposed on immigrants the ultural conditions suggested by Tamir. Even Kymlicka, rk is geared towards protecting minority cultures, makes a disti... on between the rights of immigrants and native minority nations, according far greater entitlements to the latter group. Distinguishing between immigrants and natives in this way effectively ranks people on the basis of how long their ancestors can be traced back within a territory, and this does not only disadvantage new arrivals. Translate the arguments of Miller and Tamir into contexts like Northern Ireland or Israel, and it becomes evident just how divisive they are in practice. How might one achieve peace in a divided territory if the expectation is that members of minority groups must share the historical memories of the majority nation?

For critics, the difficulty with the liberal defence of nationalism, as with any form of nationalism, is that it sustains an irrational dichotomy between outsiders and insiders. Encouraging people to be conscious of what makes them different makes it likely that a good number among them will come to regard external cultural influences or people who remain stubbornly different as an affront. As debates over immigration show, when people become sufficiently concerned about immigrants claiming welfare benefits or taking the jobs of 'natives', public opinion lurches to the right. Given the capacity of nationalism to generate ill-feeling towards outsiders, even a liberal nationalism is prone to be used as justification for precisely the sorts of nationalist policies and outcomes liberals have castigated as 'extreme'.

Conclusion

Liberal defenders of nationalism address issues the sociological literature on nationalism rarely confronts directly. We have been able to attend to only a few of these matters, but it should be clear that the areas on which they focus are integral to the sociological study of nationalism, and indeed reflect wider sociological concerns. At root, liberal defences of nationalism are reflections on the relationship between the individual and the community, on what it means for people to 'belong' to a cultural community (Kymlicka, 1991, p. 3). When analysing this relationship, liberal defenders of nationalism set themselves against what they see as a tendency within liberal thought to detach people from their cultural environment. A powerful element of the liberal defence of nationalism, therefore, is the argument that our membership of a nation, of which we are made aware through a process of socialization, shapes our self-identity in important ways. Nevertheless, Tamir, Kymlicka and Miller stress that this influence does not overwhelm the individual, and that people can and should have the ability to make choices about their national identities. Furthermore, unless cultural diversity is retained, people will not be able to choose. As Tamir remarks, the 'right to make cultural choices is only meaningful in a world where the plurality of cultures is protected' (1993, p. 30).

It is hard to dissent from the view that people should have the right to choose whether or not they wish to invest significance in their national identity. Yet, the liberal defence of nationalism faces two fundamental problems. Firstly, its exponents tend to overstate the significance of national identity for self-identity. As we have outlined, Tamir's claim that the nation ranks above all other considerations in shaping our personal identity is hard to sustain, given that we have so many attachments to various types of social groups. More particularly, we have suggested that the idea of a discernible national culture is problematic, and needs to be treated with great caution. The second problem connects more directly to the issue of personal autonomy. Nationalism is a doctrine that encourages us to 'remember' our national history, to 'respect' the nation, and to fulfil our 'duty' to the community. Nationalism rarely encourages critical reflection. In fact, many would see it as an inherently conservative ideology that presents national memories as if handed down like family heirlooms from generation to generation. The very idea of 'tradition', so central to nationalism, suggests a practice that cannot be changed; as Hobsbawm remarks, the 'object and characteristic of "traditions", including invented ones, is invariance' (1983, p. 2).

Hence it is hard to square the conception of nationalism articulated by its liberal defenders with even a moderate practical nationalism and to see how individuals are to be encouraged to respect their nations, yet at the same time reflect critically upon them. This explains why some critics question whether a nationalism that fosters critical debate about values, traditions and the common cultural bond can actually be characterized as nationalism at all (Miščević, 2001). Others argue that even in its most moderate guise, nationalism is beyond ethical defence, so that liberal nationalism must be seen as a stalking horse for something altogether more illiberal. Vincent captures this view when he writes that, like 'religious fanatics, criminal associations and large business corporations' (1997, p. 294), we might have to live with nationalism, but that does not mean we should encourage it. Elsewhere, O'Neill comments that nationalism will always involve the effort of a dominant group to impose its self-image on a wider population, and to 'call for its hegemony over others' (1994, p. 140). For its critics, then, liberal nationalism can never amount to anything but an unhappy marriage between two profoundly unsuited partners.

CHAPTER 9

The 'Challenge of Globalization': Between Nationalism and Globalism

Amid the Ridley Scott images of world cities, the writing about skyscraper fortresses, the Baudrillard visions of hyperspace ... most people still live in places like Harlesden or West Brom [areas in England]. Much of life for many people, even in the heart of the First World, still consists of waiting in a bus-shelter with your shopping for a bus that never comes.

(Massey, 1994, p. 163)

Addressing the Asian Pacific Bankers Club in 2000, Masaru Hayami (2000), Governor of the Bank of Japan, remarked that 'the move toward globalization is an inevitable reality, and not likely to be reversed'; it was a 'fact of life'. Politicians, economists and business leaders throughout the world echo these sentiments. Even among its many critics, the concern seems to be with finding alternatives to the current form of globalization, rather than abandoning it altogether. Indeed, the growth of an increasingly interconnected opposition to global capitalism itself may be understood as a manifestation of globalization. For politicians and protesters, economists and environmentalists, the 'challenge of globalization', a much repeated phrase, cannot be side-stepped. As IBM's General Manager for Europe, Middle East and Africa told participants during a 1999 symposium on the 'Impact of Globalization', 'it is a sweeping force that ... no company or no nation state can afford to ignore in any way, and it's really a sea change ... globalization without a doubt is dissolving barriers like time and distance' (Lawrie, 1999).

The idea that globalization makes political borders increasingly irrelevant is a key theme in discussions in this area. However, it is not just physical borders that are said to be eroding. Globalization is also regarded as changing the ways in which we see the world, our place in it, and our relations with others. In one of the first books to address this phenomenon (Robertson, 1992), the essence of globalization is taken to be the intensification of connections between different parts of the world *and* our increasing consciousness of this development. Globalization, in this sense, is about how we come to view the world as one place.

For this reason, it is not surprising that globalization excites considerable interest among social theorists in general and, increasingly, scholars of nationalism. If globalization transcends mental, as well as physical, barriers, then surely it must have consequences for the idea of the nation, and for national identity. In what follows we address these issues in three sections. We begin by looking broadly at the idea of globalization, focusing on how it relates to the nation-state and the nation. Next we examine the political consequences of globalization. Here we argue that while globalization may indeed bring challenges for national government, the vision of the nation-state remains important for national leaders. A final section on the cultural aspects of globalization asks whether the nation remains a meaningful social category for people across the world. We conclude that its appeal remains strong, and that national identity is still significant in terms of how people order their social world.

What is 'globalization'?

It should come as no surprise that a concept of such magnitude can be interpreted in many ways. Though there are different ways of conceptualizing globalization, nevertheless there are some discernible common themes. One is that globalization refers to the increased interconnections brought about by the global spread of ideas, images and commodities. In a poll of US citizens in 2000, of the 70 per cent who had heard the term, nearly all described it as involving growing interconnectedness across the world (PIPA, 2000). Closely related to this perception, globalization also appears to be about our changing conceptions of time and space; to use a well-worn phrase, how the world is 'becoming smaller'. As a mid-1990s advertisement for British Telecommunications' internet service declared: 'Geography is history'.

These related themes feature recurrently in the globalization literature. Giddens, whose 1999 BBC Reith Lectures highlighted a growing popular interest in the subject in Britain, comments that it is 'about the transformation of time and space in our lives', explaining that 'distant events ... affect us more directly and immediately than ever before. Conversely, decisions we take as individuals are often global in their implications' (1998, p. 31). Harvey's (1989) notion of 'time–space compression' has become especially influential in making sense of globalization. For Harvey, the world 'shrinks' as a consequence of technological innovations enabling people and commodities to travel more quickly than hitherto, and reducing distance as an obstacle to communication. These technological advances facilitate the increased interconnectedness that constitutes a core component of discussions of globalization.

The implications of these developments are hotly contested, perhaps no more so than with regard to the consequences for the nation-state, national identity and nationalism. This is not surprising, since nation-states are territorial entities, while globalization refers to processes – cultural, economic and political – believed to transcend territorial boundaries. Many of the terms used to describe the character of globalization emphasize this quality, including 'transnational' (Sklair, 1995; Hannerz, 1996; Fulcher, 2000), 'supranational' (Held, 2000) and 'supraterritorial' (Scholte, 2000).

For some, the age of the nation-state is already passing (Albrow, 1996; Ohmae, 1996). Thus, Ohmae argues that the 'nation-focused maps we typically use to make sense of economic activity are woefully misleading' (1996, p. 20). Others are far from convinced of the evidence of a burgeoning 'borderless world' (Hirst and Thompson, 1996; Rodrik, 1997; Weiss, 1998, J. Hall, 2000). Though some assert the resilience of the nation-state more vigorously than others, the general argument is made that national governments still retain many of their 'old' functions while also acquiring new ones, such as regulating transnational bodies they have helped to establish. Something of a middle ground is occupied by those who adhere to what has been termed the 'transformationalist' view (Held et al., 1999). These writers variously argue that while national governments remain significant actors, they are no longer the principal form of governance or authority. For example, a wide range of transnational actors now play important roles in global politics, including multinational corporations, global social movements and transnational bodies such as the World Trade Organization and the United Nations.

Holton's (1998) *Globalization and the Nation-State* has a good deal in common with the transformationalist view. While maintaining that economic and political processes operating above the level of the nation-state mean that national governments no longer hold a monopoly on power, Holton states firmly that globalization does not herald the end of the nation-state. He describes global politics as a 'multi-actor system' (1998, p. 107) regulated by transnational institutions, as well as by the evolving nation-state. Holton's view reflects his wider disposition that rather than an inexorable force dragging us towards a unified world society, globalization is a multi-dimensional phenomenon, in which the global, national and individual interact.

Holton therefore eschews an evolutionary reading of globalization as following a single underlying logic. He does so partly because he is at odds with accounts that see it as driven by specific historic forces, notably capitalism, or by particular regional forces, such as 'the West' or, more notably, the USA. His principal reason, however, is that he sees nothing inevitable about its development. Thus, globalization is 'better seen as a set of intersecting processes that falter as much as they advance' (1998, p. 204). Sometimes globalization can be misread as implying that values and experiences across the world are converging inexorably. Holton's attention to the cultural or normative dimensions of globalization is a useful reminder that it is not an abstract 'force' that simply acts upon us. Rather, it is a phenomenon whose meaning and trajectory is subject to debate. As he comments, 'globalization is as much about ideals and values as economic development, about ideals of what the world should be as well as what it currently is or is thought to be' (1998, p. 41). Corporate notions of the 'global village' may be countered by the 'one world' values of environmental activists. Equally, while some may view themselves as part of an emerging global community, others, although embracing perhaps some universal standards (such as on human rights), retain a view of the world as divided among nations. Therefore, while a key element of the historical development of globalization has been the way in which people have come to think of the world progressively as a single place, as with many world images developed in earlier centuries, the globe today is more likely to be imagined as 'singular yet somehow differentiated and subdivided' (1998, p. 39).

In the rest of this chapter we want to pursue this idea that the impact of globalization is complex and uneven. There are three particular points arising from Holton to which we will return below. The first concerns his 'defence' of the nation-state as an actor in global politics, and as a focus for identity. There are solid political reasons why the nation-state continues to be a key actor, such as its role in establishing the economic, political and social conditions necessary for economic growth and for attracting foreign capital. Additionally, Holton maintains that another explanation for the resilience of the nation-state relates more to the nation than to the state. Numerous social theorists argue that globalization, especially cultural globalization, calls into question the idea of discrete, national cultures. Holton nevertheless holds that the appeal of nationhood, and the idea of the *nation*-state, is far from diminishing, referring to the 'robustness and persistence of national identity and nation-focused sentiments' (1998, p. 155). As he acknowledges, this 'robustness' is as much a feature of advanced industrial nation-states as it is of developing countries.

A second point drawn from Holton is his cautious approach to the notion of cultural hybridity. 'Hybridity' refers to what Stuart Hall describes as 'identity formations which cut across and intersect natural frontiers' (1995, p. 629). The debate about the current era is largely about the intensification of cultural hybridity brought about through increased global interconnections, such as the flows of commodities and images and the movement of people across national borders. Under these conditions growing numbers of writers argue that the idea of national culture becomes difficult to sustain. Some see such hybridity as the basis for post-national identity, and as stretching the credibility of the idea of the national identity and the nation-state (Appadurai, 1996). Holton however is sceptical about exaggerating the extent and significance of cultural hybridity, especially as the basis for cultural identity.

The third point Holton makes concerns a different aspect of global mobilities. With regard to hybridity, the concern is with the disembedding of culture from place, usually facilitated by global marketing, the mass media and film, among other cultural carriers. But Holton also focuses attention on *human* mobility, whether through tourism, migration, or via membership of global diaspora. In doing so he shows how globalization and nationalism, often understood as mutually oppositional, are not necessarily so. Thus, members of diaspora populations may perceive themselves as belonging to a global community of Croatians, Irish or Greeks, retaining links with their national 'homeland' while also holding citizenship of their adopted country. Migrant populations may establish communities in new locations that reproduce elements of the cultural life of their ethnic homeland. Such instances 'throw into doubt the simple idea of a polarization between global and national identities' (1998, p. 159).

The general lesson we take from Holton is his insistence that globalization is contested and its effects complex. As he comments, 'whether globalization is to be seen as good or bad, or is given a mixed reception, depends on what we take globalization to be and which voices or interests are doing the judging' (1998, p. 197). With this message in mind, we turn to examine in more detail one of the key issues raised by Holton: the consequences of globalization for the nation-state.

Political consequences of globalization

Scholars of nationalism routinely attribute a leading role in the formation of national identity to the state. Though nationalism does not require sovereign political institutions to flourish, nevertheless the state has played a vital role in fashioning national identity as a mass public culture, through its management of the education system and, in the twentieth century, publicly controlled broadcasting. Moreover, in times of conflict, states have mobilized populations around the idea of the nation. They have also extended citizenship rights and provided varying levels of social welfare in order to engender social cohesion within the national territory. Now, however, there is mounting debate about whether the state remains committed to, let alone capable of, such management of national identity. Thus, Gibbons and Reimer (1999, p. 35) argue that globalization is contributing to a 'loosening' of the cultural bonds between state and citizen and to a 'rethinking of the role of nation state as the "natural" unit for the sense of cultural identity'. Before evaluating this assessment, we will take a closer look at some arguments about how globalization challenges the nation-state, especially the ability of the state to maintain cohesion around the idea of the nation.

The challenge of globalization for the nation-state

A common claim is that nation-states are increasingly unable to control activities within their territorial domain, especially with regard to economic affairs (Strange, 1996; Amin, 1997; Beck, 2000). Thus, it is argued that globalization has a significant bearing on the tax-raising capacities of national governments, as they become ever more keen to secure direct foreign investment, and as large corporations, aware of their economic cachet, bargain for lower tax levels as a precondition of investment (Jones, 2000). It is also suggested that the globalization of financial markets places increasing pressure on national macroeconomic policy, with the consequence, among other things, that public expenditure may have to be curbed to help control inflation. Indeed, Dean (1998) remarks that private credit assessment companies such as Standard and Poors are 'respected (and feared) by nation-states worldwide' due to their power to influence the rates at which governments borrow international capital. A country's economic and political health, or any other factors affecting its capacity to repay loans, has a direct bearing on its credit rating.

How national governments address global or supraterritorial pressures can have serious domestic consequences. Thus, weak or diminishing public services owing to reduced tax income or the need to limit public expenditure may fuel dissatisfaction with government. This may be exacerbated if nationals view the decisions determining the condition of their social goods as being taken effectively by institutions above the level of national government. Instances of civil unrest in which national governments have been targeted for their perceived complicity with the International Monetary Fund (IMF) are increasingly commonplace within developing industrial countries. Concerns about the inability of national governments to represent the 'national interest' are not just confined to these countries, as voters in the EU have demonstrated. For Horsman and Marshall, the growing unaccountability of national governments slowly erodes the very basis of the legitimacy of the nation-state: its ability to provide for the collective well-being of the national community. As they write, 'unable on its own to fashion economic policies purely in the light of "national interest", the nation-state is in danger of losing an essential element of its authority' (1995, pp. 220–1).

The second argument relates closely to the above. Not only are governments less able to regulate domestic affairs, it is also proposed that the state has become less concerned with the nation. Away from the rhetoric and bluster of defending the 'national interest', the relationship between nation, nationalism and state is deemed to be undergoing a radical transformation in which globalization is one of the principal agents of change. For Bauman (2000) the state has less need for the nation, because success in the global economy depends on the attractiveness of the country to global capital, and not on national cohesion. Delanty and O'Mahony (2002) take a similar stance. For them, the durability of nationalism until recently is explained by its role in managing cultural integration within socially and institutionally differentiated societies, thus enabling the state to secure legitimacy and to pursue political objectives. In many parts of the globe, however, globalization has diminished the attraction of the nation for the state because in an increasingly interconnected world, it makes less sense for governments to mobilize the nation against outsiders, since this will run counter to its political and economic objectives. In this argument, it is not the ability of the state to appeal to the nation that is weakened by globalization, so much as its desire to do so.

A main consequence of this argument is that while globalization makes state-sponsored nationalism counter-productive, it does not eliminate nationalism's appeal. Thus, while Bauman argues that dying for one's country today 'sounds vacuous and increasingly bizarre, if not amusing' (2000, p. 185), he does not suggest that the appeal of the nation necessarily diminishes. Indeed, it is likely that the 'function' the nation-state performed in conferring 'ultimate identity' will 'seek another carrier, and will seek it all the more ardently for the "softness" – elusiveness and contingency – of all available alternatives' (Bauman, 1992, p. 692). Similarly, Delanty and O'Mahony (2002) argue that the loss of the 'integrative function' of national culture due to globalization does not mean the end of nationalism. On the contrary, others are only too willing to step into the void left by the state to reclaim the nation against outsiders, both within and beyond the national territory.

The final argument draws on elements of the above two positions, notably that the state faces growing pressures from above and below. Here the concern is with what various writers, after Bull (1977), term the 'new medievalism' (Goodman, 1996; Jones, 2000). Though more usually used to describe the development of overlapping layers of governance within the global political system, new medievalism also refers to the increasing levels of communication between individuals, groups and movements operating within and across national borders. The term is also used to highlight the parallel growth in significance of globalist ideologies. Though not always explicitly used, the idea of new medievalism is akin to the kinds of changes social theorists describe as characteristic of globalization, such as Robertson's (1992) notion of 'glocalization' or Rosenau's (1997) 'fragmegration'. Numerous sociologists have drawn attention to the growth of movements that, while having local networks within national territories, are nevertheless part of global communities that share supraterritorial values (Lash and Urry, 1994; Castells, 1996; Urry, 2000). Albrow (1996) detects in the actions of these individuals across the world the beginnings of global citizenship. Therefore, while new medievalism refers to the limits on the authority of the nation-state as an institution of government, in the emerging global society identified by Albrow and others it is the nation-state as a locus of identity that is undermined.

Looking after the national interest

The preceding arguments point to how globalization presents a challenge to the nation-state, both as an idea and in practice. At the very least, for a good many commentators, globalization blurs the boundaries between the realms of domestic and foreign policy. Thus, for Rosenau (1997) the space created by the interaction between the domestic and the foreign, the global and the local, is 'the frontier'. The erosion of boundaries means that the current age, more than earlier periods, is marked by uncertainty, anxiety and complexity. Perhaps the only certain thing is that we have moved from a stage in which world affairs centred on the national state and international relations. Elsewhere, Held (1995) argues similarly that globalization produces a number of important 'disjunctures' – such as in the development of a growing corpus of international law – curtailing the autonomy of national states. Nowhere is this more so than in the arena of national economic policy. Global political institutions will not 'eclipse' national governments, but the latter will, of necessity, be tied increasingly into regional (such as the EU) and global institutions, able to address matters beyond national control (Held, 2000). Not everyone agrees. One of the sharpest alternative readings of 'globalization' remains Hirst and Thompson's *Globalization in Question* (1995), which questions even the existence of a global economy, which they prefer to see as an international economy. While they advocate increased multilateralism to confront international difficulties, it will be 'national governments that take the lead in any further extensions of international governance, on an ad hoc and limited functional basis rather than in terms of some comprehensive global initiative' (G. Thompson, 2003).

Even if we accept that globalization places limits on the policy options of governments, it is difficult to believe that nation-states will become an increasingly residual force in global politics. National cohesion, in the sense of a nationally self-conscious population, may not be needed to attract foreign investment, as Bauman suggests, but the credit rating of countries *does* depend on the level of domestic economic, political and social stability, and ultimately only national governments can ensure these conditions, not multinational corporations, the IMF or the United Nations. Following the economic and political turmoil that occurred in the country in the late 1990s, Indonesian Foreign Affairs Minister, Alwi Shihab (2000), remarked that before it could regain the support of the international community and foreign investors it was necessary to restore Indonesia's 'good image'. Writing about Singapore, David Brown (2000) shows how the pursuit of economic globalization and growth was underpinned by the promotion of a civic nationalism that created the appropriate domestic conditions for the state's economic strategy, including the partial suppression of political opponents. So long as national governments remain the principal or sole legislative body within national territories, they will continue to exercise major influence on both the domestic and world stages. National governments, too, still maintain extensive control over the affairs of their citizens, from schooling and criminal justice to travel and immigration.

Turning more particularly to the *nation*-state, as Holton suggests, the appeal exerted by ideas of nation and nationhood has not diminished significantly, despite globalization. As a mode of organizing political space, the nation-state has enjoyed unprecedented popularity over the last half century. From its initial membership of 51 in 1945, the United Nations (UN) now encompasses 191 nation-states. Moreover, the pursuit of nation-state status remains an objective for many groups across the world today. With regard to international relations, there is a good degree of support for Delanty and O'Mahony's view (2002) that it is counter-productive to their economic interests for many states to foster nationalistic passions that would inhibit international trade or foreign investment. However, there is scant evidence that the nation and national identity have become any less significant for national governments when mobilizing support for domestic policies, or maintaining social cohesion. Even in an age when governments are more willing to acknowledge, even celebrate, cultural diversity within national borders, the pursuit of cohesion remains important. For many political leaders, the task is to reconcile this diversity within the framework of the nation. Returning to Delanty and O'Mahony, the 'integrative function' of national culture arguably becomes more, not less, important, given the need to maintain unity in spite of diversity. In Britain, there is growing discussion about the significance of Britishness as a collective identity capable of binding a multinational country and a multicultural, multi-faith society (see Parekh, 2000). In Denmark, similar debates have taken place in recent years, leading the government to commission a study in 2000 on the integration of 'foreigners' into Danish society (Ministry of Refugee, Immigration and Integration Affairs, 2002). While political leaders remain accountable to, and responsible for, national societies, the integrative function of shared national values will remain undiminished. In his inaugural presidential address in January 2001, George W. Bush (2001b) spoke of how Americans had 'never been united by blood or birth or soil' but nevertheless were 'bound by ideals that move us beyond our backgrounds, lift us above our interests and teach us what it means to be citizens'. It is this idea of a national public culture that Berns (2001) argues needs to be further strengthened in the USA.

When transnational cultural flows increasingly expose national citizens to external influences, then defence of national values by national political leaders becomes more pressing. Perhaps it is not coincidental that a law was introduced in Japan in 1999 establishing the sun flag as the national flag and the *Kimigayo* as the country's national anthem. The Prime Minister, Keizo Obuchi (1999), stated that his desire was that 'appropriate education on the national flag and the national anthem will help instill in the minds of the children of the next generation the kind of manners required as members of the international community and thus help them grow up as Japanese who are respected'. Other political leaders have spoken more stridently of the need to defend national identity in the face of globalization. Setting out his country's *National Vision Policy* in 2001, Mahathir Mohamad, the Prime Minister of Malaysia, remarked that while it was important that Malaysia be fully integrated into the global economy, globalization should not be allowed to undermine national culture. As he commented, 'we must not only become more competent and be equipped with new and better skills, we must also ensure that foreign values and practices do not erode our national identity and heritage' (Mohamad, 2001). Elsewhere, Kofi Annan, Secretary-General of the UN, has stated that globalization has been portrayed as a 'foreign invasion that will destroy local cultures, regional tastes, and national traditions' (1999, p. 27). Concerns about the impact of transnational cultural flows are not confined to non-Western countries. When Euro Disney opened outside Paris in 1992 French critics denounced the event as a 'cultural Chernobyl' (Baughn and Buchanan, 2001).

It is also contestable whether national identities are any less important for foreign policy. Perhaps it is better to say that governments need to redefine national identity in ways that retain an element of distinctiveness, while nevertheless projecting an image of the nation that is more compatible with interdependency. In relation to British foreign policy, Wallace has argued that increased interdependency means the 'resources of soft power' – 'education, communication, cultural tradition and innovation' – become more important than military power and commercial rivalry, the conventional resources of 'hard power' (1991, p. 78). In the closing months of the Clinton administration in the USA, Condoleezza Rice, now part of George W. Bush's government, advised that the new President 'must speak to the American people about *national* priorities and intentions and work with Congress to focus foreign policy around the *national* interest' (2000). For Rice, the Clinton administration had gone too far in favouring internationalism over the national interest.

From the perspective of national governments, then, there seems little doubt that national identity remains important, both as a vehicle for seeking to manage domestic social cohesion and for relations on the world stage. Although for a variety of reasons it may be counter-productive to encourage hostility to foreign powers and other nations, security interests alone dictate that governments must maintain a sense of national unity, whether in relation to states on the other side of the world or to neighbouring countries. The critical question then is whether or not the idea of the nation-state remains as appealing to national citizens as it does to their governments.

Cultural consequences of globalization

Terms such as 'transnational', 'supranational', 'supraterritorial' and 'deterritorialization' are used with increased frequency to describe the flows of goods, ideas, communications and people across national borders. It is not just cross-border movement that prompts theorists to refer to these flows as 'transnational'. More specifically, it is the sense that through this movement the connection with place of origin is transformed, even if not necessarily entirely lost. Some theorists point to the formation of 'post-national' communities, and an evolving global civil society arising out of transnational networks (Albrow, 1996; Scholte, 2000). Others highlight how both the contents of these flows – the goods, ideas and people – and their destinations are transformed by processes Giddens (1990) terms 'disembedding' (see Appadurai, 1996; Hannerz, 1996, on their consequences).

What do these global cultural flows mean for the nation and national identity? There is no straightforward answer. Rather, as noted earlier, much depends on how we understand globalization. Certainly globalization has led to concerns about the threat to national culture and traditions. We will return briefly to this issue when considering claims that cultural globalization means advanced Westernization. We also want to consider two further perspectives on the cultural consequences of globalization.

Homogenization or Westernization

The first concerns the idea of an emergent global culture. There are numerous ways of understanding this notion, but for the moment we are concerned with the view that globalization facilitates the creation of a single global culture arising from the flows of cultural goods and images across national borders. Anthony Smith (1990, 1995a) is one of the few leading scholars of nationalism to have anything much to say about globalization. In a number of works, he explores the implications of such a culture, especially whether it can rival the affections currently more commonly associated with national identities. For Smith this global culture is 'not tied to a particular time or place, and ... does not mask a national origin and character' (1995a, p. 19). Instead, its cultural form is hybrid, the product of mass migration and mass communications, and characterized by 'mass consumerism consisting of standardized mass commodities, images, practices and slogans' (1995a, p. 20). It is also hybrid in the sense that it is a mélange of cultural practices originating from different parts of the world, a 'pastiche of traditional local, folk and national motifs and styles' (1995a, p. 20). Smith sets himself the task of deciding whether this type of 'rootless, cosmopolitan culture' (1995a, p. 22) can have mass appeal. His conclusion doubts that it can, because communities are sustained by values, myths, traditions and memories that are historically and culturally specific.

If Smith is sanguine about the resilience of the nation in the face of globalization, others are less so. Barber (2003) describes the rise of an emergent global culture – 'McWorld' – dominated by US corporations, a world in which people are reduced to individual consumers while local cultural traditions are eroded by forces that promise greater choice but that ultimately flatten cultural diversity. Like Smith, Barber identifies local reactions to the spread of McWorld: the defence of the particular – what he terms 'Jihad' – in the face of the universalizing. There are similarities, too, between Barber and Smith's references to the need to defend the nation-state. However, Barber is more pessimistic about the appeal of McWorld. As he comments, 'censorship against McWorld's flood tide can be little more than a dyke or a levee that is bound to give way when it is sodden enough ... No walls can keep out the virtual culture of McWorld' (1995, p. 18). The consequences for national difference are little short of disastrous. Contrary to arguments that even global commodities re-embed themselves in local settings in culturally specific ways, McWorld eats away at national cultures:

> McWorld does take on the colors of the cultures it swallows up – for a while: thus the pop music accented with Reggae and Latino rhythms in the Los Angeles barrio, Big Macs served with French wine in Paris or made from Bulgarian beef in Eastern Europe, Mickey speaking French at Euro-Disney. But, in the end, MTV and McDonald's and Disneyland are American cultural icons, seemingly innocent Trojan-American horses nosing their way into other nations' cultures (Barber, 1998, p. 29).

The globalizing culture alluded to by Smith, and discussed in detail by Barber, features in a second argument about globalization's cultural impact. Some view a globalizing culture as extending the hegemonic dominance of the West, or, as in Barber's case, the USA in particular. In this thesis, Western corporations are regarded as perpetuating the dominance of the West beyond the end of empire. Rather than through direct colonial rule, the power of the West is advanced now by corporate penetration and transformation of post-colonial societies and cultures. Globalization is equated with Western cultural imperialism. Tomlinson (1991; 2000), a critic of this position, summarizes the argument well: 'globalization is the enforced installation, worldwide, of one particular culture, born out of one particular, privileged, historical experience. It is, in short, simply the extension of *Western* culture' (1996, p. 25).

While one might query the extent to which multinational corporations act directly on behalf of the interests of 'the West', it can be argued that these corporations are indeed iconic of Western societies and especially of the USA (Barber, 2003; on the music industry, see Hesmondhalgh, 1998). It is undeniable that Western corporations have been able to advance their interests even, as in the case of the fast food industry, in countries that traditionally resisted the allure of the 'Golden Arches', such as Japan. On normative grounds, one might share Barber's sense of exasperation about the global impact of McWorld. Yet is the cultural impact of 'the West' really as total as advocates of the cultural imperialism thesis suggest? More broadly, thinking about the idea of global culture, is the choice between foreign and local, global and national, Jihad and McWorld really so stark?

As we have already indicated, the perceived globalization of Western culture meets considerable resistance across the globe. Even allowing for global flows of commodities and images, people still appear to be remarkably adept at taking on board external influences, even incorporating them within *their* culture, while retaining a sense of difference. The celebrated author of *The Clash of Civilizations and the Remaking of World Order* (Huntingdon, 1997) comments that what the 'West spits out won't be ingested over the longer term without being modified and refined. The Japanese have so far been a good case in point – they've absorbed the technology of modernization, but they still have a culture that is distinctly Japanese and very different from that of the West' (1995, p. 26). How people in local settings translate global cultural flows depends very much on the cultural and social backgrounds from which they come. These flows do not go in just one direction. Advances in communications technologies may spread the influence of American and British television, but, in Britain, they also allow Turkish Cypriots to access Turkish-language television (Robins and Aksoy, 2001) and Indians to tune into a world beyond the BBC via the India-based Zee TV (Tyrell, 1999).

Consider the case of young people, whom Ohmae (1996) regards as the advance guard of global consumer culture. Research in Singapore (Wee, 1999) suggests that, like their peers in Western societies, teenagers show similar interests in global corporate brands and have growing knowledge of international phenomena, yet their personal values remain strongly influenced by the society in which they live. Another study of the impact of globalization on Danish, French and Israeli children concludes that globalization is 'not a matter of oppositions. It is not globalization vs localization, international vs national, universal vs particular. Rather, globalization involves the linking of their own locales to the wider world' (Lemish et al., 1998, pp. 552–3). These children experienced little difficulty in moving between cultural worlds, as in the case of a group of 12-year-old Israeli girls adhering to strict religious beliefs while also professing a penchant for the rather more secular films of Jean Claude van Damme. As these examples underline, the relationship between the national and the global is not necessarily antagonistic. As Holton says of Smith, the principal problem with the cultural imperialism thesis and the idea of global culture as deployed by Smith and Barber is that they give 'insufficient attention to the ways in which the global and the national or local may co-exist in people's lives' (1998, p. 160). However, we do not wish to suggest things necessarily remain unchanged (nor, indeed, does Holton).

Global hybridization

The final perspective on the cultural consequences of globalization we want to consider sees the global and local fusing to create a hybrid cultural form or what some term a 'third culture' (Featherstone, 1995; Nederveen Pieterse, 1995). Here, the notion of a global culture refers not to the spread of cultural homogenization, but rather to the multitude of ways in which cultural styles, practices and beliefs originating from different parts of the world are recombined the world over. This is not just about transplanting cultural phenomena into different locations, such as the Mexican restaurants in Cardiff or Irish bars in Warsaw that feature in clichéd ideas of the 'global village'. Rather, it is about the development of new cultural forms, greater than the sum of their parts. Think of 'Thai boxing by Moroccan girls in Amsterdam, Asian rap in London, Irish bagels, Chinese tacos' (Nederveen Pieterse, 1995, p. 53). Nederveen Pieterse's examples highlight that hybrid cultures are not just the preserve of 'the rest'; they are also part-and-parcel of life in 'the West'. Furthermore, he argues that this is not unique to the current age: 'hybridization is as old as history' (2001, p. 222). Cultures are never hermetically sealed off from the rest of the world; rather our cultural worlds have always been meeting-points for cultural flows, whether or not this consciously registers with us. The significance of globalization – or what Nederveen Pieterse terms 'accelerated globalization' (2001) – is that it intensi-fies and widens the scope of hybridization. The spread of global commodities, of global leisure phenomena (music, film, food, fash-ion), the growth of global or transnational media, the physical movement of people and the advances in communications tech-nologies – together make 'transnational connections' (Hannerz, 1996) more likely. Globalization, it is argued, makes hybridization a marker of our times: 'we are *all* "Moroccan girls doing Thai boxing in Amsterdam"' (Nederveen Pieterse 2001, p. 237); that is, we are all mixing cultural elements and traces *across* places and identities.

What should we make of this argument? Friedman (2000) holds that unless people themselves acknowledge the significance of hybridity, we should not impute any causal effect on people's self-identity. However, he does point to some – a 'transnational elite'– for whom hybridity has not only become something to recognize, but also to champion. For this group, notions such as hybridity and transnationalism may *seem* like universal conditions, but they 'do not function as scientific renditions of social reality' (2000, p. 144). That we can point to a growing number of transnational connec-tions outside this limited 'transnational elite' does not necessarily mean that these affect how people perceive themselves: the global, the national and the local may coexist. Friedman therefore counters what he views as the excesses of the global hybridization perspec-tive. His argument may strike a chord with many of our everyday experiences. Especially in the advanced industrial countries, we might consume every day a host of global commodities – eat Chinese food, drive Korean cars, wear Levi jeans, drink Mexican beer – yet our lives still remain largely local. Maybe we are all 'Moroccan girls doing Thai boxing in Amsterdam', but it is difficult to know what this amounts to in terms of how we view ourselves.

It would be rash to dismiss entirely the social impact of the forces that are taken to underpin hybridity, if not the idea of hybridization itself, for a number of reasons. Firstly, to argue that territorially bounded populations retain a pure national culture, despite mass migration over time, as well as the fusion of cultural styles, is at odds with sociological reality. What *exactly* does it mean to be British, for example, when one can point now to an ethnically diverse population that embraces a wide range of religions and cultural traditions? The presence of such diversity, which in countries such as Britain is a legacy of an earlier phase of globalization tied up with imperialism, makes any idea of 'national culture' contestable. Secondly, there are undoubtedly large numbers for whom hybridity is indeed a serious matter, such as migrant populations and descendent generations. Appadurai (1996) describes how diasporic populations can have a hybrid sense of locality, created partly by the global mass media, especially electronic media, that enable them simultaneously to exist in their place of residence and to be linked to their place of birth or origin. Finally, to say that hybridization is significant only if we acknowledge it ignores how important and often basic aspects of our lives are shaped through interactions with distant places and others. Stuart Hall, who was born in Jamaica but moved to England when he went to university, writes of himself and the sugar plantations of his birth place: 'people like me who came to England in the 1950s have been here for centuries; symbolically, we have been here for centuries. I was coming home. I am the sugar at the bottom of the English cup of tea' (1991, p. 48). We might think of global hybridization in a similar way. Though they might register consciously only occasionally, the imprint of accelerating transnational connections is no less real. They affect what we eat, how we work, who we work for, and they affect what we desire, as well as what we are no longer happy to accept.

The idea of hybridization underscores the complexity of the relationship between the national and the global. More particularly, the value of the idea is that it encourages us to reflect on notions often taken for granted, such as 'national culture' and 'national values'. However, it is necessary to question some of the key implications of the argument about global hybridization, especially the claim that it takes us into a post-national era, by creating post-national cultural formations. Whatever one's view of the *idea* of the nation, there is ample evidence to demonstrate that local factors continue to filter how the global interacts with, or impacts on, people's sense of national identity. Domestic conflicts in which national identity figures prominently, or disputes with neighbouring states, can shore up awareness of nationality. Young Israeli Jews exposed to the influence of Hollywood *may* come to question the relevance of their religion, but, given the political circumstances in Israel, they will also be exposed to local, counteracting influences that maintain in them a heightened awareness of their nation and religion.

The findings of the World Values Survey, conducted in 65 countries representing three-quarters of the world's population, suggest that the influence of historically embedded cultural traditions, such as religion, remains a significant determinant of the social and cultural impact of modernization (Inglehart, 2001). As Inglehart and Baker remark: 'the fact that a society was historically shaped by Protestantism or Confucianism or Islam leaves a cultural heritage with enduring effects that influence subsequent development' (2000, p. 49). Furthermore, global hybridization can buttress not only national identity, but also the nation-state. Thus, Fernandes shows how globalization in India can be reconciled with a new nationalist narrative that accommodates modernization to Indian values. This narrative, appealing in large part to the country's middle classes, portrays India as a modern country, open to international capital and commodity flows, while also sending Indian goods out into the world. Central to the narrative's production are images that 'Indianize' foreign commodities and television formats. Overall, Fernandes remarks that while the 'subversive potential of hybridity and diaspora rests on an identification between a cultural form of hybridity and the crossing of territorial national boundaries' this notion misses the 'ideological and material conditions' shaping hybrid formations (2000, p. 622), such as the way national political leaders incorporate, or *nationalize* changes into the national narrative.

For many social theorists, this is among the greatest of the challenges globalization presents to the nation-state, since not all global phenomena can be absorbed easily, if at all, into even a revised national narrative. In many areas of the social sciences we witness moves to think outside of a national framework. It is apparent in the growing body of work on transnational communities and citizenship. Thus Soysal (1994) argues that while citizenship rights have conventionally been linked to membership of a national community, in the European Union immigrants and their descendants increasingly draw on universal discourses of individual and human rights to advance particularistic claims, such as the right to express 'one's own' culture. Elsewhere she also highlights how immigrant populations, in the EU but also, for example, Mexican-Americans in the USA, argue for voting rights in both their countries of origin and residence (Soysal, 1999). As she argues, 'membership and participation are increasingly matters beyond the vocabulary of national citizenship' (1999, p. 12). Although Soysal does not choose to think in terms of a move from national *to* transnational identities, the central themes of her work do resonate with studies of transnational communities as populations transcending national boundaries, assisted by new technologies that enable migrants easily to maintain links with their countries of origin.

The emergence of transnational communities, and the case for extending the privileges and protections of citizenship to non-nationals (see Baubcock, 2001) can be acknowledged, without discarding the centrality of the idea of the nation-state as a guide to national policies. Joppke (1999), for example, highlights the persistence of important national differences with respect to the integration of immigrants in countries such as Germany, the UK and the USA. Wimmer and Glick Schiller (2002) state that while it is right to question the 'methodological nationalism' that characterized a good deal of social science throughout the nineteenth and twentieth centuries, nevertheless we should be careful about replacing this too hastily with a tendency to see the 'transnational life of migrants constantly on the move' as the 'prototype of the human condition' (2002, p. 326). Even in the EU, where a transnational political community and form of citizenship exists, attempts to embed a transnational identity within the lives of ordinary Europeans comes up against national barriers. We are, then, a long way from a post-national world. This is not to deny that globalization does intensify global interconnectedness or that it has changed many people's perception of geography and time. Nevertheless it is salutary to remind ourselves that the cultural impact of globalization is likely to be as complex as the patterns of cultural diversity throughout the world. Just as Benedict Anderson wrote that it was the 'fatality of human linguistic diversity' that contributed to the origins of the nation as an imagined community (1983, p. 46), so today the 'fatality' of human cultural diversity mediates the cultural consequences of globalization.

Conclusion: Still waiting for a bus . . .

Massey's comment at the outset of this chapter is an important reality-check on how we conceptualize globalization. Her concern is that discussions of globalization tend to overstate the extent to which it impacts on people's sense of place, even in the heart of the advanced industrial world. Similar caution should be applied to understanding the relation between the global and the national. Where globalization and nationalism are treated together, more often than not it is in the context of discussions about how the latter responds to the former – Jihads against McWorld, to use Barber's terms. Yet, nationalism is not simply a response to globalization. Even in established, comparatively stable nation-states, attachments to the nation still run deep. In the EU, where a process of European integration has been underway for half a century, attachment to the nation remains stronger than to any other spatial entity, such as town, region, or 'Europe'. The *Eurobarometer* (CEC, 2001), a survey instrument used by the European Commission to gauge public opinion in the EU, found that nearly 90 per cent of people feel 'very' or 'fairly' attached to their country. National pride still runs very high in almost all EU member states; according to the report, in 11 of the 15 member states above 85 per cent of the population were proud to belong to their nation. In spite of claims that we live in a 'borderless world', there is still a great deal of evidence that borders remain significant, as shown in disputes between Argentina and Chile, Armenia and Azerbaijan, or in the case of the civil war in the former Yugoslavia in the 1990s. Expressions of national identity cannot simply be passed off as responses to globalization. In most instances the primary issues at dispute are local, rather than global. Global interconnectedness facilitated by communications technologies and the mass media has also enabled diasporic populations across the globe to maintain active involvement in local political disputes – what some writers term 'long distance nationalism' (B. Anderson, 1992; Skrbis, 1999).

While seeking therefore to qualify some of the arguments about the relationship between nationalism and globalization, it is our view that people *are* becoming increasingly conscious of how their lives are locked into social relations that extend beyond the borders of their country. There is no doubt that for some this has intensified a sense of cosmopolitanism (Beck, 1999). However, it is also evident that attachments to the nation remain strong throughout the world. Indeed, commitment to the nation remains vastly more widespread than any notion of global citizenship. Even so, it would be erroneous to conclude that this is because we have a natural attachment to our nation. As we have tried to show throughout this chapter, we prefer to explain the persistence of national identity in terms of local factors that ensure that the nation remains a useful category for making sense of our experiences. Conflicts over borders, disputes with other states, the rhetoric of political leaders, the influence of local cultural traditions and practices, and the pervasive 'banal nationalism' documented by Billig (1995), among other factors, together ensure that the idea of the nation remains a highly meaningful social category. In particular, these factors ensure that the influence of transnational cultural flows will be translated and adapted within local settings. There seems little prospect that the popular currency of nations and nationalism, or indeed the nation-state, will diminish in the decades to come.

Conclusion: Between Jihad and McWorld?

That we live in one world has become something of a cliché. Featherstone notes the contribution images make towards this popular globalism, and that few images are more powerful than 'photographs of the planet earth taken in space by the returning Apollo astronauts after setting foot on the moon' (1995, p. 86). These images, recorded on the historic Apollo 11 mission, furthered the globalization process by enhancing awareness that 'the world itself is a locality, a singular place' (1995, p. 92). Yet the Apollo 11 mission also offers us an interesting instance of coexistence between the 'global' and the 'national'. Memorable as images of the earth seen from space may be, just as poignant, and possibly more so for millions of US citizens watching on their televisions, was the image of the US flag planted on the moon. The decision to fly the national flag was preceded by a fair degree of political and technical preparation. NASA (National Aeronautics and Space Administration), the Nixon administration and Congress needed to heed the 1967 'Outer Space Treaty', passed by the UN (including the USA), which prohibited national claims to the moon. Thus, when Congress approved the decision, it stated expressly that it was intended as a 'symbolic gesture of national pride in achievement' and not a 'claim of sovereignty'.

The moon landing was 'supraterritorial' in a number of respects: because the moon could not be claimed for a nation; and because it was celebrated as an achievement of humanity (a 'giant leap for mankind', as Neil Armstrong, the mission's commander, famously remarked). However, as Platoff (1994) notes, the returning astronauts were lauded as 'national heroes', and the decision to hoist the US flag, rather than the insignia of the UN (which was considered), suggests that the mission was always to be seen as an achievement of the USA. Even on the moon, nationalism shared centre stage with globalism.

This coexistence seems set to continue for the foreseeable future. Some would say that 'coexistence' does not capture adequately the nature of the complex relationship between nationalism and globalization today. Barber (2003) offers a manichean view of the contemporary world in which secessionist nationalist movements and domestic ethnonational conflicts waging a 'Jihad in the name of a hundred narrowly conceived faiths against every kind of interdependence' are the flip side to a McWorld demanding ever more 'integration and uniformity' (2003, p. 4). 'Jihad' and 'McWorld' are forces in mutual opposition: one cannot live with the other. Barber's book includes numerous examples showing how present-day nationalism feeds off globalization in the guise of McWorld. Many nationalist movements and projects are intended to resist or deflect the impacts of globalizing forces, so as to retain whatever it is that is held to make the nation distinct, valuable and worthy of independent existence. Castells (1997, p. 52) notes how nationalism represents a powerful response to cultural homogenization brought about by the ideology of modernization and the power of global media, and how it tends to be built around the defence of meaning, culture and, perhaps most formidably, language.

Yet there are also many kinds of ethnonational strife that owe very little directly to 'McWorld'. Recent examples would include the genocidal struggles in Rwanda, ethnic/national conflicts on the Indian subcontinent, political efforts to set black against white Zimbabweans, or the murderous attacks upon ethnic Chinese by ethnic Filipinos described by Chua (2003). Very often, local factors are the most immediate cause of these disputes, and, at root, these struggles seem no different from the territorial and power battles fought over national boundaries and national identities for decades, if not centuries. They all pose questions about the right of some groups, rather than others, to 'belong' to the nation, and to play a part in deciding its future.

Separating national, or local, matters from international issues is never easy. Chua's discussion of disputes in the Philippines and Zimbabwe (2003) locates them in frictions between comparatively wealthy ethnic minorities who are 'market dominant', and who migrated to the territory at some earlier period, and a larger group that defines itself as the 'native' or indigenous population. Again, in a world where migration flows are becoming stronger and more complicated, there is no prospect that such conflicts will abate.

Without doubt, nationalism, and contests surrounding national identity, will continue to be one of the main ways in which such divisions and conflicts are expressed, and they will generate ample future work for scholars of nations and nationalism.

Castells is one among many authors who have been grappling with the problem of situating nations and nationalisms within the framework of a rapidly changing global environment. He does so in terms of its relationship to the dynamics of a global economy marked by 'an enduring architecture and a variable geometry' (1996, p. 145). He notes that many of the key actors and agencies today are not 'national' in any meaningful sense, but include an array of transnational or multinational organizations and corporations whose powers and resources often far outstrip those of nation-states. Few of the relationships that really matter now confine themselves to the limits of particular countries. Walby (2003) similarly points to a world in which nations take their place among a multiplicity of entities, which intertwine in complex ways. These include states, organized religions and developing 'regional' powers (such as the EU), as well as nations. Nations considerably outnumber states, and are best viewed as projects organized around ideas of common heritage or imagined community. Thus, nations are usually in a state of 'becoming', rather than fully developed, while the long view would suggest that 'at most nation-states exist for short moments of history, before being reconstructed yet again' (Walby, 2003, p. 353).

Such reflections lead Walby to wonder about the validity of conventional definitions of 'society'. The prevailing image of a society as a self-contained unit, within which economic, social, political and cultural relationships more or less coincide, is attributable, she argues, to the work of classical sociologists, and perpetuated by the writing of 'national sociologies'. The erosion of the dominance of the nation as the key social unit, and especially the nation-state, contributes towards a readiness on the part of many social theorists to rethink the concept of 'society', and its relationship with nationalism. Soysal's (1994) work on the limitations of the concept of national citizenship, and the possible emergence of 'post-national' rights and responsibilities is an example. Such arguments are elaborated by Urry in his discussion of emerging forms of global citizenship. Urry's *Sociology Beyond Societies* (2000) is a manifesto for a sociological imagination concerned less with 'society' – typically, if usually implicitly, conceptualized as the nation-state – and more with 'mobilities'. Applied to the field of nationalism, Urry's notion of a sociology of mobilities makes us reflect on what we mean by referring to 'the nation' and the concept of a single, often territorially limited, national culture. In a context where national societies appear to be losing their ability to regulate and control movements of all sorts across their boundaries, Urry contends that the notion of a single, stable and exhaustive national identity becomes increasingly implausible (2000, p. 195). When we put this alongside Castells' description of the contemporary world as made up of a bewildering jumble of nations without states, states without nations, pluri-national states and nations divided between states (1997, p. 51), we are bound to ask what has become of the universe made by nationalism. Our twenty-first century world is certainly vastly more complex, messy and fluid than that captured within debates about the 'rise of the nation', and the inexorable power of nationalism. Yet few, any longer, would be so bold as to predict nationalism's demise. Far from it, the talk is more of its resurgence, and the enormous capacity it retains to disrupt and reconfigure. We should be very careful about thinking of globalization as leading to the inevitable weakening of national states. Whatever power globalizing and internationalizing forces exert, national governments still strive to promote the 'national' interests, and to defend the sovereignty of the national space. The tensions and contradictions are well caught in the assertion of President George W. Bush that the principal thing 'free nations' can do to counter global terrorism is to make their 'homelands' safe.

Nationalism and social theory

We began this book by remarking that the study of nationalism is a field in which students of social theory should recognize some familiar terrain, but also confront some novel questions. We have shown how social theory has performed a useful role in the analysis of nationalism, by exploring dimensions that hitherto were neglected. Moreover, we have pointed to ways in which the study of nationalism is informed by the use of analytical tools developed by social theorists in discussions of other sociological phenomena. It is not surprising, therefore, that as the discipline of social theory evolves, so, too, the study of nationalism takes new turns. We have seen how the import of discussions elsewhere of gender, multiculturalism and globalization has encouraged critical reflection on the 'nation' as it is represented within classical approaches to the study of nationalism, and indeed within popular discourse. We should expect to see further challenges to conventional ways of conceptualizing nationalism.

The classical theorists of nationalism situated its analysis within the framework of mainstream classical sociological theory, and especially the writings of Durkheim and Weber. These early social theorists were preoccupied with the transition to a modern, industrial society and with understanding the repercussions of this profound social change in generating new forms of social organization and interaction. Although differing in their views as to how far pre-modern influences carried over into this new era, theorists like Gellner and Smith have sought to understand nationalism – its rise and development, and the nature of the nation as a cultural and moral community – as a product of this transition. The dialogue with Durkheim is evident in Gellner's theorization of nationalism as providing the generic culture needed to integrate societies characterized by an increasingly complex division of labour. With Anthony Smith, the Durkheimian influence lies more with his writings on religion, and their 'timeless' bearing on our understanding of ethnicity and nationalism. Nowhere is this 'timeless quality' more present than in Smith's 'defence of the nation' in *Nations and Nationalism in a Global Era* (1995). His view that by 'rehearsing the rites of fraternity in a political community in its homeland at periodic intervals, the nation communes with and worships itself' (1995, p. 155) is deeply coloured by his reading of Durkheim. However much his style of sociology might jar with the language and conventions of contemporary social theory, Smith's analysis helps us understand why the appeal of nationalism will not disappear in the foreseeable future.

As social theory has evolved in the past two decades, the debate in which Gellner and Smith engaged has become increasingly removed from mainstream theoretical developments. Just as disputes between competing nationalists over events buried deep in their past can seem out of place and irrelevant in a world networked by satellite communications and the internet, so classical contributions on nationalism seem to be about issues social theory has left behind. Nevertheless, we would caution against neglecting this important area of work. Precisely because nations are projected so often as entities whose histories stretch back into the dim and distant past, it will continue to be necessary to understand the role nationalism has played in creating nations and the significance of both for large-scale social developments. However, as Smith himself acknowledges in his scholarly survey *Nationalism and Modernism*: '[i]f the former grand narratives of nations and nationalism no longer command respect, the imperatives of the times in which we live urge us to fashion new explanations more attuned to our perceptions and to the problems that we face' (1998, p. 228).

The contributions we have placed under the umbrella of 'post-classical' theory are about more particular issues: the relationship between nationalism and 'race', gender, multiculturalism, liberal-ism and globalization. With the exception of work on globaliza-tion, these do not generally involve the kind of historical sociology that typified the classical approach. For a classical theorist, like Anthony Smith, this is disappointing. One senses that he views the issues raised as interesting side dishes rather than the main fare; the absence of general theory means that 'they illuminate a corner of the broader canvas only to leave the rest of it in untraversed darkness' (1998, p. 220). However, this charge can be countered by arguing that post-classical theorists shed light on important dimensions of nationalism insufficiently acknowledged by classi-cal theorists. To borrow from Reicher and Hopkins (2001), a strength of the post-classical contribution is to emphasize that nationalism is a 'project'; the nation is the subject of ongoing reflec-tion. This brings people, in all their diversity, back into theories of nationalism, whereas classical approaches routinely dealt with nations as mass collectivities, and abstractions. Social groups, it can be said, *never* comprise such settled, homogeneous masses. People hold multiple identities, and at any given time individuals will draw on a multiplicity of experiences to make sense of their social world. Hence the social world is considerably untidier than classical theorists would have us believe. As Brubaker (1996) argues, with some of the classical theorists in mind, there has been a tendency to mistake 'categories of practice' for 'categories of analysis'. Consequently, classical theorists implicitly partake in the reproduction of the idea of the nation as a unified human group. The advantage of the post-classical approach is that it recognizes the consequences of empirical social diversity for how we theorize nationalism, and that it can be employed to examine how the nation, *conceived* as a homogeneous population, is institutionalized (to follow Brubaker) or is constituted through discursive practices. This opens up a greater space for the consideration of human agency.

Recognizing the *contingency* of the nation, post-classical theories provide a better reflection of the empirical conditions of the proliferating multicultural, multi-faith and multinational countries across the world. In such contexts, the idea of the unified national community seems increasingly at odds with social and cultural diversity, and with the conflicting political projects that characterize these national societies. Under these conditions, as Billig (1995) advises, any cathartic dialogue among members involves coming to terms with the embedded, though often overlooked, nationalism of the established social orders. Post-classical theories of nationalism do not, then, proffer the type of developmental account we get from the classical theorists, but their contribution may be more in tune with the current 'state of the nation'. In his more recent work, Brubaker continues to argue for a focus on how the category of nation is institutionalized, but, drawing on the tenets of ethnomethodology and conversation analysis, also notes how the 'categorized appropriate, internalize, subvert, evade, or transform the categories that are imposed on them' (2002, p. 6). This turn to agency is shared by other post-classical approaches. Miller's liberal nationalism emphasizes the capacity of individuals to reflect actively on the values with which they were brought up: 'the identity is always a provisional one, and new events, or further critical thought, may cause us to revise it' (1995, p. 45). We have referred elsewhere to the 'local production' of national identities, to describe the processes through which people invoke the category of nation to make sense of their own experiences and their relations with others (Day and Thompson, 1999). In a similar vein, Reicher and Hopkins state that when examining nationalism we are 'dealing with the ways in which people understand who they are, the nature of the world they live in, how they relate to others and what counts as important to them' (2001, p. 3).

It would be misguided to abandon one of these approaches entirely in favour of the other. Classical and post-classical scholars often speak with different sociological dialects; they draw on different canons of social theory, and write about nationalism in different ways. Gellner drew for his inspiration upon Durkheim, Weber and social anthropologists such as Radcliffe-Brown. In his more recent work, Brubaker is influenced by Bourdieu, and ethnomethodology, among other sources. There is a place for both approaches in our analytical toolkit. It would be to the detriment of our broader understanding of nationalism to neglect the question of what forces have contributed historically to its rise and spread. Though no single answer will account satisfactorily for all manifestations of nationalism, or even the majority of them, it is part of the job description of the social theorist to seek connections, and underlying causal relationships, between social phenomena. Conversely, we ignore at our peril the warnings of those theorists who tell us not to treat nations abstractly, as homogeneous, internally cohesive human groupings. In much contemporary theory, it has become a rule of thumb to regard with suspicion the idea that groups have any such clear-cut identity. Instead we are urged to look at who is speaking on behalf of the group, what criteria for membership are employed, and to whom this denies entry. In the case of the nation, as Brubaker suggests (1996, p. 16), the key issue is not what the nation *is*, but rather how nationhood as a political and cultural form is institutionalized within and among states Such healthy disdain for intellectual convention is not peculiar to debates on nationalism; it is at the core of social theory.

Bibliography

Abbott, P. and Wallace, C. (1990) *An Introduction to Sociology* (London: Routledge).

Albrow, M. (1996) *The Global Age* (Cambridge: Polity).

Alexander, J. (1982) *Theoretical Logic in Sociology* (London: Routledge).

Alexander, J. (1995) *Fin de Siecle Social Theory: Relativism, Reduction, and the Problem of Reason* (London: Verso).

Allen, S. (1998) 'Identity: "Race", Ethnicity, and Nationality', in N. Charles and H. Hintjens (eds), *Gender, Ethnicity, and Political Ideologies* (London: Routledge).

Amin, A. (1997) *Capitalism in the Age of Globalization* (London: Zed).

Anderson, B. (1983) *Imagined Communities* (London: Verso).

Anderson, B. (1992) 'The New World Disorder', *New Left Review*, 1 (193): 3–13.

Anderson B. (1991) *Imagined Communities*, rev. ed. (London: Verso).

Anderson, H. and Kasperson, L.B. (eds) (2000) *Classical and Modern Social Theory* (Oxford: Blackwell).

Anderson, P. (1976) *Considerations on Western Marxism* (London: New Left Books).

Anderson, P. (1992a) *A Zone of Engagement* (London: Verso).

Anderson, P. (1992b) *English Questions* (London: Verso).

Annan, K. (1999) 'The Backlash Against Globalism', *Futurist*, 33 (3): 27–30.

Ansell, A. (1997) *New Right, New Racism* (Basingstoke: Macmillan).

Anthias, F. and Yuval-Davis, N. (1989) *Women-Nation-State* (Basingstoke: Macmillan).

Anthias, F. and Yuval-Davis, N. (1992) *Racialized Boundaries* (London: Routledge).

Appadurai, A. (1996) *Modernity at Large* (London: University of Minnesota Press).

Apter, D. (1965) *The Politics of Modernisation* (Chicago: University of Chicago Press).

Arblaster, A. (1995) 'Identity, Unity, Difference: Some Thoughts on National Identity and Social Unity', *New Community*, 21 (2): 195–206.

Arendt, H. (1973) *The Origins of Totalitarianism* (London: Harcourt Brace Jovanovich).

Armstrong, J. (1982) *Nations Before Nationalism* (Chapel Hill: University of North Carolina Press).

Aron, R. (1967) *Eighteen Lectures on Industrial Society* (London: Weidenfeld and Nicolson).

Balakrishnan, G. (ed.) (1996) *Mapping the Nation* (London: Verso).

Balibar, E. (1991) 'Racism and Nationalism', in E. Balibar and I. Wallerstein, *Race, Nation and Class* (London: Verso).

Balibar, E. and Wallerstein, I. (1991) *Race, Nation and Class: Ambiguous Identities* (London: Verso).

Barber, B. (1995) 'The Making of McWorld', *New Perspectives Quarterly*, 12 (4): 13–18.

Barber, B. (1998) 'Democracy at Risk', *World Policy Journal*, 15 (2): 29–43.

Barber, B. (2003) *Jihad vs McWorld* (New York: Corgi).

Barker, M. (1981) *The New Racism* (London: Junction Books).

Barker, M. (2002) 'Reflections on *The New Racism*', in P. Essed and D.T. Goldberg (eds), *Race: Critical Theories* (Oxford: Blackwell).

Barot, R. and Bird, J. (2001) 'Racialization: The Genealogy of a Concept', *Ethnic and Racial Studies*, 24 (4): 601–18.

Barth, F. (ed.) (1969) *Ethnic Groups and Boundaries: The Social Organisation of Culture Difference* (Boston: Little Brown).

Baubcock, R. (2001) 'International Migration and Liberal Democracies', *Patterns of Prejudice*, 35 (4): 33–49.

Baughn, C. and Buchanan, M. (2001) 'Cultural Protectionism', *Business Horizons*, 44 (6): 5–15.

Bauman, Z. (1990) *Thinking Sociologically* (Cambridge: Polity).

Bauman, Z. (1991) *Modernity and Ambivalence* (Cambridge: Polity).

Bauman, Z. (1992) 'Blood, Soil and Identity', *Sociological Review*, 40 (4): 675–701.

Bauman, Z. (2000) *Liquid Modernity* (Cambridge: Polity).

Beck, U. (1999) *World Risk Society* (Cambridge: Polity).

Beck, U. (2000) *What is Globalization?* (Cambridge: Polity).

Beck, U. and Beck-Gernsheim, E. (2002) *Individualization* (London: Sage).

Bell, D. (2001) *The Cult of the Nation in France* (Cambridge, MA: Harvard University Press).

Bendix, R. (1965) *Nation Building and Citizenship* (New York: John Wiley).

Benner, E. (1995) *Really Existing Nationalisms: A Post-Communist View from Marx and Engels* (Oxford: Clarendon).

Benton, S. (1998) 'Founding Fathers and Earth Mothers: Women's Place at the "Birth" of Nations', in N. Charles and H. Hintjens (eds), *Gender, Ethnicity, and Political Ideologies* (London: Routledge).

Berger, P. and Luckmann, T. (1967) *The Social Construction of Reality* (London: Allen Lane Penguin).

Berlin, I. (1998) *The Proper Study of Mankind* (London: Pimlico).

Berns, W. (2001) *Making Patriots* (Chicago: University of Chicago Press).

Best, S. and Kellner, D. (1997) *The Postmodern Turn* (London: Guilford).

Bhabha, H. (ed.) (1990) *Nation and Narration* (London: Routledge).

Billig, M. (1995) *Banal Nationalism* (London: Sage).

Blair, T. (1999) *National Pride – A Modern Patriotism*, speech at 'Pride of Britain' Awards, 20 May 1999. http://www.huntfacts.com

Blaut, J. (1982) 'Nationalism as an Autonomous Force', *Science and Society*, 46 (1): 1–23.

Bourdieu, P. (1977) *Outline of a Theory of Practice* (Cambridge University Press).

Bourdieu, P. (1990) *In Other Words* (Cambridge: Polity).

Bradley, H. (1996) *Fractured Identities* (Cambridge: Polity).

Bradshaw, B. and Roberts, P. (eds) (1998) *British Consciousness and Identity* (Cambridge University Press).

Brah, A., Hickman, M. J. and Mac an Ghaill, M. (eds) (1999) *Thinking Identities* (London: Macmillan).

Braudel, F. (1991) *The Identity of France* (London: Fontana).

Brennan, G. (2001) 'Language and Nationality: The Role of Policy Towards Celtic Languages in the Consolidation of Tudor Power', *Nations and Nationalism*, 7 (3): 317–38.

Brennan, T. (1990) 'The National Longing for Form', in H. Bhabha (ed.) *Nation and Narration* (London: Routledge).

Breuilly, J. (1993) *Nationalism and the State*, 2nd edn (Manchester University Press).

Breuilly, J. (1996) 'Approaches to Nationalism', in G. Balakrishnan (ed.), *Mapping the Nation* (London: Verso).

Brighouse, H. (1997) 'Against Nationalism', in J. Couture, K. Nielsen and M. Seymour (eds), *Rethinking Nationalism* (Calgary: University of Calgary Press).

Brown, A. (1999) '"The Other Day I Met a Constituent of Mine": A Theory of Anecdotal Racism', *Ethnic and Racial Studies*, 22 (1): 1–23.

Brown, D. (2000) *Contemporary Nationalism* (London: Routledge).

Brown, P. and Lauder, H. (2001) *Capitalism and Social Progress* (Basingstoke: Palgrave).

Brubaker, R. (1996) *Nationalism Reframed* (Cambridge University Press).

Brubaker, R. (1998) 'Myths and Misconceptions in the Study of Nationalism', in J. Hall (ed.), *The State of the Nation: Ernest Gellner and the Theory of Nationalism* (Cambridge University Press).

Brubaker, R. (2002) 'Ethnicity Without Groups', *Archives Européenes de Sociologie*, 43 (2): 163–89.

Brubaker, R. and Cooper, F. (2000) 'Beyond Identity', *Theory and Society*, 29: 1–47.

Bryson, V. (1998) 'Citizen Warriors, Workers and Mothers: Women and Democracy in Israel', in N. Charles and H. Hintjens (eds), *Gender, Ethnicity, and Political Ideologies* (London: Routledge).

Bull, H. (1977) *The Anarchical Society* (London: Macmillan).

Bush, G.W. (2001a) *Radio Address of the President of the Nation*, 18 August 2001. http://www.whitehouse.gov/news/releases/2001/08/20010818.html .

Bush, G.W. (2001b) *Inaugural Address*, 20 January 2001, Capitol Hill, Washington DC. http://www.whitehouse.gov/news/inaugural-address.html .

Bush, G.W. (2002) *Commencement Address at Ohio State University*, 14 June 2002. http://www.whitehouse.gov/news/releases/2002/06/20020614-1.html .

Calhoun, C. (1994) 'Nationalism and Civil Society: Democracy, Diversity and Self-Determination', in C. Calhoun (ed.), *Social Theory and the Politics of Identity* (Oxford: Blackwell).

Calhoun, C. (1995) *Critical Social Theory* (Oxford: Blackwell).

Calhoun, C. (1997) *Nationalism* (Buckingham: Open University Press).

Caney, S. (1999) 'Nationality, Distributive Justice and the Use of Force', *Journal of Applied Philosophy*, 16 (2): 123–38.

Cannadine, D. (2001) *Ornamentalism* (London: Penguin).

Carr, E.H. (1945) *Nationalism and After* (London: Macmillan).

Castells, M. (1996) *The Rise of the Network Society* (Oxford: Blackwell).

Castells, M. (1997) *The Power of Identity* (Oxford: Blackwell).

CCS (Centre for Contemporary Cultural Studies) (1981) *The Empire Strikes Back* (London: Hutchinson).

Charles, N. and Hintjens, H. (eds) (1998) *Gender, Ethnicity, and Political Ideologies* (London: Routledge).

Chua, A. (2003) *World on Fire* (London: Heinemann).

Clark, H. (2000) *Building Cultural Identity*, speech at launch of 'Building Cultural Identity' Programme, 18 May 2000. http://www.beehive. govt.nz/ViewDocument.cfm?DocumentID=7442 .

Cleary, D. (1999) *Race, Nationalism and Social Theory in Brazil: Rethinking Gilberto Freyre*, ESRC Transnational Communities Programme, Working Paper Series. WPTC-99-10. www.transcomm.ox.ac.uk/working%20papers/cleary.pdf .

Cobban, A. (1969) [1994] *The Nation-State and National Self-Determination* (London: Collins).

Cockburn, C. (2000) 'The Anti-Essentialist Choice: Nationalism and Feminism in the Interaction Between Two Women's Projects', *Nations and Nationalism*, 6 (4): 611–29.

Cohen, A.P. (1982) 'Belonging: The Experience of Culture', in A. Cohen (ed.), *Belonging* (Manchester University Press).

Cohen, A.P. (1985) *The Symbolic Construction of Community* (London: Ellis Horwood).

Colley, L. (1996) *Britons: Forging the Nation 1707–1837* (London: Vintage).

Commission of the European Communities (2000) *Perceptions of the European Union* (Brussels: Commission of the European Communities).

Commission on the Future of Multi-Ethnic Britain (2000) *The Future of Multi-Ethnic Britain* (London: Runnymede Trust).

Connor, W. (1994) *Ethnonationalism* (Princeton University Press).

Craib, I. (1984) *Modern Social Theory* (Hemel Hempstead: Harvester Wheatsheaf).

Crompton, R. and Mann, M. (eds) (1986) *Gender and Stratification* (Cambridge: Polity).

Da Silva, L.I.L. (2003) *Inaugural Address*, 1 January 2003. http://www. brazil.org.uk/page.php?cid=1499.

Daly, M. (1978) *Gyn/Ecology* (London: Women's Press).

Davies, C. A. (1999) 'Nationalism, Feminism and Welsh Women: Conflicts and Accommodation', in R. Fevre and A. Thompson (eds), *Nation, Identity and Social Theory* (Cardiff: University of Wales Press).

Day, G. (2002) *Making Sense of Wales* (Cardiff: University of Wales Press).

Day, G. and Thompson, A. (1999) 'Situating Welshness: The Local Production of National Identity', in R. Fevre and A. Thompson (eds), *Nation, Identity and Social Theory* (Cardiff: University of Wales Press).

Dean, G. (1998) 'Globalisation and the Nation-State', http://www. okusi.net/garydean/works/globalisation.html .

Debray, R. (1977) 'Marxism and the National Question', *New Left Review*, 105: 25–41.

Delanty, G. and O'Mahony, P. (2002) *Nationalism and Social Theory* (London: Sage).

Deutsch, K.W. (1966) [1953] *Nationalism and Social Communication* (Cambridge, MA: MIT Press).

Dolman, J. (2002) 'Overtaken by Events', *National Leader*, July/August: 24–5.

Dunn, J. (1993) *Western Political Theory in the Face of the Future* (Cambridge University Press).

Durkheim, E. (1960) *Division of Labour in Society* (New York: Free Press).

Durkheim, E. (1964) *The Rules of Sociological Method* (New York: Free Press).

Durkheim, E. (1979) *Essays on Morals and Education* (London: Routledge and Kegan Paul).

Elias, N. (1996) *The Germans* (Cambridge: Polity).

Elliott, A. and Turner, B.S. (eds) (2001) *Profiles in Contemporary Social Theory* (London: Sage).

Enloe, C. (1988) *Does Khaki Become You?* (London: Pandora).

Enloe, C. (1990) 'Womenandchildren: Making Feminist Sense of International Politics', *Village Voice*, 25 September 1990.

Enloe, C. (2000) *Bananas, Beaches and Bases* (Berkeley: University of California Press).

Eriksen, T.H. (1993) *Ethnicity and Nationalism* (London: Pluto).

Eriksen, T.H. (2002) *Ethnicity and Nationalism*, 2nd edn (London: Pluto).

Eze, E. (ed.) (1997) *Race and the Enlightenment* (Oxford: Blackwell).

Fanon, F. (1965) *The Wretched of the Earth* (London: MacGibbon and McKee).

Featherstone, M. (1995) *Undoing Culture* (London: Sage).

Fernandes, L. (2000) 'Nationalizing "the Global": Media Images, Cultural Politics and the Middle Class in India', *Media, Culture and Society*, 22 (5): 611–28.

Fernbach, D. (ed.) (1973) 'Introduction', in K. Marx, *The Revolutions of 1848* (Harmondsworth: Penguin).

Fevre, R. and Thompson, A. (1999) *Nation, Identity and Social Theory* (Cardiff: University of Wales Press).

Firestone, S. (1971) *The Dialectic of Sex* (London: Jonathan Cape).

Forde, S., Johnson, L. and Murray, A.V. (eds) (1995) *Concepts of National Identity in the Middle Ages* (Leeds Texts and Monographs, University of Leeds).

Fredrickson, G. (2002) *Racism* (Princeton University Press).

Freeman, M. (1994) 'Nation-State and Cosmopolis: A Response to David Miller', *Journal of Applied Philosophy*, 11 (1): 79–87.

Freyre, G. (1986) [1933] *The Masters and the Slaves*, 2nd English language edn (Berkeley: University of California Press).

Friedman, J. (2000) 'Americans Again, or the New Age of Imperial Reason?', *Theory, Culture and Society*, 17 (1): 139–46.

Fulcher, J. (2000) 'Globalisation, the Nation-State and Global Society', *Sociological Review*, 48 (4): 522–43.

Geertz, C. (1975) *The Interpretation of Cultures* (London: Hutchinson).

Gelber, H. (2001) *Nations Out of Empires* (Basingstoke: Palgrave).

Gellner, E. (1964) *Thought and Change* (London: Weidenfeld and Nicholson).

Gellner, E. (1983) *Nations and Nationalism* (Oxford: Basil Blackwell).
Gellner, E. (1988) *Plough, Sword and Book* (London: Collins Harvill).
Gellner, E. (1994a) *Encounters with Nationalism* (Oxford: Blackwell).
Gellner, E. (1994b) *Conditions of Liberty* (London: Hamish Hamilton).
Gellner, E. (1997) *Nationalism* (London: Weidenfeld and Nicholson).
Gerstle, G. (2002) *American Crucible* (Princeton University Press).
Gibbons, J. and Reimer, B. (1999) *The Politics of Postmodernity* (London: Sage).
Giddens, A. (1981) *A Contemporary Critique of Historical Materialism* (Basingstoke: Macmillan).
Giddens, A. (1984) *The Constitution of Society* (Cambridge: Polity).
Giddens, A. (1985) *The Nation State and Violence* (Cambridge: Polity).
Giddens, A. (1990) *The Consequences of Modernity* (Cambridge: Polity).
Giddens, A. (1998) *The Third Way* (Cambridge: Polity).
Gillingham, J. (2000) *The English in the Twelfth Century* (Woodbridge: Boydell Press).
Gilroy, P. (1987) *There Ain't No Black in the Union Jack* (London: Routledge).
Gilroy, P. (2001) *Between Camps* (London: Penguin).
Ginsberg, M. (1962) [1953] *On the Diversity of Morals* (London: Mercury).
Goldberg, D.T. (1993) *Racist Culture* (Oxford: Blackwell).
Goldfield, M. (1997) *The Color of Politics* (New York: New Press).
Goodman, J. (1996) 'The Shifting Stage of Politics: New Medieval and Postmodern Territorialities?', *Environment and Planning D: Society and Space*, 14 (2): 133–53, April.
Gorski, P. (2002) 'The Mosaic Moment: An Early Modernist Critique of Modernist Theories of Nationalism', *American Journal of Sociology*, 105 (5): 1428–68.
Gramsci, A. (1971) *Selections from the Prison Notebooks* (London: Lawrence and Wishart).
Greenfeld, L. (1992) *Nationalism: Five Roads to Modernity* (Cambridge, MA: Harvard University Press).
Griffin, N. (2003) *Race and Reality*. www.bnp.org.uk/articles/race_reality.htm .
Guibernau, M. (1996) *Nationalisms* (Cambridge: Polity).
Gutiérrez, N. (1997) 'Ethnic Revivals Within Nation-States?', in H-R. Wicker (ed.), *Rethinking Nationalism and Ethnicity* (Oxford: Berg).
Gutiérrez, N. (1999) *Nationalist Myths and Ethnic Identities* (Lincoln: University of Nebraska Press).
Haas, E.B. (1997) *Nationalism, Liberalism and Progress* (Ithaca: Cornell University Press).
Hall, J. (2000) 'Globalization and Nationalism', *Thesis Eleven*, 63: 63–79.
Hall, J. (ed.) (1998) *The State of the Nation: Ernest Gellner and the Theory of Nationalism* (Cambridge University Press).
Hall, S. (1991) 'Old and New Identities', in A.D. King (ed.), *Culture, Globalization and the World System* (London: Macmillan).
Hall, S. (1995) 'The Question of Cultural Identity', in S. Hall, D. Held, D. Hubert and K. Thompson (eds), *Modernity* (Cambridge: Polity).
Hanchard, M. (1994) *Orpheus and Power* (Princeton University Press).
Hannaford, I. (1996) *Race* (Maryland: Johns Hopkins University Press).
Hannerz, U. (1996) *Transnational Connections* (London: Routledge).

Harvey, D. (1989) *The Condition of Postmodernity* (Cambridge: Polity).

Hastings, A. (1997) *The Construction of Nationhood* (Cambridge University Press).

Hayami, M. (2000) *Globalization and Regional Cooperation in Asia*, speech to the Asian Pacific Bankers' Club, 17 March. http://www.bis.org/review/r000324b.pdf .

Hayes, C. (1931) *The Historical Evolution of Nationalism* (New York: Smith).

Hechter, M. (1975) *Internal Colonialism* (London: Routledge and Kegan Paul).

Heilbron, J. (1995) *The Rise of Social Theory* (Cambridge: Polity).

Held, D. (1980) *Introduction to Critical Theory* (London: Hutchinson).

Held, D. (1995) *Democracy and the Global Order* (Cambridge: Polity).

Held, D. (2000) 'Regulating Globalization? The Reinvention of Politics', *International Sociology*, 15 (2): 394–408.

Held, D., McGrew, A., Goldblatt, D. and Perraton, J. (1999) *Global Transformations* (Cambridge: Polity).

Hesmondhalgh, D. (1998) 'Globalisation and Cultural Imperialism: A Case Study of the Music Industry', in R. Kiely and P. Marfleet (eds), *Globalisation and the Third World* (London: Routledge).

Hester, S. and Housley, W. (eds) (2002) *Language, Interaction and National Identity* (Aldershot: Ashgate).

Hickman, M. (1998) 'Reconstructing Deconstructing "Race": British Political Discourses about the Irish in Britain', *Ethnic and Racial Studies*, 21 (2): 288–307.

Hirst, P. and Thompson, G. (1996) *Globalization in Question* (Cambridge: Polity).

Hobsbawm, E. (1962) *The Age of Revolution* (London: Weidenfeld and Nicolson).

Hobsbawm, E. (1977) 'Socialism and Nationalism: Some Reflections on The Break-Up of Britain', reprinted in Hobsbawm (1989).

Hobsbawm, E. (1982) 'Gramsci and Marxist Political Theory', in A. Showstack Sassoon (ed.), *Approaches to Gramsci* (London: Readers and Writers Publishing Cooperative).

Hobsbawm, E. (1983) 'Mass-Producing Traditions: Europe 1870–1914', in E. Hobsbawm and T. Ranger (eds), *The Invention of Tradition* (Cambridge University Press).

Hobsbawm, E. (1989) *Politics for a Rational Left* (London: Verso).

Hobsbawm, E. (1990) *Nations and Nationalism Since 1780* (Cambridge University Press).

Hobsbawm, E. (1994) *Age of Extremes* (London: Abacus).

Hobsbawm, E. and Ranger, T. (1983) 'Introduction: Inventing Traditions', in E. Hobsbawm and T. Ranger (eds), *The Invention of Tradition* (Cambridge University Press).

Holt, C.T. (2000) *The Problem of Race in the Twenty First Century* (London: Harvard University Press).

Holton, R. (1998) *Globalization and the Nation-State* (Basingstoke: Palgrave).

Horsman, M. and Marshall, A. (1995) *After the Nation-State* (London: HarperCollins).

Huntingdon, S. (1995) 'Ancestral Territory *vs.* the Global Nomenklatura', *New Perspectives Quarterly*, 14 (1): 26–30.

Huntingdon, S. (1997) *The Clash of Civilizations and the Remaking of World Order* (London: Touchstone).

Hutchinson, J. (1994) *Modern Nationalism* (London: Fontana).

Ignatieff, M. (1993) *Blood and Belonging* (London: Chatto and Windus).

Imhof, K. (1997) 'Nationalism and the Theory of Society', in H-R. Wicker (ed.), *Rethinking Nationalism and Ethnicity* (Oxford: Berg).

Inglehart, R. (2001) 'Globalization and Postmodern Values', *Washington Quarterly*, 23 (1): 215–28.

Inglehart, R. and Baker, W. (2000) 'Modernization, Cultural Change and the Persistence of Traditional Values', *American Sociological Review*, 65 (1): 19–51.

Inkeles, A. and Smith, D. (1974) *Becoming Modern* (Cambridge, MA: Harvard University Press).

James, P. (1996) *Nation Formation* (London: Sage).

Jenkins, R. (1996) *Social Identity* (London: Routledge).

Jenkins, R. (1997) *Rethinking Ethnicity* (London: Sage).

Jones, R.J.B. (2000) *The World Turned Upside Down?* (Manchester University Press).

Joppke, C. (1999) *Immigration and the Nation-State* (Oxford: Clarendon).

Junco, J.A. (1996) 'The Nation-Building Process in Nineteenth Century Spain', in C. Mar-Molinero and A. Smith (eds), *Nationalism and the Nation in the Iberian Peninsula* (Oxford: Berg).

Kedourie, E. (1960) *Nationalism* (London: Hutchinson).

Kerr, C., Dunlop, J., Harbison, F. and Myers, C. (1973) *Industrialism and Industrial Man*, 2nd edn (Harmondsworth: Penguin).

Kitching, G. (1985) 'Nationalism: The Instrumental Passion', *Capital and Class*, 25: 98–116.

Kohn, H. (1944) *The Idea of Nationalism* (New York: Macmillan).

Kohn, H. (1955) *Nationalism: Its Meaning and History* (Princeton, NJ: Van Nostrand).

Kolakowski, L. (1978) *Main Currents of Marxism, Vol. 2: The Golden Age* (Oxford University Press).

Kumar, K. (1988) *The Rise of Modern Society* (Oxford: Blackwell).

Kurauchi, K. (1960) 'Durkheim's Influence on Japanese Sociology', in E. Durkheim *et al.* (eds), *Essays on Sociology and Philosophy* (New York: Harper Torchbooks).

Kymlicka, W. (1991) *Liberalism, Community and Culture* (Oxford University Press).

Kymlicka, W. (1995) *Multicultural Citizenship* (Oxford University Press).

Kymlicka, W. (1997) 'The Sources of Nationalism: Commentary on Taylor', in R. McKim and J. McMahan (eds), *The Morality of Nationalism* (Oxford University Press).

Kymlicka, W. (1999) 'Misunderstanding Nationalism', in R. Beiner (ed.), *Theorizing Nationalism* (State University of New York Press).

Kymlicka, W. (2001) *Politics in the Vernacular* (Oxford University Press).

Laitin, D. (1998) 'Nationalism and Language: a Post-Soviet Perspective', in J.Hall (ed.), *The State of the Nation: Ernest Gellner and the Theory of Nationalism* (Cambridge University Press).

Langley, L.D. (1996) *The Americas in the Age of Revolution* (New Haven: Yale University Press).

Lash, S. and Urry, J. (1994) *Economies of Signs and Space* (London: Sage).

Lawrie, M. (1999) *Opening Speech* to the IBM Institute for Advanced Commerce Symposium on The Impact of Globalization, 22 March. http://www.research.ibm.com/iac/transcripts/impact-globalization/transcript-lawrie.html .

Layder, D. (1994) *Understanding Social Theory* (London: Sage).

Lemish, D., Drotner, K., Liebes, T., Maigret, E. and Stald, G. (1998) 'Global Culture in Practice: A Look at Children and Adolescents in Denmark, France and Israel', *European Journal of Communication*, 13 (4): 539–56.

Lenin, V.I. (1974) *Critical Remarks on the National Question* (Moscow: Progress).

Lerner, D. (1958) *The Passing of Traditional Society* (New York: Free Press).

Levinson, S. (1995) 'Is Liberal Nationalism an Oxymoron?', *Ethics*, 105: 626–45.

Levy, R. (1966) *Modernisation and the Structure of Societies* (Princeton University Press).

Lichtenberg, J. (1997) 'Nationalism, For and (Mainly) Against', in R. McKim and J. McMahan (eds), *The Morality of Nationalism* (Oxford University Press).

Lichtenberg, J. (1999) 'How Liberal Can Nationalism Be?' in R. Beiner (ed.), *Theorizing Nationalism* (State University of New York Press).

Lind, M. (1995) *The Next American Nation* (New York: Simon and Schuster).

Linke, U. (1999) *Blood and Nation* (Philadelphia: University of Pennsylvania Press).

List, F. (1885) *The National Systems of Political Economy* (London: Longmans, Green).

Llobera, J. (1994) *The God of Modernity* (Oxford: Berg).

Luxemburg, R. (1976) *The National Question*, ed. H.B. Davis (New York: Monthly Review Press).

Mac an Ghaill, M. (1999) *Contemporary Racisms and Ethnicities* (Milton Keynes: Open University Press).

Makdisi, S., Casarino, C. and Karl, R. (1996) *Marxism Beyond Marxism* (London: Routledge).

Mann, M. (1986) 'A Crisis in Stratification Theory?', in R. Crompton and M. Mann (eds), *Gender and Stratification* (Cambridge: Polity).

Mann, M. (1988) *States, War and Capitalism* (Oxford: Blackwell).

Mann, M. (1995) 'A Political Theory of Nationalism and its Excesses', in S. Periwal (ed.), *Notions of Nationalism* (Budapest: Central European University Press).

Mar-Molinero, C. (1996) 'The Role of Language in Spanish Nation-Building', in C. Mar-Molinero and A. Smith (eds), *Nationalism and the Nation in the Iberian Peninsula* (Oxford: Berg).

Marshall, T.H. (1950) *Citizenship and Social Class* (Cambridge University Press).

Marx, A. (1998) *Making Race and Nation* (Cambridge University Press).

Marx, K. (1953) *On Britain* (Moscow: Foreign Languages Publishing House).

Marx, K. (1961) *Capital, Vol. 1* (Moscow: Foreign Languages Publishing House).

Marx, K. (1969) *Selected Works* (Moscow: Progress).

Marx, K. (1973) *Grundrisse* (Harmondsworth: Penguin).
Marx, K. and Engels, F. (1970) *The German Ideology*, ed. C.J. Arthur (London: Lawrence and Wishart).
Marx, K. and Engels, F. (1975) *Collected Works* (London: Lawrence and Wishart).
Mason, A. (1997) 'Special Obligations to Compatriots', *Ethics*, 107 (April): 427–47.
Massey, D. (1994) *Space, Place and Gender* (Cambridge: Polity).
McCrone, D. (1992) *Understanding Scotland* (London: Routledge).
McCrone, D. (1998) *The Sociology of Nationalism* (London: Routledge).
McMaster, N. (2001) *Racism in Europe* (London: Palgrave).
Melucci, A. (1996) *Challenging Codes* (Cambridge University Press).
Miles, R. (1989) *Racism* (London: Routledge).
Miles, R. (1993) 'The Articulation of Racism and Nationalism: Reflections on European History', in J. Wrench and J. Solomos (eds), *Racism and Migration in Contemporary Europe* (Oxford: Berg).
Miliband, R. (1977) *Marxism and Politics* (Oxford University Press).
Miller, D. (1995) *On Nationality* (Oxford University Press).
Miller, D. (1997) 'Nationality: Some Replies ', *Journal of Applied Philosophy*, 14 (1): 69–82.
Miller, D. (1998) 'Secession and the Principle of Nationality', in J. Couture, K. Nielsen and M. Seymour (eds), *Rethinking Nationalism* (Calgary: University of Calgary Press).
Ministry of Refugee, Immigration and Integration Affairs (2002) *The Integration of Foreigners in the Danish Society*, Think Tank on Integration in Denmark, Ministry of Refugee, Immigration and Integration Affairs, March 2002.
Miščević, N. (2001) *Nationalism and Beyond* (Budapest: Central European University Press).
Modood, T. (1997) ' "Difference", Cultural Racism and Anti-Racism', in P. Werbner and T. Modood (eds), *Debating Cultural Hybridity* (London: Zed Books).
Mohamad, M. (2001) *The Third Outline Perspective Plan*, speech to the Malaysian Parliament, 3 April 2001. http://www.epu.jpm.my/Bi/speech/pmspeech/speech_pm.pdf .
Morokvasic, M. (1998) 'The Logics of Exclusion: Nationalism, Sexism and the Yugoslav War', in N. Charles and H. Hintjens (eds), *Gender, Ethnicity, and Political Ideologies* (London: Routledge).
Mosse, G.L. (1985) *Nationalism and Sexuality* (Madison: Wisconsin University Press).
Mouzelis, N. (1991) *Back to Sociological Theory* (Basingstoke: Macmillan).
Mouzelis, N. (1998) 'Ernest Gellner's Theory of Nationalism: Some Definitional and Methodological Issues', in J. Hall (ed.), *The State of the Nation: Ernest Gellner and the Theory of Nationalism* (Cambridge University Press).
Munck, R. (1985) 'Otto Bauer: Towards a Marxist Theory of Nationalism', *Capital and Class*, 25: 84–97.
Nagel, J. (2003) *Race, Ethnicity, and Sexuality* (Oxford University Press).
Nairn, T. (1977) *The Break-Up of Britain* (London: Verso).
Nairn, T. (1997) *Faces of Nationalism* (London: Verso).

Nederveen Pieterse, J. (1995) 'Globalization as Hybridization', in M. Featherstone, S. Lash and R. Robertson (eds), *Global Modernities* (London: Sage).

Nederveen Pieterse, J. (2001) 'Hybridity, So What?', *Theory, Culture and Society*, 18 (2–3): 219–45.

Nelson, D. (1998) *National Manhood* (London: Duke University Press).

Nicholson, P. (1999) *Who Do We Think We Are?* (London: M.E. Sharpe).

Nimni, E. (1985) 'The Great Historical Failure: Marxist Theories of Nationalism', *Capital and Class*, 25: 58–83.

Nimni, E. (1991) *Marxism and Nationalism* (London: Pluto).

Noble, T. (2000) *Social Theory and Social Change* (Basingstoke: Macmillan).

Obuchi, K. (1999) *Statement*, 9 August 1999. http://www.mofa.go.jp/announce/announce/1999/8/809.html .

Ohmae, K. (1996) *The End of the Nation-State* (London: HarperCollins).

O'Leary, B. (1998) 'Ernest Gellner's Diagnoses of Nationalism: A Critical Overview', in J. Hall (ed.), *The State of the Nation: Ernest Gellner and the Theory of Nationalism* (Cambridge University Press).

Omi, M. and Winant, H. (1994) *Racial Formation in the United States*, 2nd edn (London: Routledge).

O'Neill, J. (1994) 'Should Communitarians be Nationalists?', *Journal of Applied Philosophy*, 11 (2): 135–43.

Orridge, A.W. (1981) 'Uneven Development and Nationalism', *Political Studies*, 29 (1 & 2): 10–15, 181–90.

Özkirimli, U. (2000) *Theories of Nationalism* (Basingstoke: Macmillan).

Parekh, B. (1999) 'The Incoherence of Nationalism', in R. Beiner (ed.), *Theorizing Nationalism* (State University of New York Press).

Parekh, B. (2000) *Rethinking Multiculturalism* (Basingstoke: Palgrave).

Parsons, T. (1964) 'Evolutionary Universals in Society', *American Sociological Review*, 29 (3): 339–57.

Parsons, T. (1966) *Societies: Evolutionary and Comparative Perspectives* (Englewood Cliffs: Prentice Hall).

Pateman, C. (1988) *The Sexual Contract* (Cambridge: Polity).

Pearce, L. (2000) *Devolving Identities* (Aldershot: Ashgate).

Periwal, S. (ed.) (1995) *Notions of Nationalism* (Budapest: Central European University Press).

Peterson, V. Spike (1994) 'Gendered Nationalisms', *Peace Review*, 6 (1): 77–83.

Peterson, V. Spike (2000) 'Sexing Political Identities/Nationalism as Heterosexism', in S. Ranchod-Nilsson and M.A. Tetreault (eds), *Women, States and Nationalism: At Home in the Nation?* (London: Routledge).

PIPA (Programme on International Policy Attitudes) (2002) *Americans on Globalization*. www.pipa.org .

Platoff, A. (1994) 'Where No Flag has Gone Before: Political and Technical Aspects of Placing a Flag on the Moon', *Raven: A Journal of Vexillology*, 1: 3–10.

Poulantzas, N. (1978) *State, Power, Socialism* (London: New Left Books).

Pryke, S. (1998) 'Nationalism and Sexuality: What are the Issues?', *Nations and Nationalism*, 4 (4): 529–46.

Pulera, D. (2002) *Visible Differences* (London: Continuum).

Purvis, T. (1999) 'Marxism and Nationalism' in A. Gamble, D. Marsh and T. Tant (eds), *Marxism and Social Science* (Basingstoke: Macmillan).

Racioppi, L. and See, K. O'Sullivan (2000) 'Engendering Nation and National Identity', in S. Ranchod-Nilsson and M.A. Tetreault (eds), *Women, States and Nationalism* (London: Routledge).

Radcliffe, S. and Westwood, S. (1996) *Remaking the Nation* (London: Routledge).

Ranchod-Nilsson, S. and Tetreault, M.A (2000) *Women, States and Nationalism* (London: Routledge).

Reicher, S. and Hopkins, N. (2001) *Self and Nation* (London: Sage).

Renan, E. (1990) "What is a Nation?', in H. Bhabha (ed.), *Nation and Narration* (London: Routledge).

Rice, C. (2000) 'Promoting the National Interest', *Foreign Affairs*, 79 (Jan–Feb): 45–62.

Richter, M. (1960) 'Durkheim's Politics and Political Theory', in E. Durkheim *et al.*, *Essays on Sociology and Philosophy* (New York: Harper Torchbooks).

Robertson, R. (1992) *Globalization* (London: Sage).

Robins, K. and Aksoy, A. (2001) 'From Spaces of Identity to Mental Spaces: Lessons from Turkish-Cypriot Cultural Experience in Britain', *Journal of Ethnic and Migration Studies*, 27 (4): 685–711.

Rodrik, D. (1997) 'Has Globalization Gone Too Far?', *California Management Review*, 39 (Spring): 29–53.

Rosenau, J. (1997) *Along the Domestic-Foreign Frontier* (Cambridge University Press).

Scholte, J.A. (2000) *Globalization* (New York: St Martin's Press).

Schulze, H. (1996) *States, Nations and Nationalism* (Oxford: Blackwell).

Seidman, S. (1998) *Contested Knowledge*, 2nd edn (Oxford: Blackwell).

Seidman, S. and Alexander, J. (2001) *New Social Theory Reader* (London: Routledge).

Shafer, B. (1955) *Nationalism* (New York: Harcourt, Brace and World).

Shafer, B. (1968) *Faces of Nationalism* (New York: Harcourt Brace Jovanovich).

Shani, G. (2002) 'Review of *Myths and Memories of the Nation*', *Nations and Nationalism*, 8 (3): 398–400.

Shihab, A. (2000) *The Indonesian Foreign Policy Outlook*, speech to the Conference in Observance of Indonesian National Press Day, Jakarta, February 2000.

Silverman, M. and Yuval-Davis, N. (1999) 'Jews, Arabs and the Theorisation of Racism in Britain and France', in A. Brah, M. Hickman and M. Mac an Ghaill (eds), *Thinking Identities* (London: Macmillan).

Sklair, L. (1995) *Sociology of the Global System* (Hemel Hempstead: Harvester Wheatsheaf).

Skrbis, Z. (1999) *Long Distance Nationalism* (Aldershot: Ashgate).

Sluga, G. (1998) 'Identity, Gender and the History of European Nations and Nationalisms', *Nations and Nationalism*, 4 (1): 87–111.

Sluga, G. (2000) 'Female and National Self-Determination: A Gender Re-Reading of the "Apogee of Nationalism" ', *Nations and Nationalism*, 6 (4): 495–521.

Smith, A.D. (1971) *Theories of Nationalism* (London: Duckworth).

Smith, A.D. (1973) 'Nationalism, a Trend Report and Annotated Bibliography', *Current Sociology*, 21, pt 3.

Smith, A.D. (ed.) (1976) *Nationalist Movements* (London: Macmillan).
Smith, A.D. (1979) *Nationalism in the Twentieth Century* (London: Martin Robertson).
Smith, A.D. (1983) 'Nationalism and Classical Social Theory', *British Journal of Sociology*, 34 (1): 19–38.
Smith, A.D. (1986) *The Ethnic Origins of Nations* (Oxford: Blackwell).
Smith, A.D. (1988) 'The Myth of the "Modern Nation" and the Myths of Nations', *Ethnic and Racial Studies*, 11 (1): 1–26.
Smith, A.D. (1990) 'Towards a Global Culture?', in M. Featherstone (ed.), *Global Culture* (London: Sage).
Smith, A.D. (1991) *National Identity* (Harmondsworth: Penguin).
Smith, A.D. (1995a) *Nations and Nationalism in a Global Era* (Cambridge: Polity).
Smith, A.D. (1995b) 'Gastronomy or Geology? The Role of Nationalism in the Reconstruction of Nations', *Nations and Nationalism*, 1 (1): 3–24.
Smith, A.D. (1996a) 'Nationalism and the Historians', in G. Balakrishnan (ed.), *Mapping the Nation* (London: Verso).
Smith, A.D. (1996b) 'Nations and their Pasts', *Nations and Nationalism*, 2 (3): 358–65.
Smith, A.D. (1998) *Nationalism and Modernism* (London: Routledge).
Smith, A.D. (1999) *Myths and Memories of the Nation* (Oxford University Press).
Smith, A.D. (2000) 'Theories of Nationalism: Alternative Models of Nation-Formation', in M. Leifer (ed.), *Asian Nationalism* (London: Routledge).
Smith, G., Law, V., Wilson, A., Bohr, A. and Allworth, E. (1998) *Nation-Building in the Post-Soviet Borderlands* (Cambridge University Press).
Smyth, A.P. (ed.) (1998) *Medieval Europeans* (Basingstoke: Macmillan).
Snyder, L. (1954) *The Meaning of Nationalism* (New Brunswick: Rutgers University Press).
Soysal, Y. (1994) *The Limits of Citizenship* (London: University of Chicago Press).
Soysal, Y. (1999) 'Citizenship and Identity', *Ethnic and Racial Studies*, 23 (1): 1–15.
Sparks, C.L. (2000) 'Citizen-Soldiers or Republican Mothers: US Citizenship and Military Obligation in an Era of "Choice" ', in S. Ranchod-Nilsson and M.A. Tetreault (eds), *Women, States and Nationalism* (London: Routledge).
Spencer, P. and Wollman, H. (2002) *Nationalism* (London: Sage).
Stacey, M. (1986) 'Gender and Stratification: One Central Issue or Two?', in R. Crompton and M. Mann (eds), *Gender and Stratification* (Cambridge: Polity).
Stalin, J. (1951) *Marxism and the National Question* (London: Martin Lawrence).
Stargardt, N. (1995) 'Origins of the Constructivist Theory of the Nation', in S. Periwal (ed.), *Notions of Nationalism* (Budapest: Central European University Press).
Strange, S. (1996) *The Retreat of the State* (Cambridge University Press).
Suny, R.G. (ed.) (1993) *The Revenge of the Past* (Palo Alto: Stanford University Press).

Swain, C. (2002) *The New White Nationalism in America* (Cambridge University Press).

Taguieff, P-A. (2001) *The Force of Prejudice* (University of Minnesota Press).

Tamir, Y. (1993) *Liberal Nationalism* (Princeton University Press).

Taylor-Gooby, P. (1998) 'Will People Pay Up for Welfare?', *New Statesman*, 6 December.

Taylor-Gooby, P. (2001) 'Sustaining Welfare in Hard Times: Who Will Foot the Bill?', *European Journal of Social Policy*, 11 (2): 133–47.

Thompson, A. (2001) 'Nations, National Identities and Human Agency', *Sociological Review*, 49 (1): 18–33.

Thompson, G. (2003) 'Age of Confusion', *Open Democracy*, 25 September. www.openDemocracy.net .

Todorov, T. (1993) *On Human Diversity* (London: Harvard University Press).

Tomlinson, J. (1991) *Cultural Imperialism* (London: Pinter).

Tomlinson, J. (1996) 'Cultural Globalization: Displacing and Replacing the West', *European Journal of Development Research*, 8 (2): 22–35.

Tomlinson, J. (2000) *Globalization and Culture* (Cambridge: Polity).

Tong, R. (1989) *Feminist Thought* (London: Routledge).

Tonnies, F. (1955) *Community and Association* (London: Routledge and Kegan Paul).

Tyrell, H. (1999) 'Bollywood versus Hollywood', in T. Skelton and T. Allen (eds) *Culture and Global Change* (London: Routledge).

Tyriakin, E.A. and Rogowski, R. (eds) (1985) *New Nationalisms of the Developed West* (London: Allen and Unwin).

Urry, J. (2000) *Sociology Beyond Societies* (London: Routledge).

Varouxakis, G. (1998) 'National Character in John Stuart Mill's Thought', *History of European Ideas*, 26 (6): 375–91.

Vincent, A. (1997) 'Liberal Nationalism: An Irresponsible Compound?', *Political Studies*, 45: 275–95.

Viroli, M. (1995) *For Love of Country* (Princeton University Press).

Wade, P. (1993) *Blackness and Race Mixture* (Baltimore: Johns Hopkins University Press).

Walby, S. (1990) *Theorising Patriarchy* (Oxford: Blackwell).

Walby, S. (1992) 'Woman and Nation', *International Journal of Comparative Sociology*, 33 (1–2): 81–100.

Walby, S. (1997) *Gender Transformations* (London: Routledge).

Walby, S. (2000) 'Gender, Nations and States in a Global Era', *Nations and Nationalism*, 6 (4): 523–40.

Walby, S. (2003) 'The Myth of the Nation-State', *Sociology*, 37 (3): 529–46.

Walker, B. (1999) 'Modernity and Cultural Vulnerability: Should Ethnicity be Privileged?', in R. Beiner (ed.), *Theorizing Nationalism* (State University of New York Press).

Wallace, W. (1991) 'Foreign Policy and National Identity in the United Kingdom', *International Affairs*, 67 (1): 65–80.

Wallerstein, I. (1974) *The Modern World System* (London: Academic).

Waters, M. (1994) *Modern Sociological Theory* (London: Sage).

Weber, E. (1979) *Peasants into Frenchmen* (London: Chatto and Windus).

Wee, T. (1999) 'An Exploration of a Global Teenage Lifestyle in Asian Societies', *Journal of Consumer Marketing*, 16 (4): 365–75.

Weiner, M. (1997) 'The Invention of Identity: Race and Nation in Pre-War Japan', in F. Dikkotter (ed.), *The Construction of Racial Identities in China and Japan* (London: Hurst).

Weiss, L. (1998) *The Myth of the Powerless State* (Cambridge: Polity).

Wimmer, A. and Glick Schiller, N. (2002) 'Methodological Nationalism and Beyond', *Global Networks*, 2 (4): 301–34.

Winant, H. (1994) *Racial Conditions* (University of Minnesota Press).

Winant, H. (2001) *The World is a Ghetto* (New York: Basic).

Winddance Twine, F. (1998) *Racism in a Racial Democracy* (New Brunswick: Rutgers University Press).

Wirth, L. (1936) 'Types of Nationalism', *American Sociological Review*, 41: 723–37.

Wodak, R., de Cillia, R., Reisigl, M. and Liebhardt, K. (1999) *The Discursive Construction of National Identity* (Edinburgh University Press).

Wright, W.R. (1990) *Café Con Leche* (Austin: University of Texas Press).

Yoshino, K. (1997) 'The Discourse on Blood and Racial Identity in Contemporary Japan', in F. Dikkotter (ed.), *The Construction of Racial Identities in China and Japan* (London: Hurst).

Yoshino, K. (1999) 'Rethinking Theories of Nationalism: Japan's Nationalism in a Marketplace Perspective', in K. Yoshino (ed.), *Consuming Ethnicity and Nationalism* (Richmond, Surrey: Curzon).

Yuval-Davis, N. (1997) *Gender and Nation* (London: Sage).

Yuval-Davis, N. (1998) 'Beyond Differences: Women, Empowerment and Coalition Politics', in N. Charles and H. Hintjens (eds), *Gender, Ethnicity, and Political Ideologies* (London: Routledge).

Znaniecki, F. (1952) *Modern Nationalities* (Urbana: University of Illinois Press).

Zubaida, S. (1978) 'Theories of Nationalism', in G. Littlejohn, B. Smart, J. Wakefield and N. Yuval-Davis (eds), *Power and the State* (London: Croom Helm).

Index